STRATEGIES FOR TEACHING

LEADERSHIP

Proven Practices in Higher Education

Edited by Kurt D. Kirstein, Craig E. Schieber, Kelly A. Flores, and Steven G. Olswang

ISBN: 1497326915
ISBN-13: 9781497326910

Table of Contents

Preface

This book is the third in the Proven Practices in Higher Education series. The books all are prompted by the desire to share with the academic community the lessons learned by the faculty of a small, private nonprofit university with international experiences in the delivery of educational leadership programs. City University of Seattle has been serving traditional and adult learners throughout the world for over forty years, innovating in the manner in which it designs its curricula, the locations where its programs are delivered, and in the content of its academic offerings. CityU offers programs in education, human services and health-care administration, management, counseling, and technology, all of which are fundamentally infused with leadership curricula as the university educates its students toward leadership positions in their chosen field. More recently, it added a Doctor of Education program in Leadership that integrates practical leadership methods, theory, reflection, and critical analysis into its curriculum at the highest level.

The vast majority of the university's faculty members are working professionals who elect to teach and thereby bring real-world expertise into the classroom in conjunction with the most modern theories of the day. These seven hundred faculty members have accumulated a rich collection of valuable knowledge about leadership, which they share among themselves in institutional workshops. This volume is the written embodiment of the best of those faculty contributions, and should contribute enormously to the growing body of literature on leadership, and more importantly, how to best teach our future leaders in multiple disciplines.

Some say that leadership is not something one can learn, but it is a skill with which one must be born. Whether one enters innately with special talents or not, there are theoretical underpinnings to leadership and lessons to be learned from styles and application that can make one a better and more effective leader. It is these aspects, and how one goes about transferring those attributes and knowledge in the most efficient and meaningful way to students, on which the chapters in this book focus.

The chapters are clustered under four different headings. First is understanding several different leadership theories and the instructional integration of these leadership practices in the classroom and in the workplace. Stephen Rowley and Craig Schieber lead off this section with a clear explanation of new leadership needs and practices in the world of educational leadership in their chapter "Leadership in the Era of Disruptive Technologies: Strategies for Educational Leaders." Continuing on the educational leadership theme, Judith Gray describes several additional leadership approaches in a case study of a school district tackling enormous diversity challenges in "Distributed Leadership and Courageous Conversations." Kathleen Werner describes another leadership model for educating future school leaders in "Could Developing Servant Leadership and Emotional Intelligence Be the Key to an Effective School Leader?" A broader approach to leadership education is espoused by Sylvia Lee in "Embedding Strengths-Based Leadership into Leadership Development Programs." Following is another perspective on how to use different instructional strategies that relate leadership learning to the students' real-life experiences in "To What Degree Do Selected Instructional Strategies Create Needed Behavioral Changes in Business Professionals?" by Laura Williamson and Tom Cary. Susan Seymour adds an additional learning theory, enactivism, with a focus on coemergence practices of learning, as a methodology to integrate social justice into future leaders' decision-making processes in "Considering the Learning Theory Enactivism to Explore the Development of Socially Conscious Leaders." Finally in this section, Lenka Rábeková espouses the use of several approaches, mind mapping and neurolinguistic programming, as instructional tools to teach individuals to be more creative leaders in "Leadership—New Adaptive Methods."

A second cluster of chapters presents a focus on transformational leadership: what it requires, how it applies, and the settings in which it is best taught. Transformational leadership theory is all about leadership that creates positive change so that everyone acts in the interests of the group as a whole. In this leadership style, the leader enhances the motivation, morale, and performance of the group. The four components of the transformational leadership style are charisma, inspirational motivation, intellectual stimulation, and personal and individual attention. In

"Tell Me, Teach Me, Involve Me: Transformational Leadership, Mentoring, and You," Aaron Walter and David Griffin do a superb job of dissecting the elements of transformational leadership and applying the theory to how to utilize mentoring as a means to best teach about it. Arron Grow suggests a "whole systems" approach to teaching and using transformational leadership to accomplish organizational change in "Taking the Teflon Off Change: An Approach for Education and Application." While recognizing that transformational leadership is best implemented through "modeling, mentoring, and motivating," these same traits are identified as consistent with feminist approaches to leadership by Stephanie Brommer in "'Feminist' Is Not a Dirty Word in Leadership: How Feminist Principles Inform Transformational Leadership." Mary Mara, Matt Lechner, Tammy Salman, and Jennifer Bodley discuss, in detail, the attributes of transformational leadership and how that approach is applied in a university library setting responsible for integrating the future into instruction in "Developing Twenty-First-Century Leaders through Transformational Leadership." Laura Carrillo de Anda describes how one university has set a leadership priority of internationalization, and how a transformational leadership approach is critical to the implementation of cultural change in "Institutional Leadership for Multicultural Integration in Higher Education."

A third cluster of chapters describes leadership education in multiple different settings and instruction in multiple different subjects. Gregory Price provides an insightful description and analysis of the several phases of start-up companies and how different skill sets are needed by those who lead these organizations through different phases of development. In his chapter "Entrepreneurial Leadership Theory Supported in Business Accelerator Programs," we learn about the application of different leadership theories, and how they might be taught at the different business stages of company development. By contrast, in the nonprofit sector, different leadership talents and skills need to be developed. Arden Henley walks us through the development of an Executive Leadership program focusing on educating to these special skills in "Building Capacity in the Not-for-Profit Sector: Executive Leadership Education." Kurt Kirstein informs us in "Socially and Environmentally Responsible Leadership: A Five-Step Plan for Teaching Corporate Social Responsibility to Diverse Audiences," that in the public sector as well as the private sector, being socially responsible is good practice, and describes how to educate future leaders about incorporating the "triple bottom line" of corporate social responsibility into practice.

A fourth cluster reviews behavioral aspects of leadership starting with what Kelly Flores calls "The Dark Side of Leadership: Combating Negative Dimensions of Leadership." Everyone knows leaders who display negative dimensions of power (compulsiveness, narcissism, paranoia, grandeur), so understanding educational techniques to prevent those characteristics from holding sway are quite necessary to ensure that a leader is accepted and thus effective. Similarly, in "Managing Boundaries in the Multiple Relationships Created by Mentorship," Pressley Rankin describes the concerns inherent in close leadership mentoring situations, and suggests strategies for the mentor to operate within accepted boundaries of the mentor/mentee or teacher/student relationship. Lindy Ryan in "A New Era of Business Intelligence Education: Preparing Ethical Next-Generation Technology Leaders" notes how educating future leaders on the use of data-based management decision-making tools could cause them to lose focus on the necessity to integrate ethics into technological leadership. Finally, Rebecca Cory reminds us that whether online or in person, learning leadership inherently integrates civility and understanding of diverse communities, and that classroom/online behavior is itself a teachable feature of learning leadership in "Behavior Management for the Higher Education Leader."

As with the first two volumes of the Proven Practices in Higher Education series, all of these chapters reflect the combination of research, theory, and practice, as well as real-life experiences, of some of the best teachers and educational leaders. Good leadership can be taught, and it can be taught well. We hope these chapters help inform how to do that.

Kurt Kirstein
Craig Schieber
Kelly Flores
Steven Olswang

July 2014

Part I

Educational Leadership

Leadership in the Era of Disruptive Technologies: Strategies for Educational Leaders

Stephen R. Rowley, PhD, and Craig Schieber, EdD
Albright School of Education

Abstract

Despite the dramatic proliferation of technological innovation across society in the past three decades, American educational systems have been slow to adopt newly designed and marketed digital platforms and devices to support and improve teaching and learning. And although the instructional content taught in K–20 systems has become more rigorous and standards based in this period, the pace of implementation and impact of digital innovation on pedagogy and curriculum has been comparatively lagging. Though the content of courses taught in the K–20 systems has changed significantly, how the content is taught has not changed. Arguably, waves of the technology revolution hit the shores of K–12 education more quickly and with greater impact than higher education. But increasingly in the past decade, colleges and universities have begun to widely incorporate "disruptive technologies" such as massive open online courses (MOOCs), digital textbooks, and online learning, into mainstream instruction. As a result, traditional methods of teaching have been challenged or replaced, creating a perceptible threat to the established controls of college faculty and textbook publishers. A new breed of accredited universities offering most of their coursework online provides an entirely new structure for gaining a college degree or advanced certification. These universities not only bypass seat time in traditional classrooms, they offer programs and coursework that can be self-paced or personalized by the student. While the question of whether digital learning is more effective than traditional classroom instruction remains unanswered, what does seem evident is that digital learning and related innovations offer a quality of teaching and learning that is more efficient and more adaptable to the learning needs and lifestyle demands of a diverse array of learners, including those already in the workforce.

The ubiquity of technology and its inevitable impact on educational systems, however fast or plodding, create a challenge for both the leadership and management of complex learning systems. The pressing demand on today's leaders requires not only a knowledge of the obstacles and opportunities inherent in digital innovation, but an entrepreneurial vision and responsive capacity to adapt to or creatively forge yet-to-be-imagined ways of teaching and learning that respond to the demands and interest of a new generation of tech-savvy students.

In this chapter, the authors cite examples of disruptive technologies and how they have changed the context and boundaries of the broader educational community. The analysis leads to identification of key knowledge, skills, and dispositions necessary in the preparation of future leaders to effectively navigate this revolution in education.

Digital Innovation and the Leadership Challenge

Large organizations, like government, the military, religious organizations, and systems of education, are by their nature slow or reluctant to respond quickly to rapid changes in their environments. Indeed, their survival depends on the constancy of their values, the reliability of their services or products, and their durability under stress. Specific economic sectors or individual industries within society are by far more susceptible to external conditions that can either threaten survival or create opportunity for expansion. But just as market sectors like publishing, finance, and telecommunications have undergone major upheavals at the hand of hardship or innovation, educational institutions find themselves under pressure to respond quickly to the unprecedented impact of technology, specifically innovations in digitized learning software, mobile devices, and the Internet. Subsequently, new models of schooling arise: charter schools, online or virtual education, open-source curriculum, digital textbooks, and the blurring of the traditional boundaries between home and school, or home and office, with regard to how and when teaching and learning occurs. In the case of higher education, MOOCs have become popular and have allowed broad audiences access, often with minimal charges, to world-class teachers and curriculum. The example of MOOCs illustrates that however territory-neutral a technology may be, it can set off a firestorm of conflict and controversy, in this case, threatening the jobs and legitimacy of local professors and instructors who lack the visibility and clout of their better-known peers.

This technology-fueled sea change in teaching and learning has created new demands on leaders and leadership training. A fuller definition and discussion of disruptive technology is provided along with examples of how the structures and methods of schooling are being transformed. Postulated is an initial set of suggestions for how higher education may respond with foresight into designing leadership training that better prepares future leaders in education so that they may respond creatively to digital trends.

Disruptive Technology

In the provocative *Disrupting Class: How Innovation Will Change the Way the World Learns,* Clayton Christensen (2011) argues that innovations in technology will proliferate in the twenty-first century, generate "student-centric" forms of digital learning, create customized learning for the individual, and provide innovative alternatives or supplements to traditional, classroom-bound teaching and learning tools. Using historic examples of well-known "sustaining and disruptive technologies," Christensen predicts that while higher education and school districts will continue to make steady progress in adopting various forms of digital learning over time (sustaining innovations), the growth or use of these innovative technologies will mirror a pattern similar to the evolution of the Apple computer: a lazy J-curve—a slow, if unnoticeable or flat curve over several years, followed by a rapid, exponentially shaped upward curve at the time of widespread adoption. If at some time new innovative educational structures are created, in higher education or public education, that are more successful in delivering a high-quality, cost-effective learning experience for students, there is the possibility that they may be so disruptive as to replace or significantly change the current structures of education.

Christensen's work is based on his analysis and evaluation of the development of the computer industry. In his book, *The Innovator's Dilemma,* Christensen (2011) established the terms, "sustaining and disruptive innovations." Sustaining innovations are ones that current industries are able to develop to maintain their dominance of the industry. An example of sustaining innovations is seen in the mobile computing field as industry leaders such as Apple and Samsung are able to continually refine their products to remain as leaders in the industry. Disruptive innovations, however, are changes to the industry from new companies, markets, and ways of doing business. Christensen uses the evolution of the disk drive to portray how businesses rise and fall with the advent of new technologies. During a period of slightly over thirty years, many companies reached success through introducing a whole new development in disk technology, and then as they became stuck in their technology, new upstart companies took over the industry with new, more effective ways to store information. When a technology is significantly different enough that it is not produced quickly by industry leaders, it is considered a disruptive technology, which leads to disruptive innovations by whoever is delivering a product or determining how business is done.

In the educational world, Christensen contends that unlike examples from technology and communications where disruptive technologies eventually overtook and replaced products previously dominant in the marketplace (e.g., Apple's ascendance over the IBM mainframe), disruptive technologies such as online and digital learning will not overtake and replace the institution of public education, which he regards as a public monopoly, and as such, will remain immune from formal takeover. Indeed, he predicts that schools and school systems will continue to demonstrate a steady pattern of adoption over time. He argues, however, that the bulk of innovations in digital learning will force a user-driven "migration" away from standardized teaching practices and tools to digital products that can better customize learning for the individual student.

Time will tell how well Christensen's analysis of disruptive technology applies to the context of American schools and schooling. It is hardly news, however, that online learning and computer-based digital programs have increased greatly in the past decade or even since *Disrupting Class* was first published. Currently, four million K–12 students are engaged in some type of online learning, and that number is doubling every three years. The number of online learners is even greater in higher education. This trend of acceleration of users is also reflected in the increasing number and sophistication of digital products and services now available for use in the classroom and at home.

Paralleling the trend of the rapid expansion of digital learning products is the acceleration of other innovations in education that are having noticeable impact on schooling and school models. Whether these innovations meet the true definition of being "disruptive technologies" may be a question of semantics. They do, however, represent potent combinations of threat and opportunity to the status quo of public education's traditional content and delivery system, and now provide innovative solutions and alternatives to mainstream practice. These emergent innovations include the following:

- The charter school movement and charter management organizations focused on creating replicable school models that can be scaled across similar (racially/culturally diverse/poor) demographics.

7

- New school models that blend digital learning with traditional teaching, or new school models that blend digital learning with new school structures, or learning venues that are much less reliant on real-time direct instruction from teachers.
- The revival of the technical school model in the contemporary framework of STEM schools.
- The open-source curriculum and free online instructional resources.
- Mobile devices that help "transport" content from school to home or link the learner to the Internet through cost-efficient hardware, e.g., the iPad.

It is tempting to be overly optimistic about claims for how technology may single-handedly transform learning and the broader educational enterprise. Larry Cuban (2003) and others have offered historically grounded research to show how seductive promises of technology-based innovation repeatedly have been unfulfilled. Prior waves of technological innovation have not significantly affected the teacher, the student, or the content—the instructional core—or student performance. The inflated expectation of the impact of television on classroom learning is a classic example of the failure of new technology to transform education. Until recently, Cuban's analysis has proven to be a reliable caveat about the presumptive limits of fundamentally changing the core of teaching and learning through technology. Although computers and a variety of digital learning programs are ubiquitous in schools today, their uses have had marginal influence on the core of the instructional experience.

With this in mind, school leaders and policy makers have looked hesitatingly at digital and other types of disruptive technology solutions to help solve chronic problems related to lagging student performance. Notwithstanding this justified skepticism about hyperbolic marketing and untested products, badly needed systemic remedies to the achievement gap and the challenges of No Child Left Behind (NCLB) and Race to the Top policies understandably have commandeered the attention of school leaders in another direction. Legislatures, school boards, and superintendents have invested enormously—in terms of financial, organizational and political capital—in solutions related more fundamentally to the core of instruction: teacher training and evaluation, standards-based curriculum, school improvement planning, intervention methodologies for struggling students, student testing and assessment systems, and most recently the integration of Common Core standards into classroom practice. At the college level, as campuses have erected massive building projects, legislatures have cut public support and student tuition has skyrocketed. Nationally there is over $1 billion in student debt, but not the matching increase in intellectual value one might expect from such an investment.

A variety of these large-scale systemic solutions popularly pursued in the NCLB era—improvements to the instructional core and its context—have been adopted in some combination in nearly fifty states and fifteen thousand school districts. To be fair, it will take time to fully assess their efficacy and impact on teaching and learning. By the same standard, it may be too early to tell to what degree emergent, innovative technologies of the early twenty-first century will generally improve or transform the instructional core as we know it today.

Whether the standards movement in the United States is producing its intended outcomes and improvements in teaching and student performance is the policy question of our era. While the evidence and arguments over that question may not be resolved for many years, it is apparent that many of the innovations of the early twenty-first century are indeed demonstrating evidence of impact on the elements of the instructional core or its context, which should compel researchers and practitioners to look with a more serious eye to innovation as a potent tool for reform and transformation. At the higher education level, competency-based education is beginning to be offered across the country. The Department of Education has now set standards for "direct assessment of learning," which allows universities to offer competency-based programs in which students can receive financial aid. Universities such as Southern New Hampshire University's self-paced College for America and Capella University are now approved by the DOE to offer financial aid to students in their online competency-based programs not directly related to credits.

What compels this closer examination is not the sheer number of like technologies (e.g., digital learning programs for elementary mathematics or online or virtual secondary schools), but product features that range from best classroom practices in programming to new and effective school models that are capable of replication on a large scale. The following is a sample by category of the disruptive or innovative technologies that are having an impact on the teaching and learning process or are providing early and important signs of altering the relationships between the student, the teacher, and the content:

Blended learning—changes in the content and the "teacher" of basic skills instruction.

> Example—Rocketship Education (early funders include Reed Hastings and The Bill and Melinda Gates Foundation): Rocketship Education charter schools have gained notoriety for greatly increased test scores for their predominantly poor and non-English-speaking students through the use of a digital learning programs (math, literacy, and English learners) used outside the classroom in a classified employee-supervised learning lab for an extended school day. Rocketship currently has seven schools in the San Jose, CA, area and will expand by another twenty schools in the same area over the next four years.

> Example—The Khan Academy (early funders include Bill Gates and Google): Khan's original tutorial-based instruction now has evolved with "adaptive" learning software in mathematics, which provides re-teaching "loops" for students who are temporarily stuck or fail to learn lesson objectives. The new Khan framework is being developed and piloted in over thirty schools in 2011–12. Since much of the curriculum is introduced, taught, and reinforced by the Khan program, the role of the classroom teacher shifts from direct instructor of basic skills to special needs interventionist and teacher of higher order skills—the so-called flip of instruction. Like other emerging digital curricula, the content and delivery of the Khan program is interactive with students. To date, the Khan Academy is a nonprofit organization.

New school models that incorporate blended learning with alterations to the way teaching and learning is organized and taught.

> Example—Flex Schools (K12, Inc.): High school students attend school during normal hours but work with an academic advisor who helps them meet state graduation criteria by selecting from a catalogue of 130 online required and elective courses. Flex Schools have real-time teachers available to tutor, coach, and

ultimately grade students for satisfactory completion of course-work. The Flex School maintains a typical offering of after-hours clubs and sports.

Example—School of One (Partners include Microsoft and Wireless Generation): Grades 6–8 students and their teachers are grouped daily using a sophisticated digital algorithm program that con-tinually assesses student needs and organizes both students and teachers into a daily schedule including large group instruc-tion, small group collaboration, and independent online learn-ing. Students are allowed to progress at their own rate, placed in student groupings of mixed ages and grades. School of One is currently piloting a dozen new digital content providers in an extended-year model.

Example: Competency-based learning in higher education that changes the learning equation from time being the constant and learning the variable to learning being the constant and time be-ing the variable. The traditional Carnegie credit unit of one credit represents ten hours of seat time in a college classroom and the assumed learning that happens in that time is being challenged by a plan to award success through direct assessment of a stu-dent's knowledge and skills.

Alternative sources of the traditional teacher supply chain and train-ing, changing the traditional source of teacher induction, certification, and ongoing training.

Example—Teach for America (TFA, funded by a variety of foun-dations and entrepreneurs such as Eli Broad and Meg Whitman): Rather than go through the traditional route of training in a college of education, TFA teachers are selected directly from a competitive pool of recent college graduates and receive imme-diate and ongoing professional development from profession-als within TFA. TFA teachers may receive certification through a training and internship process not typically connected to a tra-ditional teacher college. As an example, the Reach Institute of Oakland provides induction and certification for TFA students and serves as a partner with more than a dozen charter schools or charter management organizations (CMOs) in the Bay Area. TFA teachers are placed in high-poverty neighborhood schools for two years. TFA is active in over forty urban regions and has placed over thirty thousand teachers to date, two-thirds of whom remain in education.

Open-source curriculum, which disrupts the traditional, proprietary control of curriculum content by large publishers.

Example—cK–12 Foundation (initial funder Vinod Khosla, Sun Microsystems cofounder and early supporter of Wikipedia): The curricular content of cK–12's digital FlexBooks is written by teams of contracted curriculum experts who, after being paid, do not hold copyright ownership of their work. Unlike the truer "open-source" content provider Wikipedia, the content of cK–12 is vetted and reviewed independently. cK–12 FlexBooks are currently aligned to California State standards, but allow the school or district user to select portions of the broader curricular content and can be customized by the user who may select various chapters for print or download—hence a "flexible" textbook. Recent innovations to the FlexBook's open-source model include embedded online links to the tutorials of the Khan Academy, as well as other important content links. In conjunction with Louise Bay Waters of Leadership Public Schools, cK–12 has begun to pioneer differentiated instruction in a new strand of literacy FlexBooks, embedding specific scaffolding strategies in lessons to make core high school content accessible to struggling readers, English learners, and students with learning disabilities.

There are potentially far-reaching consequences of the evolution of innovation products and services such as these. Beyond the elements of applicability and problem/solution fit that these innovations offer school leaders today, a number of external factors will further shape innovation over time. Examples include the following:

1. Corporate and private equity interest in monetized educational products and services, i.e., the profit motive.

2. Nonprofit, social venture philanthropy, and political agendas for change.
3. Private acquisition at home by users, including the increasingly digital-savvy home-school community.
4. Public antipathy for lackluster results in traditional schooling models, including the failure of secondary and post-secondary education to invigorate the job market and economy.
5. Millennial/Facebook Generation popular use and familiarity with digital learning.
6. The rising popularity of more successful education systems on the world stage.
7. The staggering cost to obtain a higher education degree.

Policy makers, historians, researchers, entrepreneurs, teachers, and school leaders in the coming years will both examine and play a role in determining the way in which these factors will influence the landscape of public schooling and higher education. Arguably, the context of education (public and private) may well be altered in the next decade and beyond, less by traditional policy initiatives and more by the market and environmental forces, some of which are mentioned above. For now, there are real consequences for practicing leaders and leadership preparation programs.

Implications for Leadership Preparation

Digital learning and other types of innovation will significantly affect the tools and context of teaching and learning in the coming decades. No one can be assured of just how great this impact will be over time. The outcomes of a generational wave of new products, services, and new methods of instructional delivery may not always create the results as intended. Indeed, they may exacerbate current problems such as the lack of equitable program quality for all students or the inaccessibility to expensive hardware, broadband capacity at home, and online college prep coursework for historically disenfranchised students.

It is foreseeable, therefore, that the growing ubiquity of digital learning in schools will also affect the traditional boundaries and roles of instructional and system leadership. Many current superintendents, principals, deans, and provosts already engage in the redesign or creation of new school models or programs that use digital learning as a part of a core instructional model. Many of these leaders now invest considerable financial and organizational capital in digital intervention systems and online programs. But just as the tools of innovation become more mature over time, the problems or challenges associated with innovation become more apparent and invasive. And what might be marginal, albeit important, management and adaptation tasks of innovation today may, in fact, become core leadership functions tomorrow.

Today, schools and universities virtually "own" or presume to control instructional content. Through staff development and instructional planning, school leaders try to cultivate "best practices" in the classroom. However, open-source curriculum provides a cost-efficient option to expensive published digital and non-digital texts. Online courses offer more variety than master schedules allow. New digital programming methodology can offer remedial instruction across a gamut of ability levels in a single classroom or lab. Students are more likely to possess mobile devices or low-cost laptop computers, which allow them to access instructional content and resources well beyond the control of teachers.

The broad and powerful label of school leader as Instructional Leader-in-Chief may not change in this future context. But just as today's leaders wear different hats (negotiator, politician, bureaucrat, financial officer), a new generation of school leaders may find themselves as instructional leaders of a new sort: the Entrepreneur-, Pioneer/Experimenter-, or Portfolio Manager-in-Chief.

Those who train future leaders for such a dynamic and unprecedented future have an essential responsibility to meet the challenges of the achievement gap, ever-declining resources, shifting federal and state regulations, inadequate new teacher training and induction, skyrocketing tuition rates, contentious school boards, faculty senates, unions, and community politics. Without a doubt, the task of preparing new leaders for these challenges and grounding them in the depths of instructional expertise and organizational leadership for the schools of today is enormous and likely will not change appreciably over time.

It would be regrettable and myopic, however, not to formally introduce aspiring school leaders to the milieu of educational innovation. Keeping abreast of the meteoric pace of early-stage innovation is a formidable job. But sheer exposure to information about innovation is insufficient.

Training new school leaders to become discerning adopters and innovators with new instructional tools and creative ways of structuring instructional delivery is critical. The modern military would not think of training its officers today without a background in technology-based weaponry and strategic planning skills for counterinsurgency warfare. Astute senior leaders in the field of education and in graduate leadership preparation programs, likewise, must arm aspiring leaders with the latest knowledge and strategic approaches for adopting the most useful digital innovations in education. Following are three ways in which leadership preparation can be improved to help meet the demands and opportunities of twenty-first-century innovation:

1. Coursework on innovation in education

Future leaders in education need an objective and reliable source of information about the products and services of the very latest innovation in digital learning or blended learning. To be worthy of inclusion in required graduate coursework, the study of innovation in education needs to embrace both inherent potential and problems of innovation by formally engaging in tough analytic inquiry and acquiring rigorous methods of assessing its utility, applicability, scalability, and equity across a broad range of learners, and measuring the genuine benefit to student learning. With this important exposure, there also needs to be the recognition that these innovations will at best provide a new, albeit compelling, array of tools and venues for learning. They may not replace the current and growing body of knowledge and skills that constitutes best practice.

2. Theoretical and actual applications of technological impacts on learning and teaching pedagogy

Responding wisely to digital innovation is not a choice between teacher-led or digitally led instruction. In many cases today, the more potent or creative application of digital innovation is the integration of face-to-face instruction with technology-based tools, i.e., "blended learning." Through case examples, problem-based learning, and creative applications of successful instructional strategies and tools, aspiring leaders need the opportunity in learning modules or internships to become creative adopters of and innovators with new digital tools or new models of schooling. Just as the most creative digital learning programmers are working to find customized or "best-fit" products, school leaders of the coming decade will have to work with teachers to find customized or best-fit digital solutions for the specific challenges of special populations, core and elective curriculum, and unique school needs. In higher education this includes a thorough understanding of the competency-based learning movement and the theories behind such phenomena as Massive Open Online Courses (MOOCs). Aspects of these ideas will spill into K–12 learning as skills-based grouping for students, which feasibly could partially or fully replace age groupings of children at some time in the future.

3. Expanding and redefining the pool of new leaders in education

Despite the potential for long-range transformation of schooling in the twenty-first century, school districts and brick-and-mortar schools will continue to exist as they are today. Schools will continue to require an ongoing supply of well-trained teachers and administrators. Colleges of education need fear only inter-program competition, including online competition, for their survival. But while competing with other programs for new students, preparation program leaders must anticipate that not all aspiring leaders will gravitate to traditional schools and school districts.

The Yahoo listserv "Edupreneurs," which is California based but posts online job opportunities nationally, displays a broad array of important leadership positions outside K–12 education. The same is also true of the job scope of education executive search firms such as Koya Consulting, Bridgestar, Bellweather Education Partners, and the K12 Search Group. Many of the positions overlap the public education sector, e.g., charter school leadership. But many also cover a growing spectrum of nonprofit and for-profit enterprises requiring knowledge of instruction, school reform, computer programming, business, fund-raising, education policy, and advocacy. These sectors, and the organizations and leaders that represent them, are powerful forces in education today.

This broad cluster of search organizations and entrepreneurial job opportunities in education typically operate in a sphere separate from traditional K–12 and higher education systems. The training for this new breed of educational leader or entrepreneur is often haphazard and not consistently based in public education values and traditions. There have been formal initiatives to meld areas such as education and business through program partnerships between the respective disciplines. This approach, however, relies on the student to integrate the intellectual capital of the education and business faculty and programs in order to develop plans for future business or nonprofit ventures in education.

It is worth considering that educational leadership programs of the future might play an important role in bridging these spheres of the traditional and nonpublic sector education leadership—fusing the intellectual capital of various disciplines under the umbrella of one educational leader preparation program. In doing so, the educational leadership sphere would profit, for example, from knowing more about interactive or adaptive programming and entrepreneurialism, while leaders in innovation would profit from knowing more about sound instructional practice and the unique learning needs of special populations.

There is no bright line to be followed in broadening the definition of what education leadership should or will be, nor is there an easy path for cultivating a leadership program that intentionally wants to integrate innovation and entrepreneurialism into core program content. The consequence for institutional reluctance to adapt to the changes in education today, however, is illustrated in the example of High Tech High in San Diego. As the first charter school organization in California authorized to offer a preliminary and professional credential to teachers, it now offers its own accredited Master's of Education program in both Teacher Leadership and School Leadership. Unable to find a leadership preparation program suited for its needs, founder and CEO Larry Rosenstock developed his own program for aspiring leaders. The potential of a large corporate entity to follow suit and develop its own accredited School of Leadership and Innovation is not far-fetched.

Regardless of whether the entrepreneurs of Silicon Valley want to foray into the business of educational leadership preparation, leaders of current leadership preparation programs should be mindful of Christensen's slow curve of adoption. Like the senior executives of IBM in the early 1980s, without appropriate foresight, today's leadership preparation program leaders may risk being overwhelmed by a quiet but visible tidal wave of a digital learning and innovation that its clients could not live without.

Conclusion

Time and the power of research will help identify which early twenty-first-century innovations or disruptive technologies will fail, which will truly transform the dynamics of the instructional core, and which will simply provide novel improvements to teaching and learning. Much will be learned from examining the trial, error, and experimentation with practicable solutions offered by disruptive technologies and other innovations to pressing and chronic problems in the field. The analysis of digital products, the adaptive strategies employed by teachers and administrators, and the trends of use by students and parents will provide valuable perspectives on the advantages and limits of innovation in improving teaching and learning. In the longer term, from a more Darwinian perspective, researchers will have a much better way to identify those who survive, perish, or adapt in the idea and product marketplace. Researchers should also reveal which of the external factors mentioned earlier may have the greatest impact on determining what survives, what perishes, and why.

In recent decades school reformers have unrelentingly decried the "school-as-industrial-factory" model that has served as the programmatic and literal architecture for most schools and school systems. Yet to date, schools and schooling appear much as they did since the mid-twentieth century. But impact of innovation on the traditional tools and methods of teaching and learning may signal a major evolutionary transformation, where the control of schools and schooling is slowly transferred from the hands of traditional public powers (legislatures, school boards) directly into the hands of users or other entities that are freed from centralized regulatory control. With reference to the theoretical framework of population ecology, these innovations may indeed trigger a new ecology of schooling in the United States or give rise to a large-scale policy shift away from the centralized initiatives of state standards, assessment, and centralized authority over schooling that dominate the landscape today.

On one hand, the relative stability of traditional schooling structures and instructional models over many decades suggests that our educational institutions will endure or integrate this current wave of disruptive technology and innovation. On the other hand, there is clear evidence that other sectors of American commerce and industry have undergone major transformation in the past two decades alone; for example, telecommunications, computing, retail, finance, the book and bookstore industry, and manufacturing. Since Christensen first presaged the impact of disruptive technologies in 2008, the smartphone, the phone app, and social networking platforms (e.g., Facebook) played enormous roles in fusing digital innovation with new and powerful methods of political campaigning. With such rapid and profound changes in our midst, the possibility of a revolution in how we educate students and the school leaders of tomorrow is not implausible.

References

Christensen, C. M. (2011). *The innovator's dilemma*. New York, NY: Harper-Collins.

Christensen, C. M., Horn, M. B., & Johnson, C. W. (2011). *Disrupting class: How disruptive innovation will change the way the world learns*. New York, NY: McGraw Hill.

Cuban, L. E., & Usdan, M. E. (2003). *Powerful reforms with shallow roots: Improving American's urban schools*. New York, NY: Teachers College Press.

Elmore, R. F. (2008). Seven Principles of the Instructional Core. In City, E. A., Elmore, R. F., Fiarman, S. E., & Teitel, L. (2009). *Instructional rounds in education: A network approach to improving teaching and learning*. Cambridge, MA: Harvard Education Press.

Hannan, M. & Freeman, J. (1977). The population ecology of organizations. *American Journal of Sociology, 82*(5), 929–964.

Ravitch, D. (2010). *The death and life of the great American school system: How testing and choice are undermining education*. Philadelphia, PA: Basic Books.

Sahlberg, P. (2010). *Finnish lessons: What can the world learn from educational change in Finland?* New York, NY: Teachers College Press.

Schwartz, R. B., & Ferguson, R. (2011, February). *Pathways to prosperity: Meeting the challenge of young Americans for the 21st century* (presentation). Cambridge, MA: Harvard Graduate School of Education.

Staker, H. (2011, May). *The rise of K–12 blended learning: Profiles of emerging models*. Mountain View, CA: Innosight Institute.

Vander Ark, T. (2012). *Getting smart: How digital learning is changing the world*. San Francisco, CA: Jossey-Bass.

Distributed Leadership and Courageous Conversations

Judith Gray, PhD
Albright School of Education

Abstract

Distributed leadership, which originally found recognition in education literature, is most commonly defined as leadership interactions and paradigms that are distributed throughout institutions involving multiple dynamic responsibilities and input of the stakeholders. Weinberger (2011) contended that, by definition, distributed leadership is a ubiquitous property and that it is decentralized so that people work for a common purpose without relinquishing their separate identities. Distributed leadership was tested in a school districted referred to throughout this chapter as the Central River School District (CRSD). A Respect Committee was formed to address district-wide inequities in student achievement related to culture and diversity. The committee modeled distributed leadership and comprised representatives from CRSD, City University of Seattle, and a regional Native American tribe. The results showed positive shifts in the area of teachers holding one another accountable for cultural sensitivity and in areas that included the school's efforts to address responsiveness to cultural inequities. This distributive leadership model resulted in many efforts to engage and promote cultural equity projects in the district's schools and ultimately, an opportunity for university involvement in collaboratively determining the future of education within this context.

Distributed Leadership

Definitions and conditions of leadership resonated urgency in David Weinberger's refreshing take on networks, knowledge, and change (Weinberger, 2011). Weinberger likened the distributive leadership and decision-making model to a micro-ecosystem (p. 166). "This world-wide ecology," he stated, "succeeds at solving urgent issues by distributing leadership as close to the ground as it can" (p. 168). Weinberger also contended that, by definition, distributed leadership is spread throughout the organization: "leadership becomes a property of a unit the way robustness is a property of an organism" (p. 166) and that distributed leadership is decentralized so that people work for a common purpose without giving up their separate identities. Finally, he maintained that distributed leadership works best when decisions require local knowledge that is fluent and diverse (p. 169). In other words, decisions that in the past have been made by the person(s) at the top of an organization's hierarchy will be increasingly made by networks of experience, wisdom, and innovation much closer to ground level.

This chapter will include discussions on applications of distributed leadership that are close to the ground in educational settings, and illustrations with action research studies (and one in particular) in a school improvement context. Distributed leadership, which originally found recognition in education literature, is most commonly defined as leadership interactions and paradigms that are distributed throughout institutions involving multiple dynamic responsibilities and input of the stakeholders. Distributed leadership as it pertains to education owes much of its evolution to James P. Spillane and his colleagues at Northwestern University (Spillane, Halverson, & Diamond, 2001). More recent research suggests positive relationships attributed to effective distributed leadership and learning gains. Woods (2012) claimed, "teacher leadership and collaborative inquiry by teachers promote professional development and new knowledge, with benefits for teacher and student learning" (p. 2). This notion of the interaction of distributed leadership and collaborative inquiry initiated the first steps of a district- and community-wide call to action.

Central River School District Respect Committee

In response to the No Child Left Behind Act, together with evidence of a significant achievement gap between native and non-native students, Washington State's Office of the Superintendent of Public Instruction (OSPI) required that school districts begin implementing cultural competence training for all administrators and teachers. In 2008 a Washington State school district, which shall be referred to as the Central River School District (CRSD) throughout the remainder of this chapter, began professional development training in cultural competence. Under the direction of the district superintendent, a collaborative CRSD Respect Committee was formed comprising district administration including the multicultural director and director of curriculum and instruction, university research faculty, and Native American tribal representatives. Each school site designed an action research project that would inform and improve the cultural competence of the teachers that would lead to increased student learning.

The following year, Site Respect Teams were formed at each school in the district. The Respect Committee facilitated the Respect work in the district by coordinating monthly professional development sessions focused on cultural competence understanding, action research skills, and site-based dilemmas. Meanwhile, the Indian Education Department of the Central River School District worked collaboratively with schools throughout the district to provide supplemental services for special education and culturally related academic needs for Indian students in the district. The *approach* for collaborative change was distributed leadership. The *catalyst* for collaborative change was the District Respect Committee, consisting of teachers and staff from each school site that met monthly as a whole. The *vehicles* for collaborative change were site-based action research projects.

Application

Project Examples

The application of the leadership model resulted in several completed action research projects throughout the school district as listed below. Moreover, one in particular will be described more fully to provide credence to the action research process as an integral component of distributed leadership in an educational setting.

- Minority students attended Measures of Academic Progress (MAP) after-school club to accelerate learning and achievement.
- Teachers were trained in skills and dispositions to better help English language learners (ELL) and special education (SPED) students succeed.
- Parents attended monthly parent-teacher meeting to address adult issues of inclusion.
- Students were involved in civic responsibilities as part of a Meaningful Work Program (MWP).
- Staff and teachers participated in tribal community events and learned traditional educational practices.

Kyak Elementary School's project. At a selected school in the CRSD, which shall be referred to as Kyak Elementary School, the principal, district multicultural director, the author Dr. Judith Gray from City University of Seattle, and five Kyak staff members prepared the work that was carried out during staff development sessions at the school throughout the 2009–10 school year. Kyak Elementary was a public, Title I school, located on an Indian reservation located within the district. As of May 2009, the date of the most recent published school demographics at that time, the school had a population of 315 students with 44.8 percent of the students being of Native American descent. The school provided special education services to a population of fifty-two students in the resource room. The members of the certificated staff met the highly qualified standards of the No Child Left Behind Act. The average duration of teaching experience was ten years with 51.6 percent of the staff holding at least a master's degree. Most recent standardized test scores indicated that the school had not met adequate yearly progress (AYP) and was currently at step two for improvement. In Washington State, AYP is a yearly measure of student progress in reading and mathematics (State of Washington Office of Superintendent of Public Instruction [OPSI], n.d.).

Kyak School was committed to a learning environment that honors cultural differences, supports differentiated learning and teaching styles, confronts bias, stereotypes, and prejudicial attitudes, and displays respect for diversity. Nevertheless, despite a highly qualified staff who implemented research-based interventions for math and reading, along with the coaching of math and literacy experts, community supports, grants tailored to improvements in education and prior research endeavors, the achievement gap concerns had not been resolved. The staff, moreover, attended regular staff meetings, professional development training as well as "neighborhood invite" meetings twice a month to discuss issues and seek solutions for underperforming students. Of greatest concern were state reports indicating that Native American students at Kyak were consistently underperforming their non-native peers on state standardized tests and local district assessments by over 50 percent.

Teachers at Kyak Elementary School were concerned by the cultural implications of the assessment data and there was reason to suspect that an underlying current of unacknowledged racism may have been a contributing factor. The purpose of Kyak's action research study was to raise the cultural awareness and responsiveness of teachers at the Kyak Elementary School site so that they could more competently serve their diverse body of students. The change process consisted of teacher conversations centered on personal perspectives about race, culture, and diversity led by the Site Respect Team, who previewed the action research intervention strategies before distribution to the staff and teachers. The Kyak Site Respect Team members also served as facilitators to oversee conversation protocols at professional development meetings. The participants in the action research study consisted of the school principal, assistant principal, K–5 teaching staff, school math and reading coaches, librarian, counselor, two special education teachers, music instructor and the Native American Liaison for a total of thirty-seven adults.

Courageous conversations. Kyak teachers met five times over a period of five months to view segments of the video, *Race: The Power of an Illusion* as well as to discuss readings from articles that pertained to race and diversity. Teachers used protocols to discuss the video and articles. Teachers were assigned a group with a facilitator. Each facilitator became a part of Kyak's Respect Committee. Kyak's Respect Committee decided to go through the process of viewing the video or reading the articles and applying the protocol to themselves before each session with the teachers. Exit slips were collected at the end of every session. These consisted of teacher responses to the prompts related to session content, relevance, and next steps. At the conclusion of the study, a cumulating reflection was administered to, and collected from, each participant. Thus, there were three main instruments employed to collect data and frame the work. The first was the *Readiness to Benefit* survey designed by the Center for Educational Effectiveness (CEE) and, in particular, the five survey items related to culture and race. (See Appendix A.) The second data collection instrument for the study comprised the exit slips distributed to the participants at the end of each session that asked the questions: "What?" and "So What?" and "Now What?" The third source of data included the culminating reflections, which comprised teacher responses to the open-ended prompts: "I used to think . . ." and "Now I think . . ."

Analysis. Results from the data-gathering instruments were analyzed collaboratively in line with the distributed leadership philosophy and model. Qualitative data (exit slips and culminating reflections) were interrogated using Richard Sagor's collaborative thematic analysis process (Sagor, 2000).

More teachers felt that they were indeed culturally responsive in their daily interactions. In other words, scores remained roughly the same (no change) for all components in the *seldom/almost never* responses to questions related to curriculum, responsiveness, teaching strategies, and training with the exception of the school's efforts to address cultural issues. This number dropped significantly from 24 percent to 15 percent.

The data interrogators teased out five dominant themes:

Awareness: Most teachers welcomed the opportunity to begin open and safe conversations about race and diversity—issues that had increasingly beleaguered the teachers over time.

Equity: Issues and concerns around equity underscored the initial teacher responses and grew more contentious over time. The teachers at

Kyak started to become more aware of the endemic nature of the inequities present in their building, and most were willing to acknowledge or consider that racism was the root cause.

Beliefs and values: As teachers developed a context of honesty and safety in their small groups, their own deeply held beliefs and values began to emerge. The early conversations were contemplative and tentative and, for the most part, were grounded in the belief that all schools are exposed to some form of racism, no matter where they were located in the district. At the start, most teachers valued the time to examine their beliefs and deconstruct their values with colleagues. However, this disposition was rejected by a small number of the teachers.

Practice/Pedagogy: Not surprisingly, some teachers were anxious to immediately apply the learning from the conversations to their own classroom practice. Teachers were impatiently motivated to do something about the problem in their classrooms as soon as possible.

Resistance: Despite the general support for, and willingness to participate in, the conversations around racism, it was possible from the first exit slips to detect elements of resistance, skepticism, and anger. Attendance, after all, was mandatory. Nonetheless, these oppositional voices provided important perspectives and a reminder that issues of racism resonate at a vulnerable personal level.

Culminating Reflections

Awareness: The post-intervention exit slips were dominated by teacher comments related to cultural awareness and sensitivity. At a personal level, teachers were intensely concerned with their own cultures. "I want to know who I am," "My plan to trace my roots back and take a walk through history," and "those barriers exist within me and I am in that journey to discover and remove them." Moreover, there was evidence of a collective consciousness of race and culture as teachers sought to constructively understand other cultures. "My understanding of my own culture and identity will help me understand others." The shifts in teachers' perceptions of culture were most significantly evident in their new appreciation for their own cultures. The contextual relationship of cultural awareness and cultural equity was raised as one of race and poverty. Overall, teachers' cultural awareness had been heightened.

Equity: Issues of equity emerged more concretely and honestly, a testament to the growth of cohesion and safety in each group. "How do we shift the system so that all groups have access?" and "I fear that in a way I am perpetuating the cycle of inequality." Changes in perceptions of cultural responsiveness were encouragingly thoughtful and profound. There was a tendency among the teachers to be more understanding, informed, and accountable.

Beliefs and values: Teachers appeared to value the conversations and the opportunity to express their beliefs and perspectives. Furthermore, they believed that they had an obligation, a "moral duty" to acquire knowledge and understanding of each student's cultural heritage. Teachers felt they needed to be clearer about their own beliefs, and they valued the personal growth associated with becoming truly culturally accepting. "We all need to value ourselves, others, individuals, and community identity." Teachers signaled an increased commitment In terms of building relationships, fully understanding the cultures in the classroom, and actively connecting with every student.

Practice/Pedagogy: There was perceptible shift in the tone of informing their practice. Rather than expressing a desire to immediately return to their classrooms to institute new ideas, teachers became more contemplative and willing to be led. "The progression for me would be to continue to explore what is needed by my students for educational equity," "I want to know what to do." A pervasive theme related to teacher practice in the post-intervention culminating reflections was one of hope and possibilities. Curriculum reform was one area where teachers felt they could make a difference.

Resistance: If anything, expressions and indications of resistance became more intractable. Two teachers declined not to complete their exit slips as a form of protest, while another claimed, "This feels superficial and very distant from my job." There was a sense of hopelessness. "We can't make people change." Teachers tended to blame parents, but this disposition came under increased scrutiny as cultural responsiveness was further deconstructed in the conversations.

Cultural Practice/Pedagogy

The habit of consciously practicing culturally sensitive, responsive, and authentic pedagogy was seen as beyond the purview of teacher practice when they first embarked on conversations about race. Nevertheless, they were willing to admit that there was cultural competency learning to be attained and skills to master. When teachers looked back in time, their initial beliefs, perceptions, and assumptions indicated that they were poised on the tip of an iceberg, some more precariously than others. That iceberg represented the true meaning of cultural competency and the ramifications for all learners at Kyak Elementary School. Overall, the prompt responses revealed significant growth and development in teacher thinking about their role in the multicultural classrooms of the twenty-first century.

In conclusion, the data analysis suggested that teachers were open to the further self-examination of their own and others perspectives on race and culture in order to increase their own awareness of the issues. During the first conversations their beliefs and values began to surface and the deeper issues of equity emerged, tentatively. There was a sense of urgency around translating the practical aspects of the conversations into immediate use with students and families. Finally, some teacher resistance was exposed in the forms of skepticism, anger, defeat, and denial. Eventually, the original small number of naysayers appeared to have diminished. Clearly, the conversations resulted in improved cultural awareness and some degree of greater openness and more intense self-searching. Notwithstanding, underneath the surface was a current of uncomfortable helplessness with the knowledge that inequities persisted and, indeed, had become institutionalized. Teachers truly believed that they had a moral duty to initiate and support cultural pedagogical changes and valued the opportunities to be open, focused, and collaborative on cultural issues. Cultural practice and pedagogy, therefore, became an unchartered area of concern and possibilities.

The culminating reflection prompts produced responses focused on cultural awareness, which in most cases was justified at this stage in the teachers' professional development of their cultural competency. Their cultural awareness grew from nebulous innocence to an almost overwhelming sense of professional and personal responsibility. The teachers' perception of *cultural responsiveness* took a steep upward curve as they realized their limitations and eventually vowed to correct and improve their responsiveness efforts. The most significant change in teacher perceptions came about in the area of *cultural curriculum*. Here, teachers voiced the need for incisive, authentic, and immediate changes in instructional content and delivery. Finally, comments regarding *cultural practice* suggested the need for building relationships with students and their families in the context of cultural respect and inclusion. Teachers agreed that there was work to be done and that they were ready and willing to increase their cultural competence.

Summary

The distributed leadership approach integrated with action research has the potential to equip future teachers with vital and requisite leadership skills. Data showed positive shifts in the area of teachers holding one another accountable for cultural sensitivity due in part to indications that teachers had become more self-aware of their cultural history and perspectives. Another small but positive shift occurred in the area that addressed the school's efforts to address issues of cultural responsiveness in its daily work more so than previously. However, there was an across-the-board moderate shift in the increase of negative responses to the questions related to the school's commitment to confronting cultural issues. This finding alone establishes fertile ground for distributed leadership growth, direction, and development. It seems fair to say that teachers were open to the further self-examination of their own and others' perspectives on race and culture in order to increase their awareness of the issues.

Much of the work prior to the action research investigations was the construction of a distributed leadership model that included educating, assembling, and training the site-based school leadership teams. These efforts ultimately resulted in several cultural equity projects in the schools. The goal is now to continue to support the application of distributed leadership with university faculty expertise, graduate student collaboration, and technical assistance. This kind of endeavor will be both viable and valuable toward building an evidence-based rich record of district-wide culturally competent practice.

References

Sagor, R. (2000). *Guiding school research with action research*. Alexandria, VA: ASCD.

Spillane, J. P., Halverson, J. & Diamond, J. B. (2001). Investigating school leadership practice: A distributed perspective. *Journal of Curriculum Studies, 30*(3), 23–28.

Weinberger, D. (2011). *Too big to know: Rethinking knowledge.* New York, NY: Basic Books.

Woods, P. A. (2012). *Structuring and restructuring schools: Critical reflections on flatter organizational structures and distributed leadership* (keynote presentation at the European Policy Network on School Leadership, Structuring and Culturing Schools for Comprehensive Learning). Berlin, Germany.

Could Developing Servant Leadership and Emotional Intelligence Be the Key to an Effective School Leader?

Kathleen Werner, EdD
Educational Leadership

Abstract

Today's public schools call for a type of leader that can take a school through the high level of change and reform. Many elementary school principals are overwhelmed with their jobs, and the level of stress sometimes reaches the point of exhaustion. Research has shown that the leadership style of a principal is important to the success of a school. Servant leadership combined with emotional intelligence has been identified as strongly correlated. Moral conviction and a calling to serve others, along with emotional stability and sensitivity to the emotional needs of others, are the behaviors needed to empower an effective principal.

Educational Leadership Challenges

Governmental demands for school reform grow stronger with each passing year (Darling-Hammond, 2007; Marzano & Waters, 2009; Ravitch, 2010; Reeves, 2006). In response, schools across the nation are changing their instructional and organizational structures in order to bring success to all students (Lezotte & McKee-Snyder, 2011; Reeves, 2006). The need for change derives from a variety of demands ranging from federal mandates, accountability through state testing, societal demands, family needs, and advances in technology, just to name a few (Darling-Hammond, 2007; Day & Leithwood, 2007). These challenges not only place demands on principals but also add more stress to an already highly stressful job (Caywood, 2007; Colbert, 2008; Fullan, 2008). The No Child Left Behind Act of 2001 and the Race to the Top Act of 2010 continue to increase challenges, thus added stress. Colbert (2008) asserted that some stress is not harmful but actually necessary, and is a normal part of life. However, high levels of ongoing stress are dangerous to a person's health. Stress in the job of a principal has caused some to seek another profession. Others love their job, but claim the demands are too much. I conducted a study with the hope that the results would identify effective leadership behaviors that help lower the stress in the life of a school principal and bring success.

Lezotte and Snyder-McKee (2011) suggested that today's public schools call for a type of leader that can take a school through the high level of change and reform. Many studies have tried to define the attributes that make a school successful (Frattura, & Capper, 2007; Lezotte & McKee-Snyder, 2011; Marzano, 2003; Odden & Archibald, 2009; Reeves, 2010). The findings showed that there is no one way and no one formula to improve the educational success of all students. However, there is an increased interest in defining what successful school principals do. The Interstate School Leaders Licensure Consortium (1996) (ISLLC) developed guidelines for principals to follow in hopes of increasing student achievement. Today, principals have a new evaluation system with similar guidelines for success. Baker and O'Malley (2008) claim that research needs to continue to examine and define the attitudes, perceptions, and practices of successful principals.

Various studies showed that a very important variable in creating an effective school is effective leadership (Lezotte & McKee-Snyder, 2011; Marzano, Waters, & McNulty, 2005; Spears, 2002). Fullan (2008) described effective schools as those with leaders who display strong core values within the work that they do. Culver (2009) characterized effective school leaders as those who have strong core values in their inner lives, which create a moral purpose around what they do. Sendjaya and Sarros (2002) identified the core values that define effective school leaders as ethical behavior and caring for others. Lashway (2003) claimed the following:

> Moral leadership has been a persistent theme in recent debates over the principal's role. While conceptions of the leader's responsibility differ widely, most discussion centers not on the need for personal ethical behavior (which is usually assumed), but on the importance of creating schools that serve a moral purpose. (p. 8)

Servant Leadership in Education

Greenleaf's (1991) study on leadership revealed a need for a better approach to leadership, in which he identified the leader as a servant of those they lead. He described servant leadership with words such as caring, compassion, empathy, listening, and encouragement (Greenleaf, 1996). Sendjaya and Sarros (2002) extended Greenleaf's definition of servant leadership, defining it as being about the heart of the leader. They described the effective leader as caring and compassionate and viewing his or her role as meeting the needs of all stakeholders. Blanchard and Hodges (2003) defined the servant leader as a person whose intent is to serve others in order to make a better world. Culver (2009), Baker and O'Malley (2008), Fullan (2008), and Hunter (2004) described effective leadership as caring for those they lead and humility in what they do.

Taylor, Martin, Hutchinson, and Jinks (2007) conducted a study looking at the practices of principals identified with servant leadership characteristics. Their findings showed that these principals who displayed servant leadership were more effective than the leaders with different styles of leadership. Fullan (2003) outlined the components of effective leadership:

having moral purpose, understanding the change process, building relationships, creating and sharing knowledge, and making coherence. Trilling and Fadel (2009) and Crippen (2007) suggested that the one key factor in developing effective school reform is a school with a principal who demonstrates servant leadership behavior.

According to Reason (2010), in order to accomplish lasting reform in schools, leaders need to have emotional intelligence, specifically the skill of emotional resiliency. Emotional resiliency refers to one's ability to adapt to stressful situations, hold on to positive emotions, and continue in their work (Reason, 2010). Goleman, Boyatzis, and McKee (2002), stated that complex times call for emotionally intelligent leaders, which they defined as those having the ability to recognize others' emotions as well as their own and to regulate their actions according to circumstances. According to Collins (2001) and other researchers (Mayer, Roberts, & Barsade, 2008; Senge, 2006; Sergiovanni, 1992; Spears, 2004), leadership is hard work because it involves an understanding of human nature and emotion.

Goleman (2006) described emotional intelligence as an intelligence model that allows a person to have the capacity to understand, perceive, and manage his or her emotions. Servant leadership is a practice and philosophy of leadership that is first concerned with serving all stakeholders, thus empowering them to identify and achieve the goals of the community (Wheatley, 2005). Spencer (2007) described the foundation of the servant leader as self-awareness. He suggested a leader must first have a solid understanding of self in order to serve others. Research has established that emotionally intelligent leaders (Cherniss, Extein, Goleman, & Weissberg, 2006; Wheatley, 2005) and servant leaders (Culver, 2009; Sipe & Frick, 2009) have a positive impact on the performance of their organization, but research on the correlation of emotional intelligence and servant leadership specific to leaders of elementary schools is still evolving. Collins (2001) discussed motivating staff to create the best school for students through a servant leadership style and the principal's ability to cope with the demands and pressures of the job through his or her level of emotional intelligence. Collins (2001) also discussed the possibility of a relationship between emotional intelligence and servant leadership within the companies that he identified as developing from being good to great.

Marzano and Waters (2009) claimed that if schools are going to have true lasting reform, there is a need to abandon the traditional leadership skills and behaviors, and instead define the skills, behaviors, and emotions that will bring lasting change and success to schools. Traditional principal leadership training programs focus on the cognitive skills needed, but this training may not be enough to give the principal all the tools he or she needs to move a school to lasting successful change (Wallace Foundation, 2007). No longer can principals depend only on their cognitive skills to bring success to their schools, but they must also develop leadership strategies and behaviors that define what they do and who they are. A better understanding of the traits and skills of effective principals is needed, and because of this, I conducted a study that looked at the relationship between servant leadership practice and emotional intelligence as it related to school principals.

Motivating staff to create the best school for students through a servant leadership style and the principal's ability to cope with the demands and pressures of the job was proposed in my study. Because servant leadership has been shown to be an effective way in which to lead a school (Black, 2007; Taylor, Martin, Hutchinson & Jinks, 2007) and emotional intelligence has been identified as necessary for improving leadership in an organization (Alston, 2009; Bardach, 2008; Cherniss & Caplan, 2001), it seemed important to investigate the relationship of the two within the role of a school principal. I conducted a quantitative, correlational study to examine if a relationship existed between teacher perceptions of emotional intelligence and servant leadership of the principal and the self-reported principal perceptions of their servant leadership and emotional intelligence behavior within elementary schools across Washington State. My study specifically examined the relationship between the elementary school principals' self-perception of their own degree of servant leadership behaviors and emotional intelligence and the emotional intelligence and servant leadership behaviors of the principals as rated by their teachers within their school building. An analysis was also conducted to determine which sub-constructs contributed most strongly to the relationship between emotional intelligence and servant leadership among the principals.

There are many factors that determine the need for strong leadership in the school system (O'Donnell & White, 2005). The job of a principal carries a high level of responsibility to the students, the teaching staff, the support staff, the parents, the central office administrative staff, the community, and society (Dufour, Dufour, & Eaker, 2008). All leaders face challenges, however, principals have a special set of challenges that are not found within other organizations. Principals must focus on accountability reform that calls for all students to pass the state testing, to analyzing and identifying areas that need improvement, and then facilitating the change needed (Reeves, 2006). Moore (2009) claimed that the task of restructuring a school calls for principals who are skilled in monitoring their own feelings in order to guide their actions. Mulford, Silins, and Leithwood (2004) claimed that the society we have and will have in the future is largely created in schools. He asserted that schools are the only institution that partners with the institution of family in the development of lifelong learning both academically and socially. The most important investment in society is seen as the education of its people, and without it, a society suffers (Mulford, Silins, & Leithwood, 2004). Principals have an enormous amount of responsibility.

The empirical literature on effective leadership in schools identified over 121 school leadership practices and standards (Leithwood, Jantzi, & Steinbach, 2002). These long lists raise a concern with the description of the role of the school leadership. According to Day and Leithwood (2007), they are impossible to fulfill and unrealistic to follow. Day and Leithwood defined these lists as mythological because they are unattainable ideals for one person. My research raised the question: Is servant leadership and its relationship with emotional intelligence a positive leadership style for a school principal?

My quantitative study examined elementary principals' self-reported emotional intelligence scores and servant leadership scores and their teachers' assessments of the principals' servant leadership behaviors and emotional intelligence behaviors. The information explains the correlations found between the independent variable of emotional intelligence and the dependent variable of servant leadership behaviors among these elementary principals. This study did not suggest that one variable caused the other, even if there was a strong relationship between the variables (Creswell, 2009). The participants in this study consisted of elementary principals from school districts in Washington State, along with teachers from each principals' building. Two surveys for principals and two surveys for teachers were used to collect the data. The teachers received observer-rated versions of both of the surveys to measure their principals' servant leadership behaviors and emotional intelligence. My study determined the relationship that existed between servant leadership and emotional intelligence in the principals' self-rating and the teachers' ratings of their principal's demonstration of servant leadership and emotional intelligence behaviors.

The data revealed that the principals' perceived themselves strong in both emotional intelligence and servant leadership behaviors. The teachers also viewed their principals strong in all areas of servant leadership behavior and emotional intelligence The highest score in the emotional intelligence scale was in Use of Emotion, and the highest score in the servant leadership factors was in Open/Participatory (delegating responsibility and nurturing participatory leadership). Self-Emotional Appraisal is the ability to monitor one's own emotional state and manage one's emotions; it is self-awareness and self-reflection of emotions (Goleman, 2002). With added pressure for reform being a common experience for principals, it was interesting to see the highest score by the principal ratings was in this area (Darling-Hammond, 2007). Others' Emotional Appraisal refers to recognizing and responding to the emotional states of others for the purpose of building relationships; teachers felt their principals did this. Research shows that relationship is what is needed in order to move a staff toward change (Lezotte & McKee-Snyder, 2011; Marzano, 2003). The twenty-first century schools are being asked to make significant changes, and that job rests on the shoulders of the principal. Bloom (2004) claimed that if a principal was going to be effective, he or she must first build and maintain positive relationships with the employees.

I conducted a Pearson correlation analysis to determine whether there was a correlation between the subscales of emotional intelligence and the seven factors of servant leadership. The subgroup factors of servant leadership are (1) Developing and Empowering Others, (2) Vulnerability and Humility, (3) Authentic Leadership, (4) Open/Participatory Leadership, (5) Inspiring Leadership, (6) Visionary Leadership, and (7) Courageous Leadership. The subgroups of emotional intelligence are Self-Emotional Appraisal (Scale 1), Others' Emotional Appraisal (Scale 2), Use of Emotion (Scale 3), and Regulation of Emotion (Scale 4).

Within the study, the principals' self-ratings of the emotional intelligence scales and the seven factors of servant leadership displayed that all correlations showed a direct positive relationship and twenty-six of the thirty-five correlations were significant. Two of the significant correlations were related to the servant leadership factor Developing and Empowering Others, which suggests that when the leader gives up power of position he/she gains the power of relationship and thus becomes more effective, this correlated with all four of the emotional intelligence scores. Salovey and Mayer (1990) proposed that the overall character of emotional intelligence was empathy. They define *empathy* as understanding others' feelings and then actually experiencing those feelings. They continued to say that the individual who could understand and sense the feelings of others was then able to develop emotional relationships with others, which was a part of developing close relationships. Servant leaders care about the feelings of others and show this by delegating and nurturing more power to the followers. Having empathy, understanding others' feelings, correlates with the servant leader's ability to build another's self-confidence.

The highest significant correlation was the servant leadership Factor 1, Developing and Empowering Others, and emotional intelligence Scale 2, Others' Emotional Appraisal, which relates to an individuals' ability to perceive and understand the emotions of the people around them. Again, leaders who rate highly in this ability are known to be very sensitive to the emotions of others as well as able to predict others' emotional responses (Law, Wong, & Song, 2004). Developing and Empowering Others in correlation with Others' Emotional Appraisal seems like two likely fits, as developing others would require the ability on the part of the leader to build relationships with his or her followers and the principal would need to see leadership as a responsibility and influence, not a position (Page & Wong, 2000; Reason, 2010). Overall, the teachers' ratings of their principal also showed a significant correlation between the principals' servant leadership style and levels of emotional intelligence. Open/Participatory, Developing and Empowering Others, and Inspiring Leadership were significantly strong in their correlation to Others' Emotional Appraisal and total emotional intelligence scores.

The strongest and most compelling finding in this study was the significant positive correlation of the teachers' ratings of their principals and the significant correlation of servant leadership behaviors and emotional intelligence. My study suggested the fact that the teachers' data showed stronger and more significant correlations than the principals' data was a great indication that the data was correct. The teachers in this study saw their principal as strong in both servant leadership and emotional intelligence with thirty-four of thirty-five constructs being significant. It was interesting that within the five largest, most significant correlations four servant leadership factors correlate with Scale 2 of emotional intelligence,

Others' Emotional Appraisal. The four servant leadership factors are Open/ Participatory, Developing and Empowering Others, Authentic Leadership, and Inspiring Leadership.

These findings seem to display Wong and Page's (2003) model of servant leadership that captures the connection of the framework; the heart of the servant, who they are; the reason they want to lead, to develop others; the method of how they lead, involving others; the impact they have as a leader, inspiring and influencing; and how others see them, modeling of authentic leadership. Russell and Stone (2002) stated that each function of servant leadership is distinct, but the functions of servant leadership also seemed too interrelated. My findings supported the literature that suggested servant leadership behavior connects to emotional intelligence (Beatty, 2007; Hannay & Fretwell, 2010; Parolini, 2005; Russell & Stone, 2002; Winston & Hartsfield, 2004; Waddell, 2008). Results from my study revealed that the application of servant leadership behaviors and emotional intelligence show promise to elementary school principal development, as both principals and teachers significantly correlated constructs of both.

Now the question arises—so what? The results of my study seem to lead to the perception that emotional intelligence has much to do with the practice of servant leadership. An area of importance in the field of education may be the inclusion of servant leadership principles combined with emotional intelligence behaviors in educational administration preparation programs. The research showed that the principal's ability to recognize and manage his or her own emotions along with those of others and to use this understanding to effectively build relationships with teachers was an important correlation with servant leadership behaviors.

Beatty (2007) suggested that principals are the ones to establish a culture that desires to learn together, and it is done through their emotional signals and emotional meaning making. Bloom (2004) and Moore (2009) claimed that principals' succeeding or not relates to their level of emotional intelligence, as all of their actions and words are closely examined by the staff and community. Moore (2009) suggested that principals need support in learning to deal with conflict that comes with implementing and leading school reform by creating high levels of emotional intelligence on the part of the principal. As Beatty stated, leadership that is practiced with a view to re-culturing our schools needs to occur through connecting with self and with others, one relationship at a time. The links between lived experiences of emotion and power, real and imagined, provide fertile ground upon which professionals can begin to understand themselves and each other and their social emotional contests in new ways (Beatty, 2007, p. 337). Darling-Hammond, Meyerson, LaPointe, and Orr's (2010) research on exemplary principal preparation programs suggests that programs need to center on problem-based learning and that the behaviors of principals are the number one factor and the beginning base for creating effective programs, thus effective principals. They also stated that there is not a shortage of principals, but there are not enough principals who have the heart that calls them to want to work in schools that are challenging.

Various studies have revealed that servant leadership was a successful behavior for school principals (Black, 2007; McClellan, 2008; Taylor, Martin, Hutchinson, & Jinks, 2007). Cherniss (2000) suggested that emotional intelligence has been studied as early as 1940, when researchers suggested that the noncognitive aspect of intelligence was important. In 1990, Goleman's *Emotional Intelligence* helped to ignite a number of research projects around the effect of emotional intelligence in the life of a leader. Today, there are studies that have been conducted that recognize the positive effects that emotional intelligence has on the school principal (Bardach, 2008; Herbert, 2010; Wells, 2010). My study demonstrated that the combination of the two has the potential to alter the behaviors of school principals, with leadership behaviors such as listening, caring for others, and building relationships combined with emotional intelligence behaviors such as creating an emotionally safe place for learning and growing as a community and creating relationships so that there is a partnership within a learning community. Bradberry and Greaves (2009) suggested that teaching skills to manage emotions for challenging situations is of number one importance, but something lacking in leadership preparation programs.

One suggestion in response to the results is to provide emotional intelligence and servant leadership coaching programs to current principals who are struggling within their role of leadership and when hiring principals, develop question criteria and assessment that includes and focuses on servant leadership behaviors and emotional intelligence. Blanchard and Hodges (2003) suggested that if leaders wish to become servant leaders, they must evaluate their behavior in order to see what changes are required in their thinking in order to become a servant leader. They also proposed that the way to recognize the difference between a self-serving leader and a servant leader was how they handle feedback. Servant leadership suggests that feedback is a gift (Blanchard & Hodges; 2007). A servant leader welcomes and uses feedback to improve. This takes the ability to handle one's emotions in order to see feedback as a positive thing and to respond in a positive way, which correlates to Mayer, Salovey and Caruso's (2004) definition of emotional intelligence; having the ability to perceive emotions and to allow that to guide a person's actions, which are the two components of emotional intelligence: awareness and management of emotions.

Another suggestion is having principals use the surveys in my study, to gain insight about their own personal levels of emotional intelligence and their servant leadership behaviors. This would give them information in order to examine the gaps between how they are viewed by their teachers and their own personal evaluation of themselves. The results could be valuable to the principals who desire to implement servant leadership and emotional intelligence into their leadership practice. The information would reveal to them where they need to grow and improve. Bradberry and Greaves (2009) suggested that emotional intelligence is something that needs to be learned and practiced on consistent bases. They describe self-awareness as understanding what makes a person tick, why certain things bring positive or negative reactions. They also suggested that with practice, anyone can become better skilled at managing and understanding emotions, and the more time spent on practicing, the quicker it is learned and incorporated. They continued to state that people who are emotionally ignorant about how emotions affect them and others would have a difficult time being successful in their leadership.

Reason (2010) proclaimed that a leader who first works at monitoring their own emotions can develop a powerful school culture that brings out characteristics of emotions such as trust, determination, and courage. With the significant high scores in the descriptive statistics from the teachers on their principals' emotional intelligence and servant leadership behaviors and the high scores on the teachers' rated relationships of these two variables within the principals' behaviors, this study implied that the teachers supported their principals, which also would suggest that principals with high levels of servant leadership and emotional intelligence create a culture where teachers feel supported. Fullan (2003) purported that having a strong, positive culture means much more than just safety and order. Fullan

(2008) described school culture, as the values, beliefs, and traditions that are formed together over time. Seven of Marzano's (2003) effective leadership traits have a common focus, which are creating and aligning the feelings, beliefs, shared purpose, and values of the stakeholder involved in the school system. School culture, according to Marzano, incorporates a feeling of well-being, purposefulness, shared vision of what the school could be, and the core values shared by everyone. Lashway (2003) claimed that principals who desire to improve and build an effective school culture create an environment that develops a shared vision and encourage shared responsibility and authority. Fullan (2008) suggested that a challenge for the leader is being able to draw out each person's values and views so that common vision, action plans, and goals are created through each person's thoughts and talents.

Summary

My study implied that the correlation of servant leadership behaviors and emotional intelligence might also be highly effective in developing a culture that aligns values and vision of purpose and mission. Again, Kouzes and Posner (2007) described the position of a school principal as one that comes with a great deal of stress. McClellan (2008) also discovered in his study that servant leaders have a higher stress level than non-servant leaders, and he suggested that servant leadership alone might not be enough. Spencer's (2007) description of servant leadership is that it is emotionally demanding; he suggested that it may require the leader to use emotional intelligence in order to implement servant leadership attributes. Blanchard and Hodges (2003) suggested that servant leadership is not a stand-alone leadership but is intended to blend the heart of the servant leader with leadership skills. The findings of this study demonstrated that servant leadership combined with emotional intelligence is strongly correlated within the setting of the elementary school principals surveyed. Reason (2010) suggested that principals need the skill of emotional resiliency when it comes to bringing the reform that is needed in schools. He suggests that a leader who has positive emotional levels is needed in order to improve learning for all. Because the leadership style of a principal is important to the success of a school, servant leadership factors combined with emotional intelligence scales are identified in this study as strongly correlated in the leadership of elementary school principals: 97 percent of the constructs (34 out of 35) correlated significantly in the teachers' ratings of servant leadership (SL) and emotional intelligence (EI), and 74 percent of the constructs (26 out of 35) correlated significantly in the principals' ratings of SL and EI. From these results, it would seem that these combinations are worth considering in the leadership behaviors of a school principal.

Beatty (2007) stated that servant leadership appears to be simple, but digging deep into the understanding of servant leadership behaviors displays that this type of leadership is probably the most profound and difficult. A possible reason for the difficulty is that it takes an inner change, not learning a set of skills, which emphasizes the importance of connecting emotional intelligence with servant leadership (Wong & Davey, 2007). Blanchard (2007) proposed that not only is servant leadership a way of life but it also takes an entire life journey to develop it.

Again, the expectations that are demanded from a school principal have become larger and more unreasonable and unrealistic (Beatty, 2006). The new criteria to evaluate principals in Washington State include the following: Lead to establish and sustain a school culture conducive to continuous improvement for students and staff. Lead the development and annual update of a comprehensive safe schools plan that includes prevention, intervention, crisis response, and recovery. Lead the development, implementation, and evaluation of the data-driven plan for improvement of student achievement. Assist instructional staff in aligning curriculum, instruction, and assessment with state and local learning goals. Monitor, assist, and evaluate staff implementation of the school improvement plan, effective instruction, and assessment practices. Manage human and fiscal resources to accomplish student achievement goals. Communicate and partner with school community members to promote student learning. Demonstrate a commitment to closing the achievement gap (Association of Washington School Principals, 2010).

It seems that moral conviction and a calling to serve others, along with emotional stability and sensitivity to the emotional needs of others, are the behaviors needed to empower an effective principal. Cherniss (2000), Goleman (1998), and Mayer, Salovey, and Caruso (1998) state that emotional intelligence does not stand alone for effective performance but is the foundation to build behaviors that provide for effective leadership. The significant correlation perceived by the principals' self-rating and the teachers' observed ratings of the principals in this study warrants a consideration of the role of emotional intelligence combined with servant leadership behaviors in the role of a school principal. Servant leadership behaviors combined with emotional intelligence enables creating a community of empathy, caring, and serving.

I close with a story told to me, a story about two communities:

> There were two rooms that were exactly the same, but the outcome was very different. Entering into the first room, you will see people sitting around an enormous round table with a large pot of savory stew set in the middle of the table. The smell is delicious, but around the pot sat desperate people who were starving. All were holding spoons with long handles that made it easy to reach into the pot, but because the handle of the spoon was longer than their arms, it was impossible to get the stew into their mouths. The people in this room were full of anguish and disparity, as their suffering was terrible.
>
> Now, enter the other room. It is identical to the first. There was a similar pot of savory stew, and the people had the same long-handled spoons, but they were well nourished, talking, laughing, and happily enjoying one another. What made the difference? The teller of the story described this room with all learning to feed one another. They were reaching across, showing empathy and care through serving one another mouthfuls of the savory stew. (Cavanaugh, 2004)

References

Alston, B. (2009). *An examination of the relationship between emotional intelligence and leadership practices* (DBA dissertation). Nova Southeastern University, Florida. Retrieved from Dissertation & Thesis: The Humanities and Social Science ProQuest Collection. (Publication N. AAT 3352390)

Association of Washington School Principals. (2010). *Evaluating principal leadership in a performance-based school.* Olympia, WA. Retrieved from http://www.awsp.org.

Baker W., & O'Malley M. (2008). *Leading with kindness: How good people consistently get superior results*. New York, NY: American Management Association.

Bardach, R. (2008). *Leading schools with emotional intelligence: A study of the degree of association between middle school principal emotional intelligence and school success*. Retrieved from Dissertation & Thesis: The Humanities and Social Science ProQuest Collection.

Beatty, B. (2006). Principals explore the emotions of school leadership. *Redress* (Association of Women Educators), *15*, 22–38.

Beatty, B. (2007). Going through the emotions: Leadership that gets to the heart of school renewal. *Australian Journal of Education, 51*(3), 328–340.

Black, G. L. (2007). *A correlational analysis of servant leadership and school climate* (EdD, dissertation). University of Phoenix, Arizona. Retrieved from Dissertations & Thesis: The Humanities and Social Science ProQuest Collection. (Publication N. AAT 3309254)

Blanchard, K., & Hodges, P. (2005). *Lead like Jesus: Lessons from the greatest leadership role model of all time*. Nashville, TN: W. Publishing Group.

Blanchard, K. (2007). *Leading at a higher level: Blanchard on leadership and creating high performing organizations*. Upper Saddle River, NJ: Prentice Hall.

Bloom, G. S. (2004, June). Emotionally intelligent principals. *The School Administrator, 61*(6), 14–17.

Bradberry, T., & Greaves, J. (2009). *Emotional intelligence 2.0*. San Diego, CA: TalentSmart.

Cavanaugh, B. (2004) *The sower's seeds: 120 inspiring stories for preaching, teaching, and public speaking*. Mahwah, NJ: Paulish Press.

Caywood, M. (2007). A principal's guide to stress relief: When principals and teachers find ways to alleviate job-related stress, their performance improves. *Leadership Compass 5*(1), 1–3.

Cherniss, C. (2000). *Emotional intelligence: What it is and why it matters* (paper presented at the meeting of the Society for Industrial and Organizational Psychology). New Orleans, LA.

Cherniss, C. (2010). Emotional intelligence: New insights and further clarifications. *Industrial and Organizational Psychology: Perspectives on Science and Practice, 3*, 183–191.

Cherniss, C., & Caplan, R. D. (2001). A case study in implementing emotional intelligence programs in organizations. *Journal of Organizational Excellence, 21*(1), 73–85.

Cherniss, C., Extein, M., Goleman, D., & Weissberg, R. P. (2006). Emotional intelligence: What does the research really indicate? *Educational Psychologist, 41*(4), 239–245.

Colbert, D. (2008). *Stress less*. Lake Mary, FL: Siloam Publishers.

Collins, J. (2001) *Good to great: Why some companies make the leap and others don't*. New York, NY: HarperCollins.

Combs, J., Edmonson, S. L., & Jackson, S. H. (2009). Burnout among elementary school principals. *Journal of Scholarship and Practice, 5*(4), 10–15.

Creswell, J. W. (2009). *Research design, qualitative, quantitative, and mixed methods approaches*. Thousand Oaks, CA: SAGE Publications.

Crippen, C. (2007). Servant leadership as an effective model for educational leadership and management: First to serve, then to lead. *Educational Publishing Co., 18*(5).

Culver, M. (2009). *Applying servant leadership in today's schools*. New York, NY: Eye on Education, Inc.

Darling-Hammond, L. (2007, September). Race, inequality and educational accountability: Irony of No Child Left Behind. *Race Ethnicity and Education, 10*(3), 245–260.

Darling-Hammond, L., Meyerson, D., LaPointe, M., & Orr, M. (2010). *Preparing principals for a changing world.* San Francisco, CA: Jossey-Bass.

Day, C., & K. Leithwood. (2007). *Successful principal leadership in times of change: An international perspective.* New York, NY: Springer.

DuFour, R., DuFour, R., & Eaker, R. (2008). *Revisiting professional learning communities at work.* Bloomington, IN: Solution Tree Press.

Frattura, E. & Capper, C. (2007). *Leading for social justice, transforming school for all learners.* Thousand Oaks, CA: Corwin Press.

Fullan, M. (2003). *The moral imperative of school leadership.* Thousand Oaks, CA: Corwin Press.

Fullan, M. (2008). *The six secrets of change: What the best leaders do to help their organizations survive and thrive.* San Francisco, CA: Jossey-Bass.

Greenleaf, R. K. (1991). *The servant as leader.* Westfield, IN: The Robert K. Greenleaf Center.

Greenleaf, R. K. (1996). *On becoming a servant-leader.* San Francisco, CA: Jossey-Bass.

Goleman, D. (1998). The emotional intelligence of leaders. *Leader to Leader,* (10), 20–26.

Goleman, D. (2002). *Primal leadership: Learning to lead with emotional intelligence.* Boston, MA: Harvard Business School Publishing.

Goleman, D. (2006). *Social intelligence: The new science of human relationships.* New York, NY: Bantam Dell.

Goleman, D., Boyatzis, R., & McKee, A. (2002). *Primal leadership: Realizing the power of emotional intelligence.* Boston, MA: Harvard Business School.

Hannay, M., & Fretwell, C. (2010). *Who will be a servant leader? Those with high emotional intelligence, please step forward!* Retrieved from www.aabri.com/LV2010Manuscripts/LV10052.pdf

Herbert, E. (2011). *The relationship between emotional intelligence, transformational leadership, and effectiveness in school principals* (PhD dissertation). George State University, Georgia. Retrieved from Dissertation & Thesis: The Humanities and Social Science ProQuest Collection.

Hunter, J. (2004). *World's most powerful leadership principle: How to become a servant leader.* New York, NY: Crown Business.

Kouzes, J. & Posner, B. (2007). *The leadership challenge,* 4th edition. San Francisco, CA: Jossey-Bass.

Lashway, L. (2002). Rethinking the principalship. *National Association of Elementary School Principals 18*(3).

Leithwood, K., Jantzi, D., & Steinbach, R. (2002). School leadership and the new right. In K. Leithwood, P. Hallinger, G. Furman, P. Gronn, J. MacBeath, B. Mulford, & K. Riley. (Eds). *Second international handbook of educational leadership and administration.* Norwell, MA: Kluwer, 849–880.

Lezotte, L. W., & Snyder-McKee, K. M. (2011). *What effective schools do: Re-envisioning the correlates.* Bloomington, IN: Solution Tree Press.

Marzano, R. J., Waters, T., & McNulty, B. A. (2005). *School leadership that works: From research to results.* Alexandria, VA: ASCD Products.

Marzano, R., & Waters, T. (2009). *District leadership that works: Striking the right balance.* Bloomington, IN: Solution Tree Press.

Mayer, J. D., Salovey, P., & Caruso, D. (2004). Models of emotional intelligence. In P. Salovey, M. Bracket, & J. D. Mayer (Eds.), *Emotional intelligence: Key readings on the Mayer and Salovey Model*. Port Chester, NY: Dude Publishing.

Mayer, J. D., Roberts, R. D., & Barsade, S. G. (2008). Human abilities: Emotional intelligence. *Annual Review of Psychology, 59*, 507–536.

McClellan, J. (2008). *A correlational analysis of the relationship between psychological hardiness and servant leadership among leaders of higher education* (PhD dissertation). Gonzaga University, 2008. (Publication N. 3302245)

Moore, B. (2009). Emotional intelligence for school administers: priority for school reform. *American Secondary Education 37*(3), 1–10.

Mulford, W., Silins, H., & Leithwood, K. (2004). *Educational leadership for organizational learning and improved student outcomes*. Boston, MA: Kluwer Academic.

Odden, A., & Archibald, S. (2009). *Doubling student performance and finding the resources to do it*. Thousand Oaks, CA: Corwin Press.

O'Donnell, R. J., & White, G. P. (2005). Within the accountability era: Principals' instructional leadership behaviors and student achievement. *NAESP Bulletin, 89*(645), 56–72.

Page, D., & Wong, P. T. P. (2000). A conceptual framework for measuring servant leadership. In S. Adjibolosoo (Ed.), *The human factor in shaping the course of history and development*. Boston, MA: University Press of America.

Parolini, J. L. (2005). *Investigating the relationships of emotional intelligence, servant leadership behaviors and servant leadership culture* (paper presented at the Servant Leadership Research Roundtable at Regent University). Virginia Beach, VA.

Ravitch, D. (2010). *The death and life of the great American school system.* New York, NY: Basic Books.

Reason, C. (2010). *Leading a learning organization: The science of working with others.* Bloomington, IN: Solution Tree Press.

Reeves, D. (2006). *The learning leader: How to focus school improvement for better result.* Alexandra, VA: Association for Supervision and Curriculum Development.

Russell, R. F., & Stone, A. G. (2002). A review of servant leadership attributes: Developing a practical model. *Leadership and Organization Development Journal, 23*(3), 145–157.

Salovey, P., & Mayer, J. (1990). Emotional intelligence. *Imagination, cognition, and personality, 9*(3), 185–211.

Sendjaya, S., & Sarros, J. C. (2002). Servant leadership: Its origin, development, and application in organizations. *Journal of Leadership and Organizational Studies, 9*(2), 57–64.

Senge, P. M. (2006). *The fifth discipline: The art and practice of the learning organization.* New York, NY: Doubleday Currency Business Books.

Sergiovanni, T. J. (1992). *Moral leadership: Getting to the heart of school improvement.* San Francisco, CA: Jossey-Bass.

Spears, L. C. (2004). Practicing servant leadership. *Leader to Leader, 34*(1), 7–11.

Spencer, J. L. (2007). *The new frontier of servant leadership* (paper presented at the Servant Leadership Research Roundtable at Regent University). Virginia Beach, VA.

Taylor, T., Martin, B., Hutchinson, S., & Jinks, M. (2007). Examination of leadership practices of principals identified as servant leaders. *International Journal of Leadership in Education 10*(4), 401–419.

Wallace Foundation. (2007). *Stanford report outlines common elements of highly effective school principal training and development programs.* Washington, DC: Stanford University. Retrieved from http://www.seli.stanford.edu/?research/?documents/?sls_final_report_pr.pdf

Wells, V. (2010). *Emotional intelligence: The heart of public school administration* (PhD dissertation), North Carolina State University. Retrieved from Dissertation & Thesis: The Humanities and Social Science ProQuest Collection. (Publication N. AAT 3442583)

Wheatley, M. J. (2005). *Finding our way.* San Francisco, CA: Berrett-Koehler.

Winston, B. E., & Hartsfield, M. (2004). *Similarities between emotional intelligence and servant leadership* (paper presented at the Servant Leadership Research Roundtable at Regent University, Virginia Beach, VA.

Wong, P. T. P., & Davey D. (2007) *Best practices in servant leadership* (paper presented at the Servant Leadership Research Roundtable at Regent University), Virginia Beach, VA.

Zhao, Y. (2009). *Catching up or leading the way.* Alexandria, VA: ASCD Products.

Embedding Strengths-Based Leadership into Leadership Development Programs

Sylvia K. Lee
School of Applied Leadership

Abstract

As leaders in business, education, health care, social work, agriculture, and many other fields direct their organizations within the context of constant and rapid change, their use of strengths-based leadership approaches can generate constructive organizational cultures and high levels of innovation, performance, and employee engagement. In contrast, continued use of the vastly more common deficit-based leadership tends to generate defensive organizational cultures and a focus on avoiding blame, maintaining the status quo, and minimizing risk, leading to low morale, low engagement, and mediocre performance. Strengths-based leadership approaches such as Appreciative Inquiry and Authentic Leadership provide leaders with practical ways to change beliefs and attitudes of themselves and others from a deficit paradigm to a strengths paradigm. Those who design and deliver leadership development programs have a moral imperative to help program participants build their strengths-based leadership knowledge and abilities, and can do so not only by teaching strengths-based leadership directly, but also by embedding strengths-based approaches into both program design and learning activities.

Embedding Strengths-Based Leadership into Leadership Development Programs

Leadership and change have been linked inextricably in the literature from ancient to contemporary writings, whether leading change in a group, organization, community or society, or helping people maintain the status quo in a changing environment. Today, both scholarly and popular literature emphasize that the rapid pace of change creates the need for agile, flexible organizations. Increasing competitiveness, the push for innovation, and for continuous improvement of goods and service quality drive new leadership decisions and actions (Gobble, Petrick, & Wright, 2012; Jamrog, Vickers, Overholt, & Morrison, 2008; Jaruzelski & Katzenbach, 2012).

Many research projects have demonstrated correlation between leadership and culture, and between culture and performance and innovation (Allard, 2010; Hartnell, 2012; Jaruzelski & Katzenbach, 2012; Katzenbach, Illona, & Kronley, 2012; Schein, 2010). Increasingly, researchers have demonstrated the efficacy of strengths-based leadership approaches in building and growing constructive cultures that engender high-performance workforces (Aguinas, Gottfredson, & Joo, 2012; Asplund & Blacksmith, 2012; Cooperrider & Godwin, 2011; Cooperrider & Sekerka, 2006; Katzenbach et al., 2012).

Strengths-based leadership has application in many leadership activities and roles, from change leadership and culture change through effective performance management and coaching, to improving employee engagement and fostering strong safety cultures. At the core of strengths-based leadership lies the constructionist philosophy that all people carry within them the need for and desire to generate positive change in themselves, their organizations, and their communities (Ngomane, 2011). Strengths-based leadership, like any leadership approach, is thus founded in relationships between leaders and followers (Carucci, 2006).

Beginning with an introduction to strengths-based leadership and a description of its roots in positive psychology and growth as a field, this chapter incorporates examples of the application of strengths-based leadership in various fields. Attention then turns briefly to two strengths-based leadership approaches (Appreciative Leadership and Authentic Leadership), an examination of the value of strengths-based leadership, and a discussion of the importance and value of including strengths-based leadership into leadership development programs. The chapter ends with some suggestions for various tools and strategies.

What Is Strengths-Based Leadership?

The deficit paradigm. To begin exploring what is strengths-based leadership, it is instructive to examine first what it is not by exploring its opposite: deficit-based leadership and the larger deficit-based paradigm. The deficit paradigm fosters a management philosophy that characterizes managers as problem solvers. Numerous job descriptions and job advertisements identify problem-solving abilities as a key job requirement. As a result, managers tend to focus on finding problems and fixing what is wrong or broken, often at the expense of understanding and leveraging what is right and working (Tombaugh, 2005).

As Cooperrider and McQuaid (2012), and Whitney, Trosten-Bloom, and Rader (2010) found, managers grounded in this deficit-based paradigm often perceive employees as problems to be fixed. This leads to performance discussions that focus on employees' weaknesses and failings (Aguinas et al., 2012; Tombaugh, 2005). In turn, this often creates a Pygmalion effect in which people find what they expect to find (Fiorentino, 2012). Fiorentino stated that asking someone to improve or to fix problems is the same as assigning a deficit-seeking task, resulting in a pervasive negativity to employees' actions. How pervasiveness is this approach? Cooperrider (2008) showed, based on a comprehensive survey, 80 percent of managers and employees around the world believe their strengths are not understood, not appreciated, and not valued.

Fiorentino (2012) emphasized the omnipresence of the deficit-based paradigm beyond organizations, and its saturation in Western societal thinking. Harry and Klingner (2007) described schoolchildren struggling to learn and therefore seen as broken, a theme on which Weiner (2006) also focused. Harris, Brazeau, Clarkson, Brownlee, and Rawana (2012) documented its presence in social work, while Ngomane (2011) wrote of its impact in agriculture. In the late 1990s, Martin Seligman, then president of the American Psychological Association (APA), discovered that almost all the articles published by the APA in the previous fifty years focused on negative psychology and people as broken and needing fixing (Seligman & Csikszentmihalyi, 2000). Similarly, a decade later, F. Luthans (2002) examined psychology literature and wrote that over 375,000 articles focused on negative emotions and concepts, while just 1,000 focused on the positives.

Cooperrider and Godwin (2011) documented the change in the organizational development field from its positive assumption roots to what they termed a massive industry based on problem-solving interventions and deficit-based change management—interventions to fix broken organizations. In a more lighthearted, but equally telling, vein, Fryer (2004) wrote of the belief of scholars, since Dante's time, that "the tortures of hell yield more interesting book material than do the blisses of heaven" (p. 22). Even before Dante, mystic, abbess, composer, and author Hildegard von Bingen (1098–1179) earned the wrath of the Constantinian church for stating that the basis of Western spirituality lay in original blessing, not original sin (Hozeski, 1985). Even as late as 1984, Hozeski reported that an article in the *National Catholic Reporter* described von Bingen as a fruitcake!

Robinson (2001) described a worldview of theology that belittles humans as sinners needing redemption, and of perceptions of those who are different as warped and broken. Robinson examined the writings of philosophers such as Marx and Nietzsche and their explorations of the concept of goodness versus badness in Judeo-Christian thinking and drew tentative links to Nazi ideologies of superiority versus inferiority. This echoes Gorski (2010), who wrote of the tendency in education to equate difference with deficit, and of an ideology focused on fixing disenfranchised children rather than the sociopolitical and systemic circumstances (e.g., economic inequities and racism) that generate disenfranchisement. Gorksi pointed to outcome inequalities such as standardized test scores that educators rationalize as addressing supposed deficiencies in students.

The impact of deficit-based leadership. The pervasiveness of deficit thinking and the deficit paradigm is clear. Such thinking permeates fields as diverse as education, business, health care, social work, agriculture, psychology, religion, philosophy, and leadership. When Cooperrider and McQuaid (2012) wrote of the majority of the world's workforce feeling undervalued, they used the term 80:20 deficit bias, or deficit ratio. They also noted that employees focus 80 percent of their energy on what is not working in an organization, versus just 20 percent on what is working well. When organizational leaders behave within the context of a deficit paradigm, those behaviors affect multiple aspects of organizational culture and practices. These include the following:

- Managers seen as and acting as problem solvers, losing sight of the need to foster innovation and leveraging opportunities.
- Managers focused on fixing inadequate employee performance rather than developing employees' skills.
- Managers and employees disliking performance discussions intensely, primarily because of the general focus on negatives (Heathfield, 2007).
- Managers finding and fixing what is wrong in the organization, resulting in improving things merely to the level of status quo (Cooperrider & Godwin, 2011).
- Overall, this culminates in the Pygmalion effect of managers and leaders expecting to find broken, underperforming employees and employees living up to those expectations (Fiorentino, 2012).

The deficit paradigm affects organizational culture, innovation, critical thinking, employee engagement, employee performance, and more. Words and terms often heard in a deficit-based organization include deficiency, deficit, broken, threats, problems, weakness, failure, low performance, and low morale (Fiorentino, 2012; Ngomane, 2011; Skerrett, 2010; Skrla & Scheurich, 2004; Tombaugh, 2005; Weiner, 2006). Employees, teachers, students, health-care patients, social work program participants, and leaders, surrounded by negativity, respond by creating negative cultures.

That response might be a passive defensive culture, featuring behaviors such as keeping heads down, avoiding making decisions, rejecting accountability, shifting blame, conforming to norms, sticking to often-ineffective rules and procedures, and management by exception (fighting fires, taking notice of employees only when things go wrong but mostly ignoring them when all is well). It might be an aggressive defensive culture, with characteristic behaviors such as challenging to undermine, exhibiting perfectionistic behaviors, deliberately looking for flaws, perceptions of those who ask for help as weak and flawed, a reliance on quality at the basic, rather than system, level, a focus on short-term over long-term goals, and attempts to be seen as working hard regardless of results. Or it might be a combination of both (Human Synergistics International, 2011). There is a clear relationship between defensive cultures and the deficit paradigm.

The strengths paradigm. In contrast to the deficit paradigm, the strengths paradigm focuses, as Ngomane (2011) indicated, on capitalizing on the inherent drive of people toward positive change. Leaders in strengths-based organizations focus on creating work environments that inspire, energize, and promote learning and openness to growth and positive change. Emphasis shifts to positive from negative, and a focus on what is working well and leveraging it (Tombaugh, 2005). In a deficit-focused organization, one hears words such as deficiencies, deficits, threats, broken, weaknesses, and problems. In a strengths-focused organization, words such as inspiring, building, opportunities, possibilities, engaging, optimism, thriving, and innovation become more common. Leaders focus on developing for performance over merely managing for performance (Fredrickson & Losada, 2005; F. Luthans, Youssef, Sweetman, & Harms, 2012; Whitney et al., 2010; Youssef & Luthans, 2007).

Basic strengths approaches are as simple as people demonstrating supportive behaviors, using positive comments, and showing appreciation rather than expressing disapproval, being critical, and assigning blame (Tombaugh, 2005). More advanced strategies involve using tools and practices that foster strengths-based leadership, designing explicitly strengths-based organizations (Cooperrider, 2008), and moving to innovation-focused and positive organizational development over intervention-focused sanctions (Cooperrider & Godwin, 2011).

According to Cooperrider (2008), strengths-based organizations have leaders who focus on combining and amplifying strengths. Positive organizational development, as envisaged by (Cooperrider & Godwin, 2011), features (a) elevating and extending individual and organizational strengths, (b) broadening and building capacity, and (c) establishing the new while eclipsing the old. This builds on the broaden and build model developed by Fredrickson and Losada (2005) in their research into human flourishing. Many authors, working in various fields, have focused on the concept of amplifying strengths (Aguinas et al., 2012; Fryer, 2004; Harry & Klingner, 2007; Seligman, Ernst, Gillham, Reivich, & Linkins, 2009). Tombaugh (2005) demonstrated improved learning and task performance when people focus on learning from success over learning from failure. As Kriflik and Jones (2002) showed, strengths-based leaders unleash potential in people, facilitating goal achievement and fostering high performance.

It is important to note, however, that the strengths-based paradigm does not ignore the existence of weakness and challenges, even though some popular literature seems to indicate such. As Whitney et al. (2010) discussed, the emphasis is on first recognizing and acknowledging weaknesses and challenges, and then on reframing them as opportunities for growth and innovation. Imagine a baby, learning to walk, and consider how, when the baby falls down, the parents do not assume the child is broken or deficient. Instead, they pick the baby up, hug her, and encourage her to keep trying and learning. They cheer when the baby stands in wobbly balance for a few seconds, proudly send photos and video clips to grandparents, friends, and anyone else who will watch when those first steps happen. They act as though their baby is the first to ever achieve such performance and radiate pride. Just a few years later, in school, the child starts to learn to operate in a deficit-based world.

The impact of strengths-based leadership. Harris et al. (2012) described the difference clients displayed in a youth substance abuse program when program leaders took a strengths-based approach. The young people began to recognize and focus on their individual strengths and see themselves as worthwhile people with a positive future. Jenson, Petri, Day, and Truman (2011), Weiner (2006), and Wisner (2011) demonstrated changes in student engagement and learning in positive education environments. Gottlieb, Gottlieb, and Shamian (2012) and Skerrett (2010) pointed to positive change in both nurses and patients following the use of strengths-based approaches to nursing.

In strengths-based organizations, people are focused on:

- leveraging strengths,
- pursuing opportunity,
- generating innovation,
- developing themselves and others,
- building hope and optimism,
- moving beyond the status quo to high performance, and
- enabling, empowering, and engaging.

This creates a different environment that generates a different culture than the defensive cultures earlier described. Far more likely is a constructive culture, featuring behaviors such as setting challenging, albeit realistic, goals and enthusiastic pursuit of those goals, fostering creativity, nurturing quality over quantity, engaging in supportive and constructive interactions with others, focusing on developing self and others, cooperating and collaborating, and empowering leadership (Human Synergistics International, 2011).

The cautions of a strengths-based approach. Like all effective strategies, strengths-based leadership is neither perfect nor a panacea. For example, managers often overuse their strengths, as Kaiser and Overfield (2011) found, identifying a strong correlation between the presence of a strength and its overuse. A manager who is adept at making quick decisions, for example, may not take needed time to analyze situations or seek input from others. In contrast, collaborative decision making may be a strength for a particular leader, for example, but become a weakness if she tries to collaborate and consult when the situation calls for immediate and decisive action. That is, overuse of strengths may lessen the use of opposing but complementary behaviors. Strengths-based leadership, or leading from strengths, requires a balanced approach and an understanding of when to use one's strengths and when to focus on less strong behaviors.

Positive Psychology: The Roots of the Strengths-Based Paradigm and Strengths-Based Leadership

Strengths-based leadership grew from the field of positive psychology. While Maslow (1954) appears to have been the first to use the term, Seligman brought it to prominence. President of the American Psychological Association in the early 1990s, Seligman began to study the change in focus of psychology over the previous fifty years, discovering that over 95 percent of research in that time had focused on the disease model (Seligman & Csikszentmihalyi, 2000). Seligman and Csikszentmihalyi contended that psychology had, since World War II, become a science of healing, focused on pathology and repairing damage, with little attention on fulfilling human functioning and thriving communities. A decade later, F. Luthans (2002) reported that he had found over 375,000 psychology articles that focused on negative emotions and just 1,000 that focused on positive concepts.

Positive psychology involves studying the conditions in which people flourish and achieve optimal functioning as individuals and in groups and organizations (Gable & Haidt, 2005). As F. Luthans (2002) wrote, in positive psychology the emphasis moves from what is wrong with people to what is right. That is, to a focus on strengths and resilience, and developing wellness and prosperity, not merely curing pathology. Seligman and Csikszentmihalyi (2000) wrote of positive psychology as centering on subjective experiences such as contentment and satisfaction with the past, happiness and flow in the present, and optimism and hope about the future. They also emphasized that positive psychology addresses both individual and group levels, with the latter about community value, citizenship, work ethic, and responsibility. F. Luthans (2002) also stressed the scientific base of positive psychology in research and sound theory compared to popular positive approaches.

Positive psychology also gave rise to positive organizational psychology and positive organizational behavior. Positive organizational psychology is the study of positive organizations and organizational dynamics that lead to development of human strengths (Donaldson & Ko, 2010). That is, the focus at the individual level is on factors such as employee flourishing and resilience, and at the organizational level on employee and organizational performance.

There are similarities between positive organizational psychology and positive organizational behavior. Bakker and Schufeli (2008) differentiated between the two, noting that the former has a positive organization perspective while the latter has a positive individual perspective. F. Luthans (2002) saw positive organizational behavior as more functional, emphasizing measurable and management performance impact.

A fourth field of study growing out of positive psychology is that of psychological capital. Again, with a heavy emphasis on individual well-being, psychological capital refers to fostering positive constructs of hope, resilience, optimism, efficacy, and happiness. According to F. Luthans et al. (2012), strong levels of positivity in an individual's predispositions, memories, goals, and motivations amplify the impact of positive events on that individual and cushions the impact of negative events. In addition to studying psychological capital in workplace settings, Luthans has also explored its relationship to effective student behaviors and performance (B. C. Luthans, Luthans, & Jensen, 2012), as has Wisner (2008). Avey, Patera, and West (2006) demonstrated that strong levels of psychological capital reduced both voluntary and involuntary employee absenteeism.

Research in all these areas of positive psychology, positive organizational psychology, positive organizational behavior, and psychological capital has demonstrated the relationship between positive human functioning and employee performance (Legier, 2007; F. Luthans, Youssef, & Avolio, 2006), student achievement (Boniwell & Ryan, 2012; Eisenman, Barnhill, & Riley, 2013; Jenson et al., 2011), and nursing effectiveness and patient health (Skerrett, 2010; Tumerman & Carlson, 2012). Other researchers have shown similar relationships in the fields of agriculture (Ngomane, 2011), organizational development (Cooperrider & Sekerka, 2006), finance (Cilliers, 2011), social work (Harris et al., 2012), and health care (Boerner & Dutschke, 2008).

If leaders in businesses, schools, hospitals, and other organizations focused rigorously on seeking and developing the best in both individuals and organizations, and on what Cooperrider and Godwin (2011) described as opportunity-rich systems, they are more likely to generate high levels of engagement, performance, and achievement. What approaches, then, can leaders take? Two leadership models rooted in positive psychology are Appreciative Leadership and Authentic Leadership.

Appreciative Inquiry and Appreciative Leadership

Appreciative inquiry takes a collaborative, participative, and system-wide approach to seeking, identifying, and enhancing the positive, or life-giving forces that are present when human performance is optimal (Elleven, 2007). It involves using a process of inquiry and dialog to generate positive change in organizations. That is, people ask questions and envision a desired future together, building constructive relationships that leverage the potential inherent in individuals, organizations, or situations (Cooperrider & McQuaid, 2012; Walker & Carr-Stewart, 2004).

The core process of appreciative inquiry features four phases, often referenced as the four Ds. First, discovering what works well in the organization, and second, dreaming, or envisioning, what could be, what could work well in the future. The third and fourth phases turn vision into application, with the third phase focusing on design, on planning and developing the desired future, while the fourth phase is the destiny, or the implementation of the design needed to achieve the vision.

Relationships are at the heart of appreciative inquiry as they are of appreciative leadership, a leadership approach founded on the principles of appreciative inquiry. Whitney et.al. (2010) defined appreciative leadership as: "The relational capacity to mobilize creative potential and turn it into positive power—to set in motion positive ripples of confidence, energy, enthusiasm, and performance—to make a positive difference in the world" (p. 3). Mantel and Ludema (2004) noted the role of conversations in those relationships, writing of language as the tool for developing appreciative leadership in organizations as they described generating sustainable positive change in an organization using both appreciative inquiry and appreciative leadership.

Mantel and Ludema (2004) have built on the appreciative concept, writing about appreciative organizational design. They described four stages of creating a rich organizational vision through collaborative processes, coupled with developing appreciative leadership skills. Mantel and Ludema focused on creating an inclusive organizational structure and leading across boundaries within that structure to create shared meaning, a common purpose, and common principles, and on continual inquiry. That is, they embedded the concepts of appreciative inquiry and leadership into the ongoing cycles of organizational operations, creating synergy between strategy creation, learning, and results generation.

Authentic Leadership

Equally rooted in positive psychology, authentic leadership builds particularly on the concepts of psychological capital. Authentic leaders exhibit confidence, hope, optimism, and resilience, and are transparent, ethical, and future-oriented. Authentic leaders place great emphasis on developing others as leaders, and use their own values, beliefs, and behaviors to model good leadership (F. Luthans & Avolio, 2003). In the field of education, Begley (2001) saw authentic leadership as a metaphor; specifically, a symbol of "professionally effective, ethically sound, and consciously reflective practices in educational administration. This is leadership that is knowledge based, values informed, and skillfully executed" (p. 353).

Authentic leaders, then, are consistent, lead with purpose and values, and have integrity. They build strong relationships based on their values, and are aware of their own and others' strengths (Avolio, Gardner, Walumbwa, Luthans, & May, 2004). They promote positive and ethical cultures, foster self-awareness and moral perspectives, and encourage balanced approaches to processing information, as well as developing relational transparency (Walumbwa, Avolio, Gardner, Wernsing, & Peterson, 2008). Authentic leadership is thus more about how a leader thinks and behaves than about a process or framework for action.

Principles of Strengths-Based Leadership

It should be clear, then, that strengths-based leadership is neither a model nor a framework, but rather an overall concept of leadership based on recognizing and leveraging the strengths of self and others. There are many ways to exhibit strengths-based leadership, and it can appear in many guises, in multiple and varied fields. There have, however, been efforts to express strengths-based leadership in a more practical way. For example, Gottlieb et al. (2012) identified eight strengths-based leadership principles:

- working with the whole,
- recognizing the uniqueness of each individual,
- creating healthy workplace environments—to develop rather than manage employees,
- helping people create meaning,
- valuing self-determination,
- recognizing integration of person and environment,
- promoting learning, and
- building effective, collaborative partnerships, negotiated goals, shared power, and mutual respect.

Incorporating strengths-based leadership into leadership development programs. Fryer (2004) wrote that a positive workplace may be the basis for organizational success, noting that organizations in which leaders amplify positive characteristics such as resilience, optimism, humility, and compassion tend to generate better organizational performance. Marzano, Waters, and McNulty (2005) suggested that increasing the leadership skills of a principal by one standard deviation (50th to 84th percentile) could increase student achievement by up to 22 percentile points. As discussed above, other researchers have shown the positive impact of strengths-based leadership in fields as diverse as health care, social work, and agriculture.

Business leaders often talk of strategic imperatives. A strategic imperative of any leadership development program today must be on developing leaders adept at leading change, not just managing it, change, fostering workforce success, building constructive and empowering cultures, and engaging employees in innovative approaches to meeting client needs. These leaders must be able to lead across boundaries and hierarchies, build effective relationships, and enable others to become high performers with a strong customer focus. As the discussion shows, deficit-based leadership cannot create the organizational cultures and environments needed, requiring leadership programs to build strengths-based leadership capabilities.

Extrapolating the thought of Fryer (2004) about positive workplaces to program environments, a leadership development program rooted in positive constructs is more likely to engage participants in their learning and empower them to become the strengths-based leaders needed in their organizations today and in the future.

One place to start when considering how to embed strengths-based leadership into programs lies in the principles described by Gottlieb et al. (2012). Many programs do, indeed, work with the whole while recognizing the uniqueness of each individual, yet there are still programs that take a narrower approach with little opportunity for participants to explore leadership within the context of their own lives and experiences and to recognize the integral nature of person and environment. Programs that help participants to create their own meaning about leadership (their own and that of others) and foster self-determination of leadership goals and dreams promote learning about self and leadership. Incorporating ample opportunity for building effective and collaborative partnerships within program assignments provides practice in negotiating goals, sharing power, and building mutual respect. That is, the fundamental design of a leadership development program should reflect strengths-based approaches.

At a programming level, programs could include courses on strengths-based leadership and building awareness of various strengths-based leadership approaches. This could include a foundation course that fosters exploration of positive psychology, positive organizational psychology, positive organizational behavior, and positive organizational development. As program participants discover the power inherent in strengths-based approaches, they can learn about its multidimensional application possibilities. These range from linking strengths-based leadership to sustainability, to citizenship (in terms of community development), and to student achievement in educational leadership.

At a practical level, many programs include exercises in which participants identify strengths, weaknesses, and challenges in a particular leadership area and then create a plan for development, but fail to create the overt link of leveraging strengths to address those challenges. How can leaders leverage strengths in others and reframe challenges as opportunities without understanding how to build on their own strengths? Helping people recognize and understand their strengths constitutes a fundamental aspect of strengths-based leadership. An additional element could be to include self-assessment strengths-based profiles into the program, giving participants the opportunity for deep reflection as well as exposing them to practical tools they can subsequently use in their workplaces.

Further, courses often include assignments in which students assess leadership capabilities in their home organizations and identify opportunities for growth. Many such exercises have an inherent focus on negativity—what is not working and what needs to be fixed. Including an element in which students assess the direct relationship between leadership strengths and organizational success could generate a different mindset, one that focuses on positivity ratios instead of negativity ratios (Cooperrider & McQuaid, 2012) and provide a basis for then assessing strengths-based leadership capabilities in the organizations.

Courses on strategic planning could introduce the strengths-based SOAR framework as a strategic tool to compare and contrast to SWOT. SOAR, founded in appreciative inquiry, stands for Strengths,

Opportunities, Aspirations, and Results, enabling participants to look beyond the limited analysis level promoted by SWOT (Strengths, Weaknesses, Opportunities, and Threats). This could lead to participants developing strengths-based strategic models for their organizations. Similarly, introducing strengths-based approaches into courses on project management, coaching, organizational design, and change leadership could enable students to compare such approaches with more traditional deficit-based approaches and understand the power inherent in strengths-based leadership.

Appreciative inquiry, in particular, used at a personal level at the beginning of a program, would help students to explore their own goals and dreams for the program while introducing them to the appreciative concept and the appreciative inquiry framework. Later in the program, students could then use appreciative inquiry in relation to their thesis work, and translate that learning to the leadership of their organizations.

Conclusion

The deficit paradigm and deficit-based leadership no longer supports and generates organizational success in a world that demands high performance from all employees. Today's employees are engaged actively in continual improvement, learning, and innovation, and have a constant focus on positive change, and the strengths paradigm and strengths-based leadership provide a solid foundation for such success. Leadership development programs must, therefore, focus on building strengths-based leadership skills as well as reflect strengths-based approaches and positive change in their design and delivery.

References

Aguinas, H., Gottfredson, R. K., & Joo, H. (2012). *Delivering effective performance feedback: The strengths-based approach*. Business Horizons, *55*, 105–111.

Asplund, J., & Blacksmith, N. (2012). Embedding strengths in your company's DNA. *Gallup Management Journal Online, 1*.

Avey, J. B., Patera, J. L., & West, B. J. (2006). The implications of positive psychological capital on employee absenteeism. *Journal of Leadership & Organizational Studies, 13*(2), 42–60.

Avolio, B. J., Gardner, W. L., Walumbwa, F. O., Luthans, F., & May, D. R. (2004). Unlocking the mask: A look at the process by which authentic leaders impact follower attitudes and behaviors. *The Leadership Quarterly, 15*(6), 801–823. doi:10.1016/j.leaqua.2004.09.003

Bakker, A. B., & Schufeli, W. B. (2008). Positive organizational behavior: Engaged employees in flourishing organizations. *Journal of Organizational Behavior, 29*, 8. doi:10.1002/job.515

Begley, P. T. (2001). In pursuit of authentic school leadership practices. *International Journal of Leadership in Education, 4*, 353–365.

Boerner, S., & Dutschke, E. (2008). The impact of charismatic leadership on followers' initiative-oriented behavior: A study in German hospitals. *Health Care Manage Rev, 33*(4), 332–340. doi:10.1097/01.HCM.0000318771.82642.8f

Boniwell, I., & Ryan, L. (2012). *Personal well-being lessons for secondary schools: Positive psychology in action for 11 to 14 year olds.* Columbus, OH: McGraw-Hill Education.

Carucci, R. (2006). Building relationships that enable next-generation leaders. *Leader to Leader, 2006*(42), 47–53.

Cilliers, F. (2011). Positive psychology leadership coaching experiences in a financial organisation. *SA Journal of Industrial Psychology, 37*(1), 14. Retrieved from http://dx.doi.org/10.4102/sajip.v37i1.933 or doi:10.4102/sajip.v37i1.933

Cooperrider, D. L. (2008). The 3-circles of the strengths revolution. *AI Practitioner* (Nov, 2008), 8–11.

Cooperrider, D. L., & Godwin, L. N. (2011). Positive organization development: Innovation-inspired change in an economy and ecology of strengths. In K. S. Cameron & G. M. Spreitzer (Eds.), *The oxford handbook of positive organizational psychology* (pp. 737–750). New York, NY: Oxford University Press.

Cooperrider, D. L., & McQuaid, M. (2012). The positive arc of systemic strengths: How appreciative inquiry and sustainable designing can bring out the best in human systems. *Journal of Corporate Citizenship, Summer 2012*(46), 71–102.

Cooperrider, D. L., & Sekerka, L. E. (2006). Toward a theory of positive organizational change. In J. V. Gallos (Ed.) *Organization Development: A Jossey-Bass Reader*, 223–238.

Donaldson, S. I., & Ko, I. (2010). Positive organizational psychology, behavior, and scholarship: A review of the emerging literature and evidence base. *The Journal of Positive Psychology, 5*(3), 177–191. doi:10.1080/17439761003790930

Eisenman, J., Barnhill, R., & Riley, B. (2013). Oil city prep: Putting positive principles into practice. *Reclaiming Children and Youth, 21*(4), 38–43.

Elleven, R. K. (2007). Appreciative inquiry: A model for organizational development and performance improvement in student affairs. *Education, 127*(4), 451–455.

Fiorentino, L. H. (2012). Positive perspectives on the profession: Reframing through appreciative inquiry. *Quest, 64*(4), 209–228. doi:10.1080/00336297.2012.723464

Fredrickson, B. L., & Losada, M. F. (2005). Positive affect and the complex dynamics of human flourishing. *American Psychologist, 60*(7), 678–686. doi:10.1037/0003-066x.60.7.678

Fryer, B. (2004). Accentuate the positive. *Harvard Business Review, 82*(2), 22–23.

Gable, S. L., & Haidt, J. (2005). What (and why) is positive psychology? *Review of General Psychology, 9*(2), 8. doi:10.1037/1089-2680.9.2.103

Gobble, M. M., Petrick, I., & Wright, H. (2012). Innovation and strategy. *Research Technology Management, 55*(3), 63–67. doi:10.5437/08956308x5503005

Gorski, P. C. (2010). *Unlearning deficit ideology and the scornful gaze: Thoughts on authenticating the class discourse in education* (p. 30). George Mason University, Fairfax, VA: EdChange.

Gottlieb, L., Gottlieb, B., & Shamian, J. (2012). Principles of strengths-based nursing leadership for strengths-based nursing care: A new paradigm for nursing and healthcare for the 21st Century. *Nursing Leadership, 25*(2), 38–50.

Harris, N., Brazeau, J. N., Clarkson, A., Brownlee, K., & Rawana, E. P. (2012). Adolescents' experiences of a strengths-based treatment program for substance abuse. *Journal of Psychoactive Drugs, 44*(5), 390–397. doi:10.1080/02791072.2012.736822

Harry, B., & Klingner, J. (2007). Discarding the deficit model. *Educational Leadership, 64*(5), 16–21.

Hartnell, C. (2012). *Leadership and organizational culture: An integrative view of leaders as culture creators and culture as social context* (PhD dissertation, Arizona State University). Retrieved from http://proxy.cityu.edu/login?url=http://search.proquest.com/docview/1010760966?accountid=1230_(ProQuest Dissertations & Theses (PQDT) database).

Heathfield, S. (2007). Performance appraisals don't work: What does? *Journal for Quality & Participation, 30*(1), 6–9.

Hozeski, B. (trans.) (1985). *Hildegard von Bingen's mystical visions.* Rochester, VT: Bear & Company.

Human Synergistics International. (2011). *Organizational culture report: The city of x*. St. Mary's, ON: Human Synergistics International.

Jamrog, J. J., Vickers, M., Overholt, M. H., & Morrison, C. L. (2008). High-performance organizations: Finding the elements of excellence. *People & Strategy, 31*(1), 29–38.

Jaruzelski, B., & Katzenbach, J. (2012). Building a culture that energizes innovation. *Financial Executive, 28*(2), 32–35.

Jenson, R. J., Petri, A. N., Day, A. D., & Truman, K. Z. (2011). Perceptions of self-efficacy among STEM students with disabilities. *Journal of Postsecondary Education and Disability 24*(4), 8–28.

Kaiser, R. B., & Overfield, D. V. (2011). Strengths, strengths overused, and lopsided leadership. *Consulting Psychology Journal: Practice and Research, 63*(2), 89–109. doi:10.1037/a0024470

Katzenbach, J. R., Illona, S., & Kronley, C. (2012). Cultural change that sticks. *Harvard Business Review, 90*(8), 110.

Kriflik, G. K., & Jones, R. (2002). *A grounded theory of the leadership process in a large government bureaucracy*. Retrieved from Research Online website: http://ro.uow.edu.au/commpapers/349

Legier, J. T. (2007). *Assessing leadership effectiveness: The relationship between emotional intelligence and leadership behaviors on group and organizational performance* (Doctor of Philosophy in Education dissertation). Southern Illinois University, Carbondale, Illinois. Retrieved from http://search.proquest.com.proxy.cityu.edu/docview/304829425 (UMI Number: 3291656)

Luthans, F. (2002). The need for and meaning of positive organizational behavior. *Journal of Organizational Behavior, 23*, 12. doi:10.1002/job.165

Luthans, F., & Avolio, B. J. (2003). Authentic leadership development. In K. S. Cameron, J. E. Dutton & R. E. Quinn (Eds.), *Positive organizational scholarship: Foundations of a new discipline* (pp. 241–261). San Francisco: Barrett-Koehler.

Luthans, B. C., Luthans, K. W., & Jensen, S. M. (2012). The impact of business school students' psychological capital on academic performance. *Journal of Education for Business, 87*(5), 253–259. doi:10.1080/0883 2323.2011.609844

Luthans, F., Youssef, C. M., & Avolio, B. J. (2006). *Psychological capital: Developing the human competitive edge.* New York, NY: Oxford University Press.

Luthans, F., Youssef, C. M., Sweetman, D. S., & Harms, P. D. (2012). Meeting the leadership challenge of employee well-being through relationship PsyCap and health PsyCap. *Journal of Leadership & Organizational Studies, 20*(1), 118–133. doi:10.1177/1548051812465893

Mantel, M. J., & Ludema, J. D. (2004). Sustaining positive change: Inviting conversational convergence through appreciative leadership and organization design. *Advances in Appreciative Inquiry, 1*, 309–336.

Marzano, R. J., Waters, T., & McNulty, B. (2005). *School leadership that works: From research to results.* Alexandria, VA: Association for Supervision and Curriculum Development.

Maslow, A. H. (1954). *Motivation and personality.* New York, NY: Addison-Wesley Educational Publishers Inc.

Ngomane, T. (2011). From a deficit-based to an appreciative inquiry approach in extension programs: Constructing a case for a positive shift in the current intervention paradigm. *Journal of International Agricultural and Extension Education, 17*(3), 57–68. doi:10.5191/jiaee.2010.17305

Robinson, M. (2001). Americans. *Theology Today, 58*(1), 72–81. doi:10.1177/004057360105800109

Schein, E. H. (2010). *Organizational culture and leadership* (4th. ed.). San Francisco, CA: Jossey-Bass.

Seligman, M. E. P., & Csikszentmihalyi, M. (2000). Positive psychology: An introduction. *American Psychologist, 55*(1), 5–14. doi:10.1037//0003-066X.55.1.5

Seligman, M. E. P., Ernst, R. M., Gillham, J., Reivich, K., & Linkins, M. (2009). Positive education: Positive psychology and classroom interventions. *Oxford Review of Education, 35*(3), 293–311. doi:10.1080/03054980902934563

Skerrett, K. (2010). Extending family nursing: Concepts from positive psychology. *Journal of Family Nursing, 16*(4), 487–502. doi:10.1177/1074840710386713

Skrla, L., & Scheurich, J. J. (2004). Displacing deficit thinking in school district leadership. In L. Skrla & J. J. Scheurich (Eds.), *Educational equity and accountability: Paradigms, policies, and politics* (pp. 107–129). New York, NY: Routledge.

Tombaugh, J. R. (2005). Positive leadership yields performance and profitability: Effective organizations develop their strengths. *Development and Learning in Organizations, 19*(3), 15–17. doi:10.1108/14777280510590031

Tumerman, M., & Carlson, L. M. H. (2012). Increasing medical team cohesion and leadership behaviors using a 360-degree evaluation process. *WMJ, 111*(1), 33–37.

Walker, K., & Carr-Stewart, S. (2004). Learning leadership through appreciative inquiry. *International Studies in Educational Administration, 32*(1), 72–85.

Walumbwa, F. O., Avolio, B. J., Gardner, W. L., Wernsing, T. S., & Peterson, S. J. (2008). Authentic leadership: Development and validation of a theory-based measure. *Journal of Management, 34*(1), 89–126. doi:10.1177/0149206307308913

Weiner, L. (2006). Challenging deficit thinking. *Educational Leadership, 64*(1), 42–45.

Whitney, D., Trosten-Bloom, A., & Rader, K. (2010). *Appreciative leadership: Focus on what works to drive winning performance and build a thriving organization*. New York, NY: McGraw Hill.

Wisner, M. D. (2008). *Psychological capital and strengths ownership as predictors of effective student leadership* (doctoral dissertation). Azusa Pacific University, Ann Arbor. Retrieved from http://proxy.cityu.edu/login?url=http://search.proquest.com/docview/304813000?accountid=1230 (ProQuest Dissertations & Theses Full Text database).

Wisner, M. D. (2011). Psychological strengths as predictors of effective student leadership. *Christian Higher Education, 10*(3/4), 353–375. doi: 10.1080/15363759.2011.576223

Youssef, C. M., & Luthans, F. (2007). Positive organizational behaviour in the workplace: The impact of hope, optimism, and resilience. *Journal of Management, 33*(5), 774–800. doi:10.1177/0149206307305562

To What Degree Do Selected Instructional Strategies Create Needed Behavioral Changes in Business Professionals?

Laura E. Williamson, MBA, EdD, and Tom Cary, JD
School of Management

Abstract

The leadership literature is clear in its suggestion that learners process information differently. The literature discloses that delivery and design practices for leadership instruction have traditionally been determined by common sense, not cognitive or learning theory. This is largely true because until recently, neither cognitive science nor educational theory have generated sufficient findings to permit extensive application to either consideration (Sweller, 1990).

Based on a study conducted at a global institution of higher learning, headquartered in the western United States, the challenges and strategies of teaching leadership to business professionals were examined. As a result, instructional designers and trainers of leadership must consider their instructional strategies and employ those strategies that reduce or eliminate the need for the learners to use cognitive resources and therefore limit their ability to attend to schema acquisition. Where instruction focuses on behavioral change, as is typically the case with leadership curriculum, creating a takeaway that applies learning theory is perhaps even more critical. It is noted that instead of lecturing to students about the theory of behavioral change in the workplace, materials should be created (specifically, takeaways used immediately on the job) that allow for schema acquisition, thereby increasing self-awareness and therefore creating the needed behavioral change in leaders.

Instructional Strategies Needed for Behavioral Change: A Study

As the traditional delivery of leadership instruction makes way for alternate methods, the question of to what degree selected instructional strategies create the needed behavioral changes in business professionals naturally occurs.

Cognition and Behavioral Change

Richard E. Mayer's cognitive theory of multimedia learning (1996, 1997, 2001) suggests that meaningful learning occurs when the learner engages in three basic kinds of cognitive processes: selecting, organizing, and integrating. *Selecting* involves paying attention to relevant aspects of the presented material (such as steps in a procedure), *organizing* involves constructing a coherent structure (such as a cause-and-effect chain in curriculum design), and *integrating* involves building connections with existing knowledge (such as relating course content to concrete experiences).

Mayer's basic hypothesis is that learners seek to make sense of the material presented by building coherent mental representations. He bases this hypothesis on the human information processing system, which he describes in his theory as diagrammed in Figure 1.

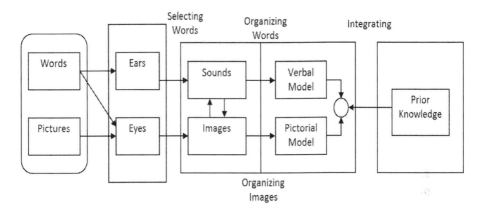

Figure 1. Cognitive Theory of Multimedia Learning

Mayer (2001) states that humans process information in what he terms the presentation modes view of multimedia learning. The presentation modes view proposes that learners are able to use various cognitive coding systems to represent knowledge, such as verbal and pictorial knowledge representations. This theory is consistent with Paivio's dual-coding theory (Paivio, 1986, 1991; Clark & Paivio, 1991; Sadoski & Paivio, 2001; Mayer & Sims, 1994), which assumes that individuals have separate processing channels for verbal and pictorial knowledge.

Schema Acquisition and Leadership

According to Anderson (1973), a schema (singular) represents generic knowledge. A general category (schema) will include slots for all the components, or features, included in it. Schemata (plural) are embedded one within another at different levels of abstraction. Relationships among them are conceived to be like webs (rather than hierarchical); thus, each one is interconnected with many others.

A question is how to support the learner to attend to schema acquisition. Cognitive load theory has some suggestions (Sweller & Chandler, 1994; Sweller & Chandler, 1991). The theory notes that schema acquisition is the building block of skilled leadership performance and may be summarized as follows: (a) Schema acquisition requires attention directed to problem states and their associated moves; other cognitive activities must remain limited and peripheral so as not to impose a heavy cognitive load that interferes with learning. (b) Encouraging or requiring learners to engage in means-ends search or to integrate multiple sources of information misdirects attention and imposes a heavy cognitive load. (c) Because integrating multiple sources of information misdirects attention and imposes a heavy cognitive load, schema acquisition cannot commence until disparate sources of information have been mentally integrated. (d) Material with reduced or unitary sources of information will reduce or eliminate the need for learners to use cognitive resources to restructure material into a form suitable for schema acquisition. (e) Learning is enhanced when learners are allowed to attend to schema acquisition rather than to information reformulation, which is the case with leadership performance.

Beyond schema acquisition, Sweller and Chandler (1994) reveal two important points to deconstruct with respect to the instructional strategy of *integrating*: the material and the method of delivery. To illustrate their point about the material, the authors provide an example.

> A student learning elementary algebra must learn how to multiply out the denominator of one side of an equation in order to isolate a single pronumeral in the numerator on that side. The student needs to learn what to do when faced with an equation such as $a/b = c$, solve for a. To learn this process, the student must learn that, when multiplying by b, the numerator on the left-hand side is multiplied by b, giving ab; the two bs on the left-hand side cancel out, leaving a isolated; because the left-hand side has been multiplied by b, the right-hand side must also be multiplied by b; multiplying the right-hand side by b gives cb in the numerator on the right-hand side; the denominator remains unchanged at 1, which is not shown in the equation; the net consequence is $a = cb$, which meets the

goal of isolating the numerator on the left-hand side of the equation. (p. 189)

Each step in the algebra equation must be learned in conjunction with the others, because in isolation, they do not make mathematical sense. To know how to multiply out a denominator, the learner must understand how to perform the other operations. The authors call this feature of the material *high element interactivity*. The suggestion is that the interaction between each step is essential to understanding the equation. Material with high element interactivity requires a higher resource or "load" of cognition. Sweller and Chandler note that "complexes of elements that are irreducibly large because they consist of many connecting elements may tax our limited processing capacity and so impose a heavy cognitive load" (p. 189).

The implementation of specific instructional strategies designed to engage the learner in three basic kinds of cognitive processes: selecting, organizing, and integrating and to attend to schema acquisition can positively affect learning. Additionally, there are differing conclusions in the literature regarding the best application of these strategies for the purposes of instruction. Where instruction focuses on behavioral change, as can be the case with leadership instruction, applying these theories is perhaps even more critical.

The Takeaway: Meeting Skills Checklist and Questionnaire

This study examined the degree to which selected instructional strategies can create the needed behavioral changes in business professionals to move organizations forward.

The instructional strategy examined in this study was the "takeaway"—creating a student experience outside of class that will lead to behavioral changes. The takeaway involved giving students an exercise to apply at their workplace that requires a reflection of the effectiveness of the exercise. The takeaway is designed, according to Clark (2001), to allow for schema acquisition (mental representation) as the building block of skilled performance. Further, Mayer (2001) suggests that attention must be focused on the content of learning and that materials need to be developed and presented in a way that integrate the necessary learning, allowing for schema acquisition, which is especially the case with leadership.

Specifically, the takeaway was designed to increase schema acquisition, thereby opening an individual to self-awareness and subsequent behavioral change. A premise was that behavior will not change unless the awareness of the need for change is present. A simple example is a coworker who is too loud. The coworker can be well aware of the benefits of workplaces without loud employees, without having any idea that this issue may apply to him/her. An exercise that brings self-awareness of the volume of the coworker (for example, having the employee record noise in the workplace), and then having them reflect on the experience, might lead to the self-awareness that he/she is too loud. An instructor can also guide the student to specific realizations if the instructor perceives areas of needed change. Of course, changing the volume of one's voice is easier to do than the subtler behaviors that can improve motivation at a workplace and increase an individual's leadership ability.

It is also important to look at the measurement of the effectiveness of takeaways. The variety of strengths and weaknesses of each student mandates that takeaways are more or less effective for each individual. Some people need a lot of work; some are well on their way to being effective leaders in the workplace. After the students practice the takeaway in their workplace for a week, they are asked to evaluate the effectiveness of the takeaway, both in the workplace and for themselves. It is this self-reflection part of the takeaway exercise that is designed to cause the increase in self-awareness that will lead to positive behavioral change.

The study looked at a number of different takeaways used in the leadership training course. The goal was to pick out one that was narrow, specific, and measurable. Ideally, it would be in an area that is most in need of improvement. The specific takeaway chosen was one designed to improve meeting behavior. This takeaway was chosen because every day, 83 million people attend 11.5 million meetings (Smart, 2010). Many of these meetings suffer from a variety of behaviors that make the meetings unproductive. According to Bradford D. Smart (2010), the following are the most common unproductive behaviors:

- 83 percent—Drifting off the subject
- 77 percent—Poor preparation

- 74 percent—Questionable effectiveness
- 68 percent—Lack of listening
- 62 percent—Verbosity of participants
- 60 percent—Length
- 51 percent—Lack of participation

Three standing university committees were selected, and each member was given a specific takeaway. For this study, it was a Meeting Skills Checklist that, according to Scholtes (2003), outlined five specific behaviors that can improve meetings (see Exhibit 1).

Each member was given a series of questions to reflect on in a Participant Meeting Questionnaire prior to receiving the Meeting Skills Checklist. They were asked to reflect on the strengths and weaknesses of the last meeting they attended (see Exhibit 2).

After filling out the Participant Meeting Questionnaire, each member was asked to review the Meeting Skills Checklist, and self-evaluate how much they modeled the five guidelines for effective meeting participation. The member was asked to submit both instruments anonymously.

The chairs of each committee were also asked to use a similar questionnaire and checklist to reflect on the most recent meeting they had led, answering the same questions, but about the committee members, not themselves (see Exhibits 3 and 4).

A baseline of responses from members of the committees and from the chair of each committee about the behavior of the members of the committees and the productivity of the meeting itself was established.

The final step was the Post-Meeting Questionnaire to evaluate the meetings and meeting behavior after the takeaway was reviewed. Both the members (see Exhibit 5) and the chairs (see Exhibit 6) were asked to evaluate the meeting they attended after the takeaway to see what effect, if any, occurred in the individual behavior or in the meeting productivity itself.

Productive and Unproductive Behaviors

The results of the study are detailed below. There was valuable feedback from the participants on the positive and negative meeting behaviors prior to the takeaway review. The observations about the negative outweighed the positive, and were more specific, covering more issues.

Participant feedback from the pre-meeting questionnaire is detailed in the sections below.

Responses to: *Please list 2-4 productive meeting behaviors you observed. Please do not give specific names.*

- Chair started and ended meeting on time.
- Chair sent out notes for review in advance of meeting and set expectations.
- Chair kept meeting focused on purpose.
- Participation by all was encouraged.
- Well facilitated, kept things moving, and ended on time. Reviewed tasks as related to charge to maintain focus.
- On time.
- Open discussion.
- Task-oriented.
- Some kudos are shared with faculty.
- I have learned new information that I didn't know from this meeting.
- Started on time.
- Time for Q & A.
- Had guest speaker who educated the team about another area of the university.
- Followed the agenda.
- Everyone gets a chance to talk and be heard.

Responses to: *Please list 2-4 unproductive meeting behaviors you observed. Please do not give specific names.*

- One member had minimal participation.
- Occasionally going off topic, but generally this is roped in pretty quickly.
- There are some negative comments and/or snark from some committee members, but it is not endorsed by the committee at large.
- A few members rarely participate, which denies the group their perspectives.
- Stay focused on agenda items.
- Do not encourage off-task conversations, as it wastes time.

- Schedule one time-efficient meeting per month.
- This meeting could be meaningful and informative.
- Did not end on time.
- People talking with one another while the main speaker was presenting.
- Discuss issues/technologies that we know we don't want but feel we have to give everything its proper amount of time.
- Let people talk too much.
- Talk topics to death.
- Let people talk off topic.
- Chair or members many times push her/his own agenda or desires.
- Many times you feel the decisions are already made but going through the motions.
- Hour and a half is too long. Attention span dwindles.
- Agenda items are not always pertinent to all members or members don't have the knowledge to make judgments.
- Should bring in folks who have the knowledge or who it affects.

The chairs of the meetings also noted a number of positive actions along with some significant concerns with general meeting protocols and member behavior. Those concerns are detailed in the sections below.

Responses to: *Please list 2-4 productive meeting behaviors you observed*

- Agenda was posted.
- Personal greetings to all before start.
- Several attendees asked probing questions.
- Redirecting "bird walks" back to the agenda.
- Asking questions to seek understanding.
- Seeking agreements on work.
- Committee members asked questions about the information that was shared to gain clarification.
- Committee members contributed concerns they had about specific projects to ensure their feedback is considered and included in the final solution.
- Committee members contributed ideas and shared in the work necessary to develop a student communication on the coming e-mail migration.

Responses to: *Please list 2-4 unproductive meeting behaviors you observed.*

- Many phone attendees did not give indicators that they were listening or attending to the topic.
- Leader did not specifically ask individual phone attendees for input.
- Some attendees did not have Collaborate running, so couldn't see PowerPoint or other docs.
- Side conversations.
- Multitasking not related to meeting (electronic).
- Committee member ranted about lack of coordination for content management across the university without providing any recommendation on how the committee could contribute to a positive solution.
- Committee member admitted to full knowledge of the content management issue, to attempting to recommend a solution in their first one to two years on the job, then giving up any further attempts despite understanding the negative impact on CityU.
- Committee members sometimes uncertain as to how to proceed with improvements to student-facing systems that are managed outside their departments.

Conclusion

The literature is clear in its suggestion that learners process information differently. As a result, instructional designers and trainers of leadership must reconsider their instructional strategies and employ those strategies that reduce or eliminate the need for learners to use cognitive resources and therefore limit their ability to attend to schema acquisition. Where instruction focuses on behavioral change, as is typically the case with leadership curriculum, creating a takeaway that applies learning theory is perhaps even more critical.

The issue of the power of suggestion was also revealed in the study. The meeting chairs perceived meetings improved, even though the participants did not. This might be a useful direction for further research in leadership instruction.

Exhibit 1

Meeting Skills Checklist
Takeaway Study

Instructions: Think about your last meeting and reflect upon your meeting behavior. Fill out the **Meeting Skills Checklist**, noting *Never, Occasionally*, or *Often* where appropriate.

Behavior	Never	Occasionally	Often
1. I suggest new ideas, activities, problems, or courses of action.			
2. I initiate attempts to redefine goals, problems, or outcomes when things become hazy or confusing.			
3. I ask others for information and/ or opinions.			
4. I relate my comments to previous contributions.			
5. I ask speakers to explain the reasoning that led them to particular conclusions.			

Exhibit 2

Participant Meeting Questionnaire

Committee Name: _____
Date: _____

Participants: Thank you for your willingness to participate in this improvement effort. We are looking at ways to improve meeting effectiveness, and the chair was kind enough to let us try it out on this committee. Please review the questions below and respond accordingly. Drop your questionnaire and checklist by **March 4**. Thank you.

All responses will be confidential and any identifying characteristics will be removed.

1. Consider your last meeting in February.

    - Please list 2–4 productive meeting behaviors you observed. Please do not give specific names.
    - Please list 2–4 unproductive meeting behaviors you observed. Please do not give specific names.

2. Now, review the attached Meeting Skills Checklist.
3. Think about your last meeting and reflect upon your meeting behavior. Fill out the Meeting Skills Checklist, noting *Never*, *Occasionally*, or *Often* where appropriate.
4. Submit the Checklist and Questionnaire.
5. There will be another brief activity after the March meeting.

Exhibit 3

Meeting Skills Checklist—Chairperson
Meeting Study.

Instructions: Think about your last meeting and reflect on the meeting. Fill out the Meeting Skills Checklist, noting *Never, Occasionally,* or *Often* where appropriate.

Behavior	Never	Occasionally	Often
1. Participants suggested new ideas, activities, problems, or courses of action.			
2. Participants initiated attempts to redefine goals, problems, or outcomes when things become hazy or confusing.			
3. Participants asked others for information and/or opinions.			
4. Participants related their comments to previous contributions.			
5. Participants asked others to explain the reasoning that led them to particular conclusions.			

Exhibit 4

Chairperson Questionnaire

Committee Name: _____
Date: _____

    Chairperson: Thank you for your willingness to participate in this improvement effort. We are looking at ways to improve meeting effectiveness. Please review the questions below and respond accordingly. Submit your answers by **March 4.** Thank you.

> All responses will be confidential and any identifying characteristics will be removed.

1. Consider your last meeting.
   - Please list 2–4 productive meeting behaviors you observed.
   - Please list 2–4 unproductive meeting behaviors you observed.
2. Now, review the Meeting Skills Checklist—Chairperson.
3. Think about your last meeting and reflect upon the meeting behavior. Fill out the Meeting Skills Checklist, noting *Never, Occasionally*, or *Often* where appropriate.

Exhibit 5

Post-Meeting Questionnaire

Committee Name: _____
Date: _____

Participants: Thank you for your willingness to continue participating in this improvement effort. Please review the questions below and respond accordingly. Drop this questionnaire by **March 15.** Thank you.

All responses will be confidential and any identifying characteristics will be removed.

After your most meeting, please reflect on the following questions:
On a scale of 1–4, did your behavior in the meeting change having reviewed the Meeting Skills Checklist? (please circle the number that best reflects your view)

1	2	3	4
My behavior did not change at all.	I noticed a slight change in my behavior.	I adopted some of the behaviors listed in the checklist.	I adopted most or all the behaviors listed in the checklist.

a. If your behavior changed, how did it change?
b. On a scale of 1–4, did the meeting as a whole seem to be more productive?

1	2	3	4
The meeting did not change at all.	I noticed a slight change the productivity of the meeting.	The meeting was noticeably more productive.	Most productive meeting ever.

    a.   If you noticed any changes, please describe below:

Exhibit 6

Post-Meeting Questionnaire—Chairs

Committee Name: _____
Chair: _____

Participants: Thank you for your willingness to continue participating in this improvement effort. Please review the questions below and respond accordingly. Drop this questionnaire by **March 15**. Thank you.

All responses will be confidential and any identifying characteristics will be removed.

After your most recent meeting, please reflect on the following question:

a. On a scale of 1–4, did the meeting as a whole seem to be more productive?

1	2	3	4
The meeting did not change at all.	I noticed a slight change the productivity of the meeting.	The meeting was noticeably more productive.	Most productive meeting ever.

b. If you noticed any changes, please describe below:

References

Anderson, R. C. (1973). Learning principles from text. *Journal of Educational Psychology, 64* (1), 26–30.

Clark, R. E. (Ed.). (2001). *Learning from media: Arguments, analysis, and evidence.* Greenwich, CT: Information Age Publishing.

Clark, J. M., Paivio, A. (1991). Dual coding theory and education. *Educational Psychology Review, 3*(3), 149–210.

Mayer, R. E. (1996). Learning strategies for making sense out of expository text: The SOI model for guiding three cognitive processes in knowledge construction. *Educational Psychology Review, 8,* 357–371.

Mayer, R. E. (1997). Multimedia learning: Are we asking the right questions? *Educational Psychologist, 32,* 1–19.

Mayer, R. E. (2001). *Multimedia learning.* Cambridge, UK: Cambridge University Press.

Mayer, R. E., Sims, V. K. (1994). For whom is a picture worth a thousand words? Extensions of dual-coding theory of multimedia learning. *Journal of Educational Psychology, 86*(3), 389–401.

Paivio, A. (1986). *Mental representations: A dual coding approach.* Oxford, England: Oxford University Press.

Paivio, A. (1991). Dual coding theory: Retrospect and current status. *Canadian Journal of Psychology Outstanding Contributions Series, 45*(3), 255–287.

Sadoski, M., Paivio, A. (2001). *Imagery and text: A dual coding theory of reading and writing.* Mahwah, NJ: Lawrence Erlbaum Associates, Publishers.

Scholtes, B. (2003). *The team handbook* (3rd ed.). Madison, WI: Joiner and Associates.

Smart, B. (1974). *Achieving effective meetings—not easy but possible* (Smart in a survey of 635 executives.) American Society for Training and Development.

Sweller, J., Chandler, P., Tierney, P. & Cooper, M. (1990). Cognitive load as a factor in the structuring of technical material. *Journal of Experimental Psychology, 119*(2), 176–192.

Sweller, J., Chandler, P. (1991). Evidence for cognitive load theory. *Cognition and Instruction, 8*(4), 351–362.

Sweller, J., Chandler, P. (1994). Why some material is difficult to learn. *Cognition and instruction, 12*(3), 185–233.

Considering the Learning Theory Enactivism to Explore the Development of Socially Conscious Leaders

Susan R. Seymour, PhD
Director, Office of Institutional Effectiveness

Abstract

We live in challenging times and are faced with economic, ecological, political, and social strife that threatens to overwhelm individuals and turn them toward apathy or selfish individualism. Since resolution of social problems relies on strong leadership grounded in social awareness, educators who teach future leaders must ask themselves if their curriculum and the focus of their pedagogy fosters growth of social consciousness in their students. This research explores learning related to the development of leaders' social consciousness and interrogates how they come to care about social justice causes and why they commit to certain causes but not others. This learning is considered through the lens of enactivism, a biologically based learning theory; pedagogical implications and strategies for the development of social consciousness are considered.

Description

A disposition toward social justice is often a strong focus in educator training programs (Spalding, Klecka, Lin, Odell, & Wang, 2010). Mills and Ballantyne (2010) determined the critical factors necessary for teachers to embrace a social justice orientation, while others investigated ways in which educators can be taught to enact a social justice disposition in their teaching practices (Agarwal, Epstein, Oppenheim, Oyler, & Sonu, 2010; Chubbuck, 2010). While this literature is helpful in considering how to promote social justice dispositions in educators, it does little to inform an understanding of how social justice orientations grow "organically" or whether social justice orientations "stick" when faced with real-world difficulties and applications. In other words, we do not know enough about social consciousness to know how it is learned, if it can be taught, if it is stable over a lifetime, and what factors and life events shape its unique expression.

While social consciousness can have many definitions (Ammenthorp, 2007; Berman, 1997; Giddings, 2005; Schlitz, Vieten, and Miller, 2010), for this research it was defined as an evolving understanding of others' perspectives and realities, an awareness of how personal actions may affect others, and an increasing sense of agency toward promoting equity and responsibility. This definition roots social consciousness in both knowledge and action. It implies that it is not enough to know that inequity exists—one must act on this knowledge. The participants in this research were female nonprofit leaders who have committed their lives to social action; life history methodologies were used to explore learning related to the development of their social consciousness.

The Learning Theory Enactivism

Learning theories such as behaviorism, constructivism, and social constructionism represent learning through psychological or sociological constructs that explain human responses related to the acquisition, application, or reproduction of knowledge (Ernest, 2010). This consideration of learning says nothing about how our lived experience, the embodied nature of knowing, shapes what we know or how we can come to know. Thus, when Varela and his colleagues introduced enactivism to the field in 1991, the biologically based theory provided an alternative view into how learners make sense of their world and are shaped by their interactions within it. In the purist sense, enactivism is a theory of human interaction and evolution.

Enactivism is a theory of learning in which embodiment is seen as the fundamental axis of knowledge, cognition, and experience. This means that the learner is not a blank slate capable of learning, interpreting, and representing objective realities. Rather, the learner is shaped by the multitude of lived experiences from her history—she does not see the world as it is, she sees the world as she is, or rather as she has become. Consequently, this embodied understanding has the potential to shape, enable, or limit her learning.

Enactivism offers unique learning insight because it considers the internal structures, or worldview, of an individual and how these structures interact and evolve within the learner's environment. Worldviews are each individual's understanding of the nature of reality through her genetic tendencies, culture, geography, experiences, attitudes, values, and relationship to her environment. By considering how these internal structures (worldviews) interact and evolve within an environment, we move beyond mere psychological understandings of learning to contextualized psychological understandings. Adaptive systems, such as human beings, can change their structures in response to internal or external pressures or stimulus, and because adaptive systems embody their history in their structure, they are seen as evolving (Davis, 2004). "Structure in this sense is both caused and accidental, both familiar and unique, both complete and in process" (Davis & Sumara, 2006, p. 13). However, it is *not* the environmental stimulus that creates changes to the structure. Rather, it is the nature of the structure that determines the changes that happen, or if change happens at all. As Proulx (2004) stated, "You get triggered by what you CAN get triggered by" (p. 115). In other words, the environment is not the place were decisions arise, but it is through an individual's interaction with an environment that her "internal dynamics can recognize potential triggers in it and get triggered by them. Learning is not determined by the environment, but it depends on it" (Proulx, 2004, p. 117).

Within an enactivist framework, cognition depends on experiences that come from having a body with various sensorimotor capacities that are embedded in biological, psychological, and cultural environments. This embedment is multidirectional in that learners adapt and learn from their environment as their environment "learns" from them. This phenomenon is called "coemergence" (Varela, Thompson, & Rosch, 1991) and represents a "structural coupling" between the learner and the environment, which enacts change in both. Structural coupling is defined as the engagement of two or more systems, such as a human being, a culture, or a specific environment that provides certain levels of mutual cohesion and development potential (Maturana & Varela, 1987). As long as the interaction between a system and the environmental medium remain viable (non-threatening to system's identity), they are said to be structurally coupled and they coemerge. It is important to understand that coemergence does not mean that the system (individual) and the environmental medium (for example, classroom) are becoming more fully adapted to each other. All that is asserted is that their structures allow them to interact and *affect* each other.

Structural coupling represents a domain of possible interactions in which a learner can enter into, but this domain is "specified, and potentially limited, by its own organization, identity, understanding and history" (Baerveldt & Verheggen, 1999, p. 196). Furthermore, it is important to recognize that while the structural coupling between learner and environment is mutual, the learner specifies the structural changes and signifies which elements from the environment constitute acts of cognition. As Proulx (2008) noted, "the environment acts 'as a trigger' for the species to evolve—as much as species act as 'triggers' for the environment to evolve" (p. 16). Davis and Sumara (1997) describe coemergence through the analogy of a conversation. Although individuals may enter a conversation with a set viewpoint about what will be discussed, those involved respond to the conversation while simultaneously shaping it. We shape the conversation and the conversation shapes us, just as learners are shaped by the learning environment and, in turn, the learning environment is shaped by the learners.

Enactivism claims that the internal organization of a structure precludes understanding. Therefore, the ability or inability of a system to respond to, or be triggered by, an environment is shaped by the system's organization (identity) and represents the limits of what action an entity can take in its environment and what it can come to know (Maturana & Varela, 1987). *Thus, it is not the environment that determines learning, but the internal structure of the individual.* Learning happens when there is *structural coupling* between the biological and experiential structures because something from the environment "triggered" something in the individual, and her structural organization "allowed" this trigger (Davis et al., 2008; Maturana & Varela, 1987).

This interactivity with environment, or coemergence, is unique because it moves beyond a consideration of present-day interactions with one's environment, to a consideration of how evolution within multiple environments (i.e., history) shapes the present. In other words, the evolution of the human species is grounded in its historical interaction with its environment, just as each learner's evolution is grounded in a history of interactions with her lived environments. Proulx (2008) asserted that one's history either enables or limits interactions with environment, and articulates this dynamic when he writes, "I—my structure—allow the physical world to be brought forth. If these attributes of the physical world are outside my structure, outside of my capacity to make sense of them, I cannot distinguish them and cannot perceive them. In other words, they cannot 'trigger' anything in me" (p. 21). This quote offers some insight into the learning process and why some individuals commit to social action and others do not. Because individuals coemerge within their environment, they are both shaped by this environment and shape and direct it in return.

Significant Life Events and Circumstances

This research studied the lives of socially conscious leaders in order to gain a deeper understanding of how their learning processes influenced the development of their social consciousness. In other words, how do people come to enact caring about social justice causes and why do they enact caring about certain causes but not others?

The life history narratives of leaders interviewed indicated major life events in childhood created structural organization (identity) that influenced the way they enacted their social consciousness (Maturana & Varela, 1987; Varela et al., 1991). For one leader, these structures were hard work, frugality, and altruistic suffering. For another, the structures were based on mental illness, abandonment, and a desire for authentic self-expression. Additional structures included social mobility, responsibility to others, and the desire for personal connections.

What is interesting about all of the organizing structures is the degree to which they emerged in early childhood, had little or nothing to do with social justice per se, remained constant throughout life, and shaped the participant's interaction to social justice causes. In other words, it doesn't seem to matter what an individual's internal organizing structure is, as long as it provides a viable opportunity to structurally couple to social justice impulses. Thus, structures unrelated to social consciousness, such as frugality, a need for attention, responsibility, or a desire for socialization, can all provide viable structures that might couple with social justice endeavors, but do not represent typical perceptions of social justice motivation. Structures act as enabling factors through which motivations can be enacted.

A theme affecting the development of identity structures related to social consciousness was family or subconscious influences occurring in childhood but subverted during adolescence and early adulthood. For example, two leaders referenced dramatic pictures they saw in childhood that influenced them:

> From my earliest memory as a child, I wanted to go to Africa and plant corn. I think maybe I saw Save the Children or something on TV—kids starving, Ethiopia . . . drought, whatever. I don't know and that's just always stayed with me.

> I think that image in *Life* magazine—the news story when they were spitting on little [black] girls—that just really got in my mind.

Another leader recognized a social consciousness that was introduced in her family of origin, but had remained "dormant for many, many years." Finally, a fourth leader acknowledged the influence of her mother who was "very socially conscious" and "carried the guilt of the Southern whites." From these statements and from the structures created in childhood, it appears the forces that influence social consciousness are both deliberate and random, and that the leaders in this study were shaped by media images and by their parents' politics. However, they seemed to be most powerfully and permanently shaped by the lived experiences and personal identities that required them to structurally couple to environments that enabled them to enact their social consciousness in uniquely personal ways.

All the leaders interviewed for this study felt they should make a difference in the world, but this compulsion went beyond mere wishful thinking to action. For each woman, the opportunities that enabled this action were specific to the structural organization of her social consciousness that was shaped in childhood but enacted in adulthood through opportunities presented in viable environments. When an environment "triggered" (Proulx, 2004, 2008) an opportunity for one of the participants to express her social consciousness, then both the leader and the environment coemerged in a dynamic whole (Davis & Sumara, 1997; Sumara & Davis, 1997). The enactment of social consciousness is not only specific to the social causes with which a leader identifies but also the specific skills and knowledge she brings to the environment, as well as the opportunities the environment provides. Put differently and in enactivist terms, the boundary of a system is specified by its operations (Baerveldt & Verheggen, 1999).

Value

How is social consciousness learned? This question and its answer extend far beyond this chapter, but it appears the foundations of social consciousness are laid in childhood through the everyday interactions of media, family politics, relationships, trauma, and opportunity. By coupling unique internal structures (worldviews) to environmental opportunities, social consciousness is learned through embodied experiences and co-emerged explorations of interests, needs, talents, fears, curiosities, beliefs, and other personal expressions. This coupling advances an individual's ability to explore her or his own identity within a complex environment of self, other, and opportunity. Even though structural dynamics related to social consciousness emerged in childhood and remained relatively stable over time, social consciousness becomes enacted in increasingly complex ways as the underlying structural dynamics that shape its enaction co-emerge with opportunity in environments. In this way, learning related to social consciousness is "occasioned" (Davis et al., 1996) rather than caused.

If learning is occasioned rather than caused, how should we envision educational environments designed to promote social justice orientations? The first step requires an understanding of complex systems, where complex systems have three characteristics (Sumara & Davis, 1997). First of all, complex systems are adaptive and have the capacity to evolve within changing environments. Secondly, they have the capacity to self-organize and in the process of self-organization, become more than themselves. In other words, a complex system is more than the sum of its parts. Thirdly, complex systems cannot be understood by analyzing the component parts the way in which a complicated system can be understood. A computer is complicated and can be understood by analyzing its individual pieces and parts and their relationships to each other. A plant is complex and can only be understood by considering its relationship to its environment.

Increasingly educational environments are viewed as complicated, which results in efforts to break teaching and learning down to component parts in order to teach and measure learning associated with each part. Once educational environments are conceptualized as complex rather than merely complicated (Davis & Sumara, 1997; Davis et al., 2000; Sumara & Davis, 1997), an understanding of how or if challenging concepts (such as social consciousness) can be taught begins to emerge. Davis and Sumara questioned the belief that learning can be predetermined and caused by linear practices such as teaching to a concept and offer instead "an interpretation of human activity as relational, codetermined, and existing in a complex web of events" (p. 112). For them, learning should not be based on a linear dynamic of cause and effect, objective and outcome, but rather should be understood to occur in nonlinear relationships between collectives and individuals, truths and emergent possibilities. As they state, "Trying to establish a causal relationship between one event and another, or between a teaching action and a learning outcome confuses essential participation with monologic authority" (Sumara & Davis, 1997, p. 412). Similarly, enactivists conceptualize learning in three states:

First that knowledge unfolds in systems, whereby cognition co-emerges with environment, individuals and activity. Second, that understanding is embedded in the conduct and relationships among systems and subsystems, rather than the minds of individual actors. Third, that learning is continuous invention and explorations linked to disequilibrium in systems and amplified with feedback loops. (Fenwick, 2001, p. 251)

These states recognize learners as more than *situated* within particular contexts and render problematic educational theories and practices that are inattentive to the evolving relationships between learner and environment. In complex systems, the learner and environment are intertwined in a mutually specifying relationship where one affects the other. As the learner learns, the context changes, simply because one of its components has changed and as the context changes, so does the learner. Thus, learning and teaching cannot be understood monologically, "there is no direct causal, linear, fixable relationship among various components of any community of practice" (Sumara & Davis, 1997, p. 414).

If complexity theory and enactivist frameworks render causal teaching relationships problematic, what are educators who are committed to fairness and social justice supposed to do? First and foremost, educators must be reflective of their own social justice orientations and motivations to educate for the development of social consciousness. Fenwick (2000) critiqued "impositional educators who presume to determine what comprises false consciousness and then undertake to replace it." She claims this primarily occurs due to a lack of self-reflexivity as shown in an unwillingness to explore "their own intrusions and repressions and [acknowledge] their own inscription by dominant discourses and their own will to power" (p. 260). Buttressed by this postmodern critique and armed with her own strong commitments to social justice causes, Tara Fenwick proposed a model for teaching social justice that is informed by her research in complexity thinking and enactivist frameworks. This model rejects a "hero-rescuer motif . . . [and] grand utopias of social responsibility for adult education" (2003, p. 134) in favor of teaching environments based on three conditions necessary for complex, coadaptive systems to flourish. These conditions are the induction of coemergence, listening, and playing the role of disturber.

Fenwick indicates an effective role for educators is to induce coemergence by influencing classroom conditions that may make it possible for students to acknowledge or exercise their social consciousness. Specific practices aimed at influencing coemergence are occasioning social justice interactions, decentralizing control and liberating constraints. As Fenwick explains, inducing coemergence "involves open-ended design but not control: making spaces, removing barriers, introducing and amplifying disturbances" (2003, p. 136).

Listening is the mechanism by which educators decentralize power, gain awareness of their students' social justice orientations, and recognize when coemergence between student and environment is occurring. When coemergence occurs, educators need to create "space" for the experience to emerge without the need to reshape, redefine, or emancipate it. As Fenwick notes, "Too often, educators might be suspected of approaching others with an anthropologist's gaze—with external 'expert' knowledge attempting to penetrate and represent the internal knowledge of a community to which they do not belong" (2003, p. 136). Instead, educators are encouraged to bear witness to enfolding stories, dynamics and relationships, and help interpret diverse individuals' experiences to one another, enabling each participant's stories and understandings to mutually specify awareness, action, and shifts in identity.

Finally, Fenwick suggested that systems must be subject to disturbances if they are to evolve. Educators committed to promoting systems that are more just and equitable are well positioned to construct "deviances that generate a system's disequilibrium" (2003, p. 137). In this context it is understood that the development of social consciousness cannot happen without challenging the status quo, and it is the educator's responsibility to do so. In making such a statement, Fenwick cautions against anarchy, but rather encourages a view of social justice education that can "help reclaim and re-embody the signifier of experiential learning, to restore its poetry and its complex entanglement in expanding spaces that resist fragmentation and control" (2003, p. 137).

This model for promoting social justice education in the classroom is worth considering, but it is important to recognize that this is not a cause-and-effect teaching/learning model. As such, it is worth noting that social consciousness is probably something educators cannot teach but can influence through exposure to social issues and questions of justice. Thus, an enactivist view of social justice education recognizes social consciousness is not caused by, but may be occasioned in, learning material that triggers reactions within students and enables their identities to couple and coemerge within the learning environment.

Summary

For educational programs aimed at developing socially conscious leaders, this approach holds several implications. Leadership programs should develop flexible curriculum and assessments that enable students to enact their social consciousness in a way that is most meaningful to them. One student may react and connect to the fair and ethical treatment of immigrants, whereas another student may feel ethical business practices hold the most hope for creating social change. There cannot be a one-size-fits-all approach to the expression of social consciousness and leadership educators should create space for a plurality of student engagement options. Engagement options can include, but should not be limited to, case studies, service learning, research papers, and the design and development of capstone projects aimed at solving social problems.

In addition to curriculum and assessments that enable diverse leadership learning projects, learning environments can and should contain mechanisms that help enact social consciousness. These mechanisms include modeling fair and just behaviors in classrooms and creating space for coemergent explorations of what it means to be socially just. These educational practices are in alignment with Fenwick's (2003) model for social justice education, which suggests listening, playing the role of disturber, and inducing coemergent opportunities for learning. Aside from utilizing these pedagogical practices, educators must divorce themselves from the expectation of actually creating socially conscious learners, or at the very least opening their minds to what social consciousness looks like in a variety of learners. As this research suggests, each human being enacts her social consciousness in a way she is structurally able to at any given time. Therefore, educators must provide a wide variety of opportunities for learners to couple their identity structures to social justice causes, but beyond that they must trust that future leaders will enact and develop their social consciousness through their own lived experiences.

References

Agarwal, R., Epstein, S., Oppenheim, R., Oyler, S., & Sonu, D. (2010). From ideal to practice and back again: Beginning teachers teaching for social change. *Journal of Teacher Education, 61*, 237–247.

Ammentorp, L. (2007). Imagining social change: Developing social consciousness in an arts-based pedagogy. *Critical Social Studies, 1*, 38–52.

Baerveldt, C., & Verheggen, T. (1999). Enactivism and the experiential reality of culture: Rethinking the epistemological basis of cultural psychology. *Culture & Psychology, 5*, 183–206.

Berman, S. (1997). *Children's social consciousness and the development of social responsibility*. Albany, NY: State University of New York Press.

Chubbuck, S. (2010). Individual and structural orientations in socially just teaching: Conceptualization, implementation, and collaborative effort. *Journal of Teacher Education, 61*, 197–210.

Davis, B. (2004). *Inventions of teaching: A genealogy*. Mahwah, NJ: Erlbaum.

Davis, B., & Sumara, D. (1997). Cognition, complexity and teacher education. *Harvard Educational Review, 67*, 105–125.

Davis, B., & Sumara, D. (2006). *Complexity and education: Inquiries into learning, teaching and research*. Mahwah, NJ: Erlbaum.

Davis, B., Sumara, D., & Luce-Kapler, R. (2008). *Engaging minds: Changing teaching in complex times*. New York, NY: Taylor & Francis.

Davis, D., & Butler-Kisber, L. (1999, April). *Arts-based representation in qualitative research: Collage as a contextualizing analytic strategy* (paper presented at the American Educators Research Association annual meeting). Montreal, Quebec, Canada.

Ernest, P. (2010). Reflections on theories of learning. In B. Sriraman & L. English (Eds.), *Theories of mathematics education* (pp. 39–47). Heidelberg, Germany: Springer-Verlag.

Fenwick, T. (2000). Expanding conceptions of experiential learning: A review of the five contemporary perspectives on cognition. *Adult Education Quarterly, 50*, 243–272.

Fenwick, T. (2001). Work knowing "on the fly": Enterprise cultures and co-emergent epistemology. *Studies in Continuing Education, 23*, 243–259.

Fenwick, T. (2003). Reclaiming and re-embodying experiential learning through complexity science. *Studies in the Education of Adults, 35*, 123–141.

Giddings, L. S. (2005). A theoretical model of social consciousness. *Advances in Nursing Science, 28*, 224–239.

Maturana, H., & Varela, F. (1987). *The tree of knowledge: The biological roots of human understanding*. Boston, MA: Shambhala.

Mills, C., & Ballantyne, J. (2010). Pre-service teacher's dispositions towards diversity: Arguing for a developmental hierarchy of change. *Teaching & Teacher Education, 26*, 447–454.

Proulx, J. (2004, September). *The enactivist theory of cognitive and behaviorism: An account of the processes of individual sense-making* (paper presented at the American Educators Research Association annual meeting). Montreal, Quebec, Canada.

Proulx, J. (2008). Some differences between Maturana and Varela's theory of cognition. *Complicity: An International Journal of Complexity and Education, 5*(1), 11–26.

Schlitz, M., Vieten, C., & Amorok, T. (2008). *Living deeply: The art and science of transformation*. Berkeley, CA: New Harbinger.

Schlitz, M., Vieten, C., & Miller, E. (2010). Worldview transformation and the development of social consciousness. *Journal of Consciousness Studies, 17*, 18–36.

Spalding, E., Klecka, C., Lin, E., Odell, S., & Wang, J. (2010). Social justice and teacher education: A hammer, a bell, and a song. *Journal of Teacher Education, 61*, 191–196.

Sumara, D., & Davis, B. (1997). Enactivist theory and community learning: Toward a complexified understanding of action research. *Educational Action Research, 5*, 403–422.

Varela, F., Thompson, E., & Rosch, E. (1991). *The embodied mind: Cognitive science and human experience.* Cambridge, MA: The MIT Press.

Leadership—New Adaptive Methods

Lenka Rábeková
VSM, School of Management, Bratislava, Slovakia

Abstract

This paper is focused on the meaning of the competitive advantage, utilizing leadership, knowledge, and the importance of creativity. At present, creativity is becoming the most important instrument of successful leaders, whereas knowledge is a fundamental economic source and production instrument. Therefore, the people who dispose of knowledge that can be deepened and shared are the crucial leaders for every enterprise. Education (learning) is one of the ways to acquire a competitive advantage, but under one basic condition: one must be quicker to learn and educate faster than competitors. The need for education with minimum time investment and maximum knowledge utilization is derived directly from the practice.

The fact that the leaders are inwardly motivated to learn presents a competitive advantage for an organization. It is possible to naturally increase the motivation in teaching made to measure, since the theory and practice are directly interconnected. To become the creator of curriculum, a developer needs to learn the tools for adaptive methods to analyze the knowledge needs of a particular student using mind maps and analyzing mental processes (by neurolinguistic programming).

Introduction

What gives a competitive advantage? Knowledge is one of the crucial competitive advantages. The people who dispose of knowledge that can be deepened and shared offer an important competitive advantage for every organization.

In gaining knowledge, it is very important to explain the whole content of the term *knowledge*, where, from the point of knowledge management, knowledge is divided into explicit and tacit. Explicit knowledge is structured and can be easily expressed in words or symbols. Its communication and sharing in formal language is also easy, as well as its capture and representation in documents, databases, or information systems. Tacit knowledge can be characterized by the words of the philosopher M. Polanyi (1966): "We know more than we can express." The ability to come up with new ideas, creative solutions of problems, or the ability to ask the right questions belongs among the tacit knowledge.

Creative Leadership, Creative Organizations

Future leaders need to be innovators and pioneers, all in one. They will need to adopt an attitude toward such concepts as think big, inspire innovation, support sharing, take the adventure, develop creativity, challenge status quo, create together, and make positive change. The difference between traditional leadership and innovative leadership is in the creativity.

Traditional leadership can be characterized as concerned with being right, following the manual, loves to avoid mistakes, and open to limited feedback. In contrast, creative leadership can be characterized as interactive, concerned with being real, improvises when appropriate, loves to learn from mistakes, hopes to be right, and open to unlimited critique.

One of the objectives of knowledge management is to support education and performance in an organization. An organization is a place where people improve their abilities to achieve required results, where people continuously learn how to learn with others, where people realize how they can participate in the creation of reality and how they can change it. This type of organization is called a learning organization. From an organization defined in such a manner, an organization can be considered as an ideal, target, desired, or dreamed organization. In such organizations people are brought to the fore. The main aim is to create an inspiring working environment where the central key is progress; success is the creativity and uniqueness of every person. Such organization creates strong creativity culture and in its daily practice (e.g., at business meetings, company meetings), it uses the methods of thinking such as mind mapping and neurolinguistic programming. It stimulates its employees by teaching them how to learn effectively by a correctly selected style of education.

Tools for the Adaptive Methods of Education

An old Chinese proverb says: "Give a man a fish and you feed him for a day. Teach a man to fish and you feed him for a lifetime." To prepare future leaders, their ability to learn on their own must be enhanced. Students can use the tools such as mind maps and neurolinguistic programming during study, as well as during performance of work studies."

What are mind maps? Mind maps are an excellent organizational instrument of our brain. They represent a creative and effective way of taking notes in our mind, which is word for word "mapping" of our reflections. They act as a simple tool for penetrating the information into or from our brain, allowing us to see a global view of a subject or field. Further, mind maps enable a plan of educational progress, i.e., we know where we are and where we would like to be.

The goal of mind mapping is for a student, a future leader, to learn to plan time better by mental mapping (as, for example, time spent on education), improve organizational abilities, develop the ability to communicate, be more creative, be able to collect himself, remember more information, and learn more effectively.

What is neurolinguistic programming (NLP)? This technique provides practical knowledge and practices of self-improvement. NLP techniques can maximize human potential and provide a complex of knowledge, skills, and habits, under which an individual is responding to inner and outer impulses of the environment, in which she lives. NLP teaches one the recognition of responses to reality, segregation of out-of-date and inefficient reactions from the new ones. The efficient reactions are helpful in performing the expected results. It thus fosters the possibility for personality change. NLP facilitates analyzing the successful models (of people): "learning by success of the best" (models of people who have learned and mastered some knowledge in a fast and thorough manner, elaborating their ways and forms of education).

The goal of neurolinguistic programming: a student can obtain valuable knowledge by analyzing mental processes and then modifying them into a higher level of activity that can be used in the most effective way in several areas, including education. Under the title of the workshop "Effective Negotiation Skills," participants were exposed to using mind maps. Instead of giving students direct tips on how to negotiate effectively, the first step is to draw their own mind map about themselves. Using NLP programming, real situations were created, analyzing the successful models of real people, excellent negotiators. Participants were asked to analyze their knowledge and find the pattern and imitate it. Using tacit knowledge–oriented coaching, participants were instructed to create their own questions and their own answers without evaluating them. The following step process is used in creating a mind map and neurolinguistic programming.

There is a procedure for how to create a mind map. A series of questions are internally asked, for example:

- Who? (boss, colleague, supplier, children, partner)
- What? (work position, money, time, price and amount of goods, free time, cooking)
- Where? (office, meeting room, corridor, coffee machine, desk, home, shop)
- Why? (I do not agree, I need to persuade others about my point of view)

- How? (clear arguments, calm tone of voice, shouting, persuading by giving examples, pointing at mistakes of counter party, pointing at good points of counter party, listening more, expressing my point of view more)
- When? (morning, afternoon, evening, Mondays–Wednesdays, weekends)

Then a series of additional questions are asked about the topic, for example, negotiation:

- If I want to influence something, first I need to know some details about it.
- If I want to influence my negotiating skills, first I need to know about me.

Think and then answer the following questions:

- Do I like negotiating?
- How does it affect my life?
- What is my usual position when negotiating?
- What are my characteristics—what kind of negotiator am I?
- What are my feelings when negotiating?

Above-mentioned practices lead individuals to draw their own mind map. They could see what their real position was in relation to negotiation. Afterward there is a possibility to build on this information and extend the knowledge.

Procedure: How to Use NLP Programming

Step 1. NLP is teaching and training how to reach the following:

- If you want to be successful in negotiation, what do you need?

Students are asked this question, and with the guidance of the lecturer answer the following:

- GOAL: we need to know what we want; we need to have clear imagination of the result in every situation.
- PERCEPTION: we need to be attentive to what we gain.
- ELASTICITY: we need to be elastic, flexible because we need to change our behavior until we gain a successful result.

Step 2. Analyzing the principles of NLP:

The map of the world. Every person has his or her own imagination of the world, i.e., the map of the world. We expect that the other people have the same map of the world, but every map is singular. If we do not want to get lost in the maze of communication with other people, we need to know our map deeply and learn how to use it correctly.

- Another series of activities help focus students on the creative use of mind maps: Think about your own map in connection to the work life.

The right decision. Life is directly connected to the activity. Plans and dreams come true when there is an actor who creates them. Just as realization can examine the factuality of our plans and the power of dreams, it uncovers our real abilities. The future is happening in this moment; there is only the need to make a first step.

- Task for students: Think of the plan or dream in your mind and then think of the first step that is needed in order to realize it (exactly and clearly).

The same step means the same result. People do the same things again and again even though these things might not work. When something does not work, try something new! The change is the answer.

- Task for students: Think about the situation in negotiation at work when you use the same strategy of negotiation, but it does not work properly. What can you change? What can you make different?

Communication. People communicate verbally and nonverbally. More than 90 percent of communication is nonverbal. Have you ever experienced the situation in which you were quiet but still received a response from the other person?

- Task for students: Think of your subliminal nonverbal way of communication, try to identify it.

Positive approach. Searching for the positive approach and looking at other people from the positive point of view brings people closer to one another.

- Tasks for students: Think of why it is good to understand and feel closer to the other people, e.g., at the negotiation meeting?

Ability to influence everything. History shows that the person who was able to orient quickly and adapt to changing surroundings was the one who became a leader. The person with the most flexible thinking reaches maximum success.

- Task for students: Is flexible thinking important when negotiating? Why?

If somebody has reached something before you, you can reach it as well. From the point of neurological fundament, every human being is the same. Therefore, you can reach everything that was reached before.

- Task for students: Think about this question—Do you believe that with the right manual, you can reach anything? Do you know any successful negotiators? Why are they successful?

People can reach what they can imagine. Every individual creates an assumption to imagine what he wants to realize. When you have an idea that has not been realized yet, somebody needs to be the first. Why not you?

- Task for students: Do you know anyone in the history who thought that his/her imagination was only sci-fi? And finally, few years later somebody made this imagination come true? Can you imagine yourself as an excellent negotiator? How do you feel about it? What clothes do you wear?

The loss does not exist. The loss does not exist, because every loss is just an experience. When we connect with this experience, we gain the overall context and the result is the lesson. We have learned something new. The most difficult thing to do is to learn from our own "mistakes." The most efficient is to learn from the "success of the best."

- Task for students: Have you ever imitated another person? Is there anyone who has reached something that you would like to reach? (success at work, private life, sport and similar)

In analyzing the successful models of how people learn, by "success of the best" (models of people who have learned objective skills and knowledge in fast and thorough manner, elaborating their ways and forms of education). Listening to the real situations (real problem solving), participants could learn from observing, analyzing, and imitating practices of the best (the most successful). Coaching is a part of NLP as well. It is based on the structural talk that supports the participant's thinking, helps positive changes, and identifies inspirational goals and the ways to get them by stimulating thinking and learning. People usually know more than they think they know, e.g., in extreme situations, unknown human power can be found.

Participants work with their inner observer and learn a lot about themselves utilizing this approach. They could uncover their tacit knowledge and are able to solve difficult tasks they had in their professional life in an easier way. New tools, instruments, and knowledge about how to be successful in the future can be gained. This process is based on sustainable learning.

Summary

It is inevitable that there will be creative ways developed to better educate future leaders. The speed of gaining new and right knowledge and the ability of leaders to learn represent a competitive advantage for every organization.

Various forms of adaptive methods of education in organizations help people to learn about themselves, maximize their potential, and allow learning professionally oriented knowledge, which can be used directly in practice. Such new methods may save time and can give a competitive advantage. The competitive advantage in this field means to learn something or to gain new knowledge quicker than a competitor.

By using tools such as mind maps and NLP programming, participants can realize what kind of knowledge they need at that real moment, and/or which kind of knowledge is relevant to their present work project or task. It is also legitimately used in the education of future leaders. In this way, the lecturer is able to structure the neurolinguistic programming and offer just that information which is sufficient for students. Students are creators of the amount of the information that is given by the lecturer. The amount and quality of offered information is equal to the real needs of students. Some needs are obvious and conscious, but some are subliminal and hidden. To realize both, several tools are available for the adaptive methods of education.

Albert Einstein said: "The definition of madness is to do the same thing repeatedly and expecting different results." With the innovation of educational methods, a creative view and practical way of human potential development have become available. That is why it is necessary to research and test new methods of education (even though they may be known but only applied in other fields), because just the right mix of them can lead to improvement and progress.

References

Buzan, T. (2012). *Myšlenkové mapy: Druhé vydanie*. Brno: Albatros Media a.s.. ISBN 978-80-265-0030-8.

Durikova, K. *Aký mám učebný štýl*. (n.d.) Retrieved from http://www.gymmrssam.edupage.org/files/aky_mam_ucebny_styl.doc [cit.2014-03-15]

Durlach, P. J., & Lesgols, A. M. (2012). *Adaptive technologies for training and education*. Cambridge, UK: Cambridge University Press.

Good Morning Creativity. (n.d.) Retrieved from http://www.goodmorningcreativity.com/sk [cit. 2014-03-15]

Hvorecky, J., Kelemen, J. (Eds.) (2011). *Readings in knowledge management.* Bratislava, Slovakia: Iura Edition.

Hvorecky J., Lichardus B. (2012, May). *Rationality and irrationality in knowledge management.* International Scientific Conference & International Workshop, Present-Day Trends of Innovations, Łomża, Poland.

Kalina, P., Klinec, I. (2007). *Využívanie znalostného manažmentu k zvyšovaniu konkurencieschopnosti firiem v globálnom turbulentnom prostredí.* Retrieved from http://www.fondstodola.sk/znalostna_spolocnost. htm [cit 2013-05-01]

Katuscakova, M. (2009). *Znalostný manažment.* V Informačné technológie a knižnice. Retrieved from http://itlib.cvtisr.sk/archiv/2009/4/znalostny-manazment.html?page_id=1060 [cit. 2014-03-15]

Knight, S. (2011). *NLP v praxi.* Tretie vydanie. Praha, Czech Republic: Management Press. ISBN 978-80-7261-231-4

Nonaka, I., & Takeuchi, H. (1995). *The knowledge-creating company: How Japanese companies create the dynamics of innovation.* New York, NY: Oxford University Press.

Oravec, V. (2008). *Znalostný manažment v meniacom sa svete.* Retrieved from http://www.efocus.sk/images/archiv/file_1130_0.pdf [cit 2013-05-01]

Polanyi, M. (1966/1967). The tacit dimension, in L. Prusak (Ed.), *Knowledge in organizations.* Newton, MA: Butterworth-Heinemann, 135–146.

Senge, P. (2007). *Pátá disciplína.* Prvé vydanie. Praha, Czech Republic: Management Press. ISBN 978-80-7261-162-1

Sicinsky, A. (2012). *Negotiation tactics.* Retrieved from http://www.mindmapart.com/negotiation-mind-map-adam-sicinski/ [cit 2013-05-01]

Stenmark, D. (2002). *Data, information, and knowledge* (KM, p. 3). Retrieved from http://w3.informatik.gu.se/dixi/km/chap3.htm [cit. 2006-05-12]

Stenmark, D. *Tacit knowledge: The fundament for knowing* (KM, p. 6). Retrieved from http://w3.informatik.gu.se/dixi/km/chap6.htm [cit. 2006-02-02]

Veljacikova, Z. (2011). *Aplikácia učebných štýlov vo vyučovaní anglického jazyka*. Metodicko-pedagogické centrum, Bratislava, Slovakia. Retrieved from http://www.shared.mpc-edu.sk [cit.2014-03-15]

Part II

Transformational Leadership

8

Tell Me, Teach Me, Involve Me: Transformational Leadership, Mentoring, and You

Aaron Walter, PhD, and David Griffin
School of Management and VSM Slovakia

Abstract

"Millennials," born between 1977 and 1997, are a unique group, characterized by an approach to work and social media that is more integrated with their lives. The millennial generation uses technology to obtain and transfer information. Popular social media sites such as Twitter and Facebook have become the go-to source for shared knowledge. This knowledge extends beyond the textbook and blogosphere. These young users are logged in and active in a perpetual state of communication. The integration of this technology has become part of their identity and expression. With this realization, there is opportunity for educators to harness this influence and effectively incorporate it into teaching. Old models of teaching and learning need to be reconsidered and mentoring techniques are among the most effective means of reaching the millennials in the classroom. In addition, many elements of transformational leadership are better transferred via experiential activities in the classroom, aided by mentoring approaches. Ultimately, a list of best practices is developed to provide instructors with concrete approaches to mentoring.

Introduction

"Tell me and I forget, teach me and I may remember, involve me and I learn."
—Liu Xiang

Educators have a difficult role in the classroom. It is their responsibility to convey knowledge of the topic with a mixture of non-bias, humor, sympathy, and sensitivity to various learning types. Educators are accountable to education standards, curriculum requirements, and supervisor comments. This has been the environment within academia for several decades.

However, in the professional environment, the workforce has undergone a significant change. Nearly half the employees today were born between 1977 and 1997. These people, known as millennials, share in common with their successive generations a view of work different than the past generations of workers. This view is that work is a part of life, not a separate activity. Job satisfaction is directly linked to personal fulfillment. Friendships are created, skills are learned, and there is a connection between work and a purpose. Motivation is vital in attaining job satisfaction.

While the approach of mentoring in companies has shifted to the line employees, it is those line employees that come directly from the halls of higher education. The younger generation of scholars must have a better understanding of how business connects to both the theory and practical aspects of their classroom experience. One way to make this connection is through transformative leadership. Transformative leadership enhances the motivation, morale, and performance of followers through a variety of mechanisms including idealized influence, intellectual stimulation, and individual consideration, the psychological mechanisms that underlie transforming and transactional leadership (Bass & Riggio, 2008).

Transformational Leadership and Motivation

"I am not a teacher, but an awakener." —Robert Frost

Transformational leadership is one way leaders and followers help one another advance to a higher level of morale and motivation (Burns, 1978). This same idea also applies to teachers whose strength of personality and vision causes inspiration and motivation for students to work toward common goals. However, the scope of motivation and mentorship is different than years past. Higgins and Kram (2001) believed that the idea of a career confidante is not attractive, leading some to believe that younger workers and students are less respectful. Higgins and Kram believe this is a misrepresentation. Moreover, they think that youth are not less respectful; rather, how they display cognitive recognition of concepts has evolved.

This evolved cognitive recognition needs to be understood in the context of mentoring. According to Jeanne Meister, co-author of *The 2020 Workplace, quoted in Khidekel's (2013) BusinessWeek* article, "The Misery of Mentoring Millennials, "today's new mentorship models are more like Twitter conversations than the long-term relationships of days past. They're short-term and quite informal. And they end before it becomes a chore for either party—like moving on from a just-OK date." Respect remains through leadership and genuine interactions between the student and instructor.

Four Elements of Genuine Interactions

Riggio (2009) discussed four elements of transformational leadership related to genuine interactions: two dealing with a leader's charisma and the other two are what Riggio (2009) referred to as charisma-plus.

Individualized consideration. The first element, individualized consideration, speaks to the psychological side of being a mentor. The mentor offers empathy and support, listens, and places challenges before the followers. Individual contribution is celebrated, which in turn Riggio (2009) believed gives followers aspirations for self-development and intrinsic motivation tasks. The classroom provides ample opportunity for applying individualized consideration.

The apprentice model is academic mentoring. Faculty members impart knowledge, offer guidance, and provide support to student protégés on academic and nonacademic issues (Jacobi, 1991). Professional identity is fostered if mentoring facilitates a psychological adjustment (Austin, 2002) that directly benefits the workplace (Kram, 1985) where both personal and professional growth occurs.

Intellectual stimulation. The second element discussed by Riggio (2009) is known as intellectual stimulation. In the classroom, students can be encouraged to be both innovative and creative. In this setting, new ideas emerge if criticism is kept constructive or private (as suggested within the workplace). If such criticism is over a mistake, the focus is on "what" rather than "who." Innovation is fostered by applying practical examples to the lesson plans, including the use of computerized modeling and business simulations.

Inspirational motivation. The third element, inspirational motivation, is where the leader articulates a vision. As Peter Drucker advised executives to create a vision that would be compelling enough to set the tone, spirit, and values for the company, so too should teachers set the vision as transformational leaders. When teachers have a vision, they are able to inspire students.

When teachers inspire, motivate, and challenge students to leave their comfort zones, students will invest more effort in tasks and will be more optimistic about their abilities. This visionary aspect of transformational leadership will convey the purpose, provide energy, and help students make progress on their goals. To motivate students, teachers must allow for creative thinking and innovation (Walter, 2010).

Instructors are uniquely positioned within academia to be a mentor precisely because they also serve as role models. Burns (1978) stated, "the transformational leader . . . recognizes and exploits an existing need or demand of a potential follower . . . [and] looks for potential motives" (p. 4). Instructors can use their own skills and charisma to influence students through the method of mentoring. Mentoring allows for subtle influence to happen.

Idealized influence. The fourth element, according to Riggio (2009), is idealized influence. Here the transformational leader offers respect and encouragement, a positive behavior that is mimicked by students to others. This repeated positive behavior offers admiration and reciprocated respect between the instructor and the students (Liu, 2013). Instructors, as transformational leaders, give students a sense of meaning and challenge fostering the spirit of teamwork and commitment with optimism. The classroom gives instructors opportunities to provide the encouragement (that graduates might not later get in the workplace) to pursue leadership roles (Khidekel, 2013).

These four elements provide a foundation of respect, encouragement, and influence. To motivate students, instructors must allow for creative thinking and innovation by moving beyond the traditional business school models and examples. Instructors' professional experience and personal aspects of their lives need to be incorporated into the instruction through genuine interaction and stories. Incorporating personal stories add legitimacy to the lessons, and are often retained long after the course is completed.

Foundation of Mentoring: Tacit Knowledge

While some principles of leadership can be taught in a traditional academic environment, there seems to be an intangible element to leadership that is more difficult to transfer via traditional teaching methods, called *tacit knowledge*. Tacit knowledge is the sixth sense, or the "gut feeling" great leaders have about the right decision that needs to be made on the spur of the moment, for no apparent reason. Tacit knowledge, or the unknowable part of these decisions, is an essential element of leadership development. The problem with tacit knowledge is that it is from the subconscious, elusive and rather nebulous. So how can this leadership skill be communicated or taught?

Mentoring provides opportunities for tacit knowledge learning to take place, especially among millennials. However, for this type of learning to be successful, three components are needed:

- First, a school's administration must create an environment conducive to the mentoring situation. The administration must allow the space and freedom for faculty to do what they need to do, and an academic model must be in place that allows for diverse approaches to teaching and learning.
- Second, the curriculum has to be flexible enough to allow for the needs of the mentors and students to be accommodated. Curriculum and assessment practices that allow for multiple pathways to achieve learning outcomes that can also be demonstrated in various ways would be the best approach. Mentoring is one example of high-level faculty involvement on the "front lines," so having a large stake in the curriculum development and assessment-design processes, with a flexible outcomes-based model, is key to supporting the mentoring classroom.
- Third, to grow the ideal mentoring situation is to implement teacher training that includes solid elements of leadership training and modeling, psychological approaches to nontraditional learning in the classroom, emotional intelligence training, and techniques for fostering critical thinking.

Best Practices for Mentoring in the Classroom (and Beyond)

An essential outcome of this chapter is to provide a list of best practices to foster the development of transformational leadership in the classroom via tacit knowledge enhancement through mentoring. Generally, activities that replicate real-life experiences where the instructor can embrace the mentoring role are ideal. Here are some examples of proven practices:

Case studies. Realistic, detailed case studies can mimic real-world analysis and decision-making processes. Case studies have long been used in business schools, laws schools, medical schools and the social sciences, but they can be used in any discipline when instructors want students to explore how what they have learned applies to real-world situations. Case studies come in many formats, from a simple "What would you do in this situation?" question to a detailed description of a situation with accompanying data to analyze. By presenting a series of case studies that have a certain level of overlap and parallels, students can be taught to recognize patterns that eventually become internalized and become part of their core body of tacit knowledge. The case study process can also include a reflective component.

Role-playing. Like case studies, role-playing helps students mimic the decision-making process, but adds a context that enhances the use of tacit knowledge. It takes the case study out of a strongly text-focused environment into one where the decision-making process imitates life and allows students to think in the moment and react to a "live" situation. Role-playing, the "physicalization" of which Simsarian (2003) described as taking "brainstorming to bodystorming," includes the following benefits: (a) it brings "teams onto the 'same page' through a shared vivid experience that involves participant's muscle memory" (p. 1012) and (b) it creates "the ability to viscerally explore possibilities that may not be readily available in the world" (p. 1012). To maximize the effectiveness of role-playing in terms of its development of tacit knowledge, the background reading and discussion of the situation and roles can be done before coming to the class session where the role-play is to be enacted, either at home or in the prior class session. The students should be instructed to be in their role for the entire class and immerse themselves in their roles. The more such "realistic" conditions are created, the more likely it will be that the students will delve into the thought processes and practice the tacit elements of transformational leadership. A key component of role-playing is to reflect individually and debrief as a group once the exercise is over. This additional reflective step will enhance both learning and retention, and serve to further internalize the indefinable elements of leadership.

Discussions. The process of discussion itself can aid in the acquisition of leadership skills. How students conduct themselves in discussions, especially when considering controversial topics or when controversy arises during a debate, is intrinsically a good opportunity to develop transformational leadership skills. The key here is in mentoring with moderation. The skilled teacher will know when to intervene, and when to let things carry on unimpeded, as both situations can lead to great learning. There are many resources on how best to moderate discussions, but it is important to allow students to take the lead and solve problems, both individually and collectively, to maximize the potential for development of tacit knowledge elements. Moderation of discussions, then, needs to include timely, probing questions, and less "preaching" toward a specific agenda. Again, a discussion's real-time-based nature encourages students to rely more on intuition and gut instincts, rather than theory. This context supports the transfer of the tacit aspects of transformational leadership.

Teams/cohorts. With the two-heads-are-better-than-one approach, students can play off one another's ideas and learn from each other. The communication skills necessary to analyze a problem within groups can assist with the development of social intelligence. Most companies have team units within their organizational structure, so working in teams provides another real-life situation. Hansen (2006) pointed out that one of the main downfalls of running teams in the classroom is that there is not enough guidance, which is where the teacher's involvement can make or break the success of the team experience and tilt the balance in favor of a positive learning experience. In more well-established, long-term cohorts, students can develop similar skills over the long term, which can bring a richer interplay as they learn how to function as a more integrated unit.

Problem-based learning (PBL). In problem-based learning, teams focus on problem solving, collaboration, and self-learning, as they are guided by an expert. Hmelo-Silver et al. (2007) asserted that "the PBL learning environment is highly effective and promotes cross-disciplinary approaches, and pushes students to explain their thinking to help them build a casual explanation or identify the limits of their knowledge. This helps support students in sense making and in articulating their ideas" (p. 101). Similarly, a micro-environment can be set up over a longer period in the classroom to foster these skills; however, it might make more sense to put the students in internship positions instead.

Internships. Internships do not just replicate a real-world business environment but are the real world. Provided the internship is properly overseen, administered, and mentored, students can have the added benefit of the combined practice component and a classroom-based component that focuses on the experiential learning of the internship. Knouse and Fontenot (2008) stated that internships "may create satisfying experiences that motivate students to continue along a career path" (p. 61) and may also "create realistic expectations about the world of work and help clarify students' career intentions" (p. 61). A highly organized approach to internships, where a considerable amount of time is spent debriefing the experiences and reflecting on the learning, can be quite effective.

Business simulations. In a way, computer-based business games, like Capsim, are a form of problem-based learning. While relatively simplified in comparison to a real business setting, simulations do provide opportunities to make informed decisions in relatively short spans of time, which enhances tacit leadership skills. Peterkova (2011) noted that business simulation games provide "support for development of [a] student's creative abilities," enhancing their "fluency," "flexibility" and "originality," and ultimately develops the "intuition" of the players (p. 459). If the simulation is enacted in groups, it combines the advantages of team learning with the advantages of the simulation, and can provide opportunities to develop negotiation skills and leadership skills within the team dynamic.

Leadership modeling. Modeling can either take place in the classroom, with the teacher modeling leadership behaviors, or via a job-shadowing arrangement, when a student can observe firsthand a leader in action. Again, reflection and debriefing are important to enhance the transfer of tacit knowledge in relation to leadership skills. In the case of job-shadowing, it is possible that leaders might not be able to articulate why they made certain decisions, so an analytical discussion of what happened can be eye-opening to all.

Guest speakers. Bringing in an experienced manager to present in class can bring the tacit elements of transformational leadership to the forefront, especially if the students have the opportunity to interact with the speaker in a question and answer forum. According to Griffin (2012):

> Some experienced business leaders are able to articulate what goes through their minds when faced with

situations where they have to make snap decisions based on intuition or "instinct." If students have an opportunity to interview the speaker, they can participate in the exploratory process firsthand, and their line of questioning (as a guided learning experience) can help them understand the process of tacit knowledge acquisition.

Reflection and journal keeping. Many teachers reflexively roll their eyes when they hear professional development trainers suggesting that learners reflect on something they want their audience to think about and explore further. While stopping to reflect on an experience annoys many teachers and businesspeople, and they criticize it as "too touchy-feely," there is some value to looking back at something that happened in the classroom or workplace and thinking further about it, analyzing what happened and why it happened. Hiemstra (2001) stated that journaling "becomes a tool to aid learners in terms of personal growth, synthesis, and reflection on new information that is acquired" (p. 20). He also noted that there "is the potential for a journaling technique to promote critical self-reflection where dilemmas, contradictions, and evolving worldviews are questioned or challenged"—in other words, it's how students can work things out in their minds. Further, keeping a journal is one effective way to track tacit elements, especially if written at the time of a critical decision that was made in a seemingly intuitive manner. Reflection also helps students see both the details of the situation and better understand the big picture.

Break it down/big picture approach. In mentoring situations, teachers need to get students closer to examine the details of the situation, and farther away to view the big picture and understand the broader meaning and application of what they've experienced, "sort of like taking a close look at the pixels and then stepping back to view their overall effect" (Griffin, 2012). The teacher can strategically use questions to guide students to both a better understanding of the minutiae of the situation and the broader significance and applications that can be extrapolated or generalized to a different context.

Field trips/shared experience. Rather than talk about operations management in the classroom, instructors can take students on a tour of a production plant and ask the managing supervisor some relevant questions. Greene, Kisida, and Bowen (2014) underscored the enhancement of critical thinking skills, empathy, and tolerance in students as beneficial outcomes of field trips. The shared experience of the group on the field trip also has lasting learning value for the mentor since it can be used extensively and broadly to explore a number of related concepts that help foster transformational leadership skills.

Technology to enhance the mentoring experience. Millennials are often connected via social media, including chatting, Facebooking, WhatsApping. Teachers can use these social media forums to promote learning. Using Facebook or other social media that many students regularly monitor is one way to strengthen and enhance the mentoring experience. In these environments, students have been known to quickly take over, posting links to articles, videos, and web pages that are relevant to the course topics. The advantage over online teaching platforms, like Blackboard or Moodle, is that almost all the students are already tuned in, and participate naturally as just another aspect to their social media lives. Posts are quickly seen by the majority of the students in the course, and these forums lend themselves to more engaging materials (e.g., funny videos related to the topic). Instructors can steer discussions toward "educational" content, and toward topics that enhance the mentoring role. The "cool factor" of these forums enhances student engagement.

A Final Word

One common trait of millennials is that they are well connected to technology, constantly texting, tweeting, and talking in online forums. And yet, many traditional instructors often try to teach students through conventional means such as lectures, slide presentations, and other one-way, uni-dimensional, text-based means. Even in online teaching platforms, where we have the world of the web at our fingertips, we often try to teach them in an overly text-heavy environment.

To reach millennials, and to more effectively address a wide range of learning styles, it is important to move beyond text-centric approaches to teaching. Good teachers know that each "new" teaching technique or approach can be added to their toolbox, to be used at the appropriate times. The approaches discussed in this chapter, to enhance the transfer and development of tactic knowledge in support of mentoring transformational leadership skills, are simply more tools that can be added to the toolbox. The sophisticated task of moving ideas into a different medium can support the development of tacit knowledge, and, by extension, can aid in the fostering of those intangible transformational leadership skills. Any mentoring approach should be filled with visual and tactile opportunities for all types of learners, but especially for millennials.

References

Bass, B. M., & Riggio, R. E. (2008). *Transformational leadership*. Mahwah, NJ: Lawrence Erlbaum Associates, Inc.

Burns, J. M. (1978). *Leadership*. New York, NY: Harper and Row.

Editorial Staff at e-Bim. (2010, February 4). *Producing innovation: A systems approach*. Retrieved from http://www.humanresourcesiq. com/Columnarticle.cfm?externalID=1880&Columnid=3&showne wswindow=1&mac=HRIQ_BusinessExchange_SMO_2010&SID= BusinessExchange&utm_campaign=BusinessExchange&utm_ medium=SMO&utm_source=e-bim&utm_content=Feb12news

Frost, R. (n.d.). *Quotes*. Goodreads. Retrieved from http://www.goodreads. com/author/quotes/7715

Greene, J., Kisida, B., & Bowen, D. (2014, April). The benefits of culturally enriching field trips: Taking students to an art museum improves critical thinking skills and increases historical empathy. *Education Next*, 4–13.

Griffin, D. (2012). *Teaching tacit knowledge: The role of "intuition" or "transrationality" in the educational administration, curriculum development and faculty training at post-secondary schools*. International Workshop on Knowledge Management (7th Annual), VSM School of Management, Trencin, Slovakia.

Hansen, R. (2006, September/October). Benefits and problems with student teams: Suggestions for improving team projects. *Journal of Education for Business, 82*(1), 11–19.

Hiemstra, R. (2001). Uses and benefits of journal writing. In L. M. English & M. A. Gillen (Eds.), *Promoting journal writing in adult education* (New Directions for Adult and Continuing Education, 90, 19–26). San Francisco, CA: Jossey-Bass.

Higgins, M. C., & Kram, K. E. (2001). Reconceptualizing mentoring at work: A developmental network perspective. *Academy of Management Review, 26*(2), 264–288.

Hmelo-Silver, C., Duncan, R., & Clark, A. (2007). Scaffolding and achievement in problem-based and inquiry learning: A response to Kirschner, Sweller, and Clark (2006). *Educational Psychologist, 42* (2), 99–107.

Khidekel, M. (2013, March 14). The misery of mentoring millennials. *Businessweek*. Retrieved from http://www.businessweek.com/articles/2013-03-14/the-misery-of-mentoring-millennials

Knouse, S., & Fontenot, G. (2008, June). Benefits of the business college internship: A research review. *Journal of Employment Counseling, 45*, 61–66.

Liu, C. (2013, August 21). The role of the role model. *Time*. Retrieved from http://business.time.com/2013/08/21/the-role-of-the-role-model/#ixzz2uyjTdCqr

Meister, J., & Willyerd, K. (2010, May). Mentoring millennials. *Harvard Business Review*. Retrieved from http://hbr.org/2010/05/mentoring-millennials/ar/1

Peterkova, J. (2011). *Best practices in the use of managerial simulation games-based learning*. (Proceeding of the European Conference on Games Based Learning), 457–464.

Riggio, R.E. (2009). Are you a transformational leader? The best in current leadership research and theory, from cultivating charisma to transforming your organization. *Psychology Today*. Retrieved from http://www.psychologytoday.com/blog/cutting-edge-leadership/200903/are-you-transformational-leader

Simsarian, K. (2003). Take it to the next stage: The roles of role playing in design process. *CHI 2003: New Horizons*, 1012–1013. Retrieved from http://dsoftware.stanford.edu/readings/p1012-simsarian.pdf

Walter, A. (2010). *Meeting the management challenges in the 21st century: Innovation in 21st-century business schools* (conference paper, 2nd International Scientific Conference Management Challenges in the 21st Century), Vysoká škola manažmentu.

Zellman, M. (2009). The advantages of transformational leadership style. Retrieved from http://smallbusiness.chron.com/advantages-transformational-leadership-style-18809.html

Taking the Teflon Off Change: An Approach for Education and Application

Arron Grow, PhD
School of Applied Leadership

Abstract

This chapter provides a review of scholarly perspectives on change management and a recommendation for managing transformational change that is based on this review. A review of the literature reveals that most research into change management can be placed into one of four areas. These four areas are (1) how to involve people in organizational change, (2) how to use theory- or model-based approaches in organizational change, (3) a focus on specific parts of an organization for successful change, and (4) case studies that explore experiences in change management. Examples from each of these four perspectives are reviewed. Following this review, the chapter presents a model-based approach that addresses leadership needs, organizational components, and the involvement of organizational members in the planning and deployment of an organizational change. This whole-system view is then discussed from two perspectives: first, as a pedagogical strategy recommended for leadership educators to use in their training on change management; second, how change leaders can apply the presented method in organizational settings.

Introduction

An ongoing concern in organizational change management (CM) is that enacted changes can, and often do, return to a former (or similar to former) state. In CM literature, estimates of CM failure rates vary but are not uncommonly quoted to be 70 percent—a percentage that was twice identified in two separate *Harvard Business Review* articles (Beer et al., 1990; Kotter, 1995). Though Hughes (2011) questions this percentage and provides an extensive review of the use of this figure in CM literature, it is not a figure that is out of line when compared with other CM failure estimates. Burnes (2009), for example, finds that change failure estimates commonly fall between 60 percent and 90 percent. Though the frequency of CM failure may be in question, it seems safe to say, as Burnes (2011) puts it, "That many organizations do seem to struggle to implement change successfully" (p. 446).

In framing a discussion around CM failure, Burnes (2011) poses three questions. The first question Burnes asks is, "How reliable is the data on change failure?" Though a more precise understanding of this information can be helpful for benchmarking purposes, an answer to this question does not, in and of itself, help advance a strategy for improving CM success rates. Burnes asks two additional questions which are more to the point for this article:

- Why does change fail?
- What can organizations do to improve their CM success rate?

In Burnes (2011), the author asks these questions as part of his preface for the edition of the *Journal of Change Management* that was dedicated to the question of CM failure. He ends this preface by introducing three articles. Hughes (2011) explores the question of how reliable failure rate data is. McClellan (2011) discusses the roll of communication and its impact on change in an organization. Raelin and Cataldo (2011) examine the experiences of one organization's failed change initiative to promote what they see as the vital role of middle management in a successful change process.

Both McClellan (2011) and Raelin and Cataldo (2011) are examples of two of the different types of articles found in CM literature; the former being an article that focuses on how organizational members are or can be involved in the process, and the other focusing on one organizational component as this same golden key. In the case of Raelin and Cataldo, the key being, how middle management is used in a change process. It is, to at least a small degree, somewhat ironic that researchers and authors who purport to be looking at a subject as large as change within an organization select as their focus only one element of an organization and call whatever they are addressing a key to greater success in change management. Yet, this proclivity is not a new one.

Both research-based and non-research-based writings about organizational change and change management tend to fall into one of four areas: (1) interpersonal elements in organizational change, (2) how to use theory- or model-based approaches in organizational change, (3) a focus on specific parts of an organization for successful change, and (4) case studies that explore past experiences in change management. Reviewing a few examples of each type of article will help build the foundation for the present work. After a review of examples in each of the four categories, a composite model will be offered as a whole-system-type approach to change management planning and process. The chapter will conclude with both a recommendation for how to teach this approach and a strategy for applying this approach in the field.

A Review of Change Management Literature

Interpersonal Elements-Based Works in CM Literature

Reporting on the role employees accepted while re-engineering services at the Ohio State University Libraries, Schlosser (2013) espouses what she called a "grassroots planning process." Schlosser reported a number of principles that aided in the success of this faculty-led effort. Grassroots characteristics listed by Schlosser included such things as executive committee support, voluntary participation, using a "phased" process, and use of appreciative inquiry method. For Schlosser's, it was the combination of these people-centric items that led to a successful change experience with the OSU Libraries.

Referred to earlier in this article, McClellan (2011) reviews a failed change initiative that took place at a college of art and design. Reporting an opposite experience from that of Schlosser (2013), McClellan's case study documents a change effort in a college of art and design wherein organizational members did not have fluid communication during the initiative. Lack of sufficient dialogue between different groups within the organization led to the eventual demise of the change. One may say that no matter how one looks at CM, the success of any CM effort lies, ultimately, in the people within an organization, for what is an organization but a collection of people? Still, as other investigations focus on different elements, the review of these other elements is worth identifying.

Continuing this theme, Levasseur (2013) suggested that involvement in effective change management practices can "facilitate the development of soft skills, such as self-awareness, communication, collaboration, and leadership." Levasseur's focus is not on how to involve people in the change management process, his writing notes phenomena that few would disagree with; that effective involvement of team members in organizational change projects will, in fact, help team members develop themselves as well. Though Lavasseur's work is indexed as one in the CM realm, here again emphasis is on the people within an organization rather than on the organization itself.

For the most part, when articles of CM discuss people, they are usually written about either the leadership (Harris, 2010), or about the involvement of organizational team members (McClellen, 2011; Schlosser, 2013). Recommendations for how to engage team members vary by article. Considering this category of CM literature, recommendations for involving team members regularly list the following six actions:

- Education
- Communication
- Participation

- Involvement
- Facilitation
- Support

One thing is clear throughout this segment of the literature, full leadership backing and full team member buy-in lead to the best chance at lasting transformational change. The level at which these things are missing in an organizational change effort, may very well indicate the likelihood that the intended change will not last.

Theories, Concepts, and Models-Based Works in CM Literature

A number of works in the CM-based literature focus on theories, concepts, and models and their utility in preparation of or application to CM work.

A good example of this is the work of Boga and Ensari (2009). Boga and Ensari studied the role of transformational leadership and its connection to perceived success in organizational change. To investigate this, they reviewed the survey responses of eighty-two individuals who worked in a variety of organizations. Participants were asked questions about their experiences with change in their respective organizations. Researchers also asked questions that helped them identify the leadership types of respondents' supervisors (transactional or transformational). Boga and Ensari found that those who reported to transformational leaders reported organizational changes as more successful compared to those supervised by transactional leaders. Note that the researchers in this case were not interested in measuring actual CM effectiveness, but only the perceived success of the change for the organization.

There are numerous examples of theoretical applications to CM in the literature. Driscoll and Morris (2001) explore rhetorical devices and cultural change management. Jones and Wallace (2005) investigate the role of ambiguity in change management. Complexity theory and its implications for CM were looked at by Cilliers (2000). Appreciative intelligence (Thatchenkery, 2013) has also been cited as useful for informing CM practice. Focusing on this aspect of CM literature, Graetz and Smith (2010) provide one of the most extensive reviews of philosophies that have been connected to CM research. Graetz and Smith provide a review of eleven different philosophical/conceptual models that appear in CM literature. For those looking for the best understanding of how theoretical models have been applied in CM research and writing, work by Graetz and Smith would be a good place to start.

The question of invoking theory, concepts, and models over empirical evidence to guide CM efforts has itself been raised. Cruickshank and Collins (2012) call attention to this as a weakness in CM-related literature. They find a "predominant theoretical focus on process" (p. 213), which provides more about the use of theory for academic inquiry than they do finding solutions to ROI or other tangible impacts on organizations with respect to change. Using theory, concepts, or models as a launch point for CM work can be done, but if practitioners find that results based solely on ideas do not generate consistent, beneficial results, organizational development specialists need to look for more productive foundations for their work.

Cruickshank and Collins (2012) feel that in the absence of empirical evidence to support theoretical underpinnings to CM, models that are more readily applicable may have more value. In *The Fifth Discipline*, Senge (2005) speaks not of change management specifically, but of organizations as a whole, literally, an interconnected whole. Senge's work applies to the idea that other CM-focused researchers have called out— that a change made in one area of an organization will indeed touch other parts of the organization. Though a change in one area of an organization may have only a small degree of impact on other parts of an organization, there will, nonetheless be an impact. Few can argue the logic of this. Of all theories that may be applied to change management work, it seems most appropriate to apply those that have intrinsic reason, such as Senge's systems thinking. Theories that team members can understand, are more likely to be agreed with and used in CM efforts.

Components-based works in CM literature. Though Senge (2005) speaks of organizations as systems, they are nonetheless systems made up of individual parts. There is a great deal of research into change efforts in isolated areas of organizations. Research that focuses on one component of an organization and its specific help to CM efforts is most commonly found not in journals dedicated to change management but in those journals that are dedicated to specific aspects of an organization. IT, HR, and leadership are just a few of the examples of organizational components that have their own collections of research journals. CM research that is connected directly to specific organizational areas is most commonly found in the journals dedicated to these areas. Here are a few examples of this type of writing.

In a review of how a county transportation service found cost-saving measures, Harris (2010) focused on how two separate teams, leadership and training, worked together to benefit their organization. Fickenscher & Bakerman (2011) reported on the efforts of IT professionals in the process they would use to improve the IT component in a health-care services organization. Ruta (2005) provided a similarly concentrated look at change being taken on in a human resources department. Another example of this type of CM research was of a change management effort for the facilities department of a large manufacturing operation (Voordijk, 2013). There are many examples of this type of article in the CM literature. As this type of work is more concerned with helping specific industries rather than the field of organizational development as a whole, one might consider this type of work to be of limited value to OD, but thinking this way would not be wise.

Articles that inform on lessons learned from CM work within specific elements of an organization can still be informative to the larger field. Reviewing CM work in specific organizational areas has at least two benefits. One benefit of reviewing work done in specific areas of an organization is that it gives those not in these areas of the organization eyes into the unique concerns of that part of the operation. Added information can foster greater understanding for areas of an organization in which one does not typically work. Another benefit of reviewing CM work done in a specific area of an organization is that it highlights new possibilities and approaches for CM work that a reader may not have otherwise thought of. For these reasons, those who are interested in doing the best they can in CM work should want to explore the CM experiences of others as much as possible.

Speaking not in terms of a departmental or functional roll, but in terms of targets for change, Schermerhorn, Osborn, Uhl-Bien, & Hunt (2012) identified eight "change targets" that CM leaders should look to when planning for and initiating change within an organization. Three components—purpose, objectives, and technology—are more the type to be set by organizational leaders. The five other components of an organization identified by Schermerhorn are strategy, structure, culture, tasks, and people. Others have also voiced this same key for CM success. Church and Rotola (2013), for example, though they did not speak specifically of Schermerhorn's five elements in their writing, understood and espoused the importance of involving multiple parts of an organization in a CM effort.

Case study-based works in CM literature. Case study work is another category of work in the CM literature database. Similar to the writing discussed in the previous section, case studies are documented to help organizational development professionals learn from the experiences of other individuals and other organizations. With this goal in mind, Bamford and Daniel (2005) documented the experiences of one department's change efforts within the National Healthcare System (NHS), a prominent organization in the United Kingdom. Their intent was to study changes this group experienced in order to identify recommendations that could be useful for those managing change in other organizations. Harris (2010) had a similar motive in documenting the use of cross-functional teams to help improve efficiency in another organization. Though the effort was initiated in response to funding cuts in the public transportation system that he studied, Harris found a longer-term benefit to the organization due to the changes proposed by the cross-functional teams. Cited earlier in this chapter, Schlosser (2013) is a third example of a case study in the CM literature. Learning about the strategies reported by Schlosser and other case studies like this can provide insight for other CM professionals to use as they go about their own CM work.

Case studies about organizations that experience positive results in their change efforts are not the only case studies found in CM literature. Case studies that report change failures can also be informative. Drawing lessons from one such less successful CM effort was McClellan (2011). Referred to earlier in this chapter, McClellan's investigation is a case study. McClellan's investigation of a college of art and design focused on organizational member discourse during a change effort. He found that in not giving faculty and staff sufficient input on a change process, challenges in the change process arose that may otherwise have been prevented. Raelin and Catoldo (2011) is another case study discussed earlier in this review.

Both of these studies highlight the fact that there can be overlap in categorizations. In fact, these two studies could be placed in three of the four categories. Both studies are (1) case studies that (2) focus on people, and (3) focus on a specific part of an organization. McClellan's work reminds university-based CM strategists to not forget the faculty (a seemingly obvious issue) while Raelin and Catoldo emphasize the importance of leveraging middle managers in CM work. Regardless of the lesson learned, the volume of case studies found in CM literature makes it clear that this use of case study research and review is instructive for both education and application purposes.

Summarizing the Literature

A review of the literature reveals three common themes:

Leadership. Though many articles and research reports have different focal areas, numerous works touch on leadership as a key element in successful change management. Whether the author's point is to document the importance of active leadership involvement (Harris, 2010), the role of mid-level leadership compared to executive-level leadership (Raelin & Catalod, 2011), the need for leaders to set direction (Boga & Ensari, 2009) or any one of a number of other points, the conclusion of each is the same: the chance for any change effort to result in lasting transformational change is closely tied to the seniority and activity level of the sponsoring leadership. The higher the level of leadership involved and the more active they are in the change effort, the more likely a change effort will "set" (Bamford & Daniel, 2005; Cilliers, 2000).

Interconnectedness. Organizations are made up of multifaceted, interconnected structures. In most cases, a change made in one area of an organization will likely affect other parts of the organization. Though this notion of all things being connected is not new to ancient native cultures, the application of this idea to organizational development work is relatively recent. Senge (2005) is one whose work is most noted in this field of inquiry. Research and reviews of CM work in specific organizational areas typically calls out the need to watch for impact in other areas of an organization (Ruta, 2005; Fickenscher &

Bakerman, 2013; Voordijk, 2013). Senge reminds us that this should be a regular consideration for all CM leaders. Schermerhorn et al. (2012) discuss specific interconnected parts of an organization that should be considered in change management efforts.

Schermerhorn et al. (2012) identified eight components of organizations. Though three of the five targets are more set by leaders (Purpose, Short-Term Objectives, and IT), the five remaining elements (Strategy, Structure, Culture, Tasks, and People) are very much a part of (or should be a part of) CM planning. CM leaders who understand the interplay of each of these elements within an organization and utilize this dynamic for organizational improvement will have a better chance of success in their work. In speaking of how to create lasting change for diversity and inclusion in an organization, Church and Rotolo (2013) put it this way: "This means integrating every aspect of diversity and inclusion into traditional development and feedback processes and tools such as performance management, leadership competencies, and 360 feedback, organizational surveys, workgroup climate assessments, talent scorecards, and internal talent deployment efforts" (p. 246). What Senge and Church and Rotolo find makes sense for any organization looking to create long-term transformational change.

Organizational member engagement. Leadership and interconnected components of any organization necessarily involves organizational members. The emphasis being brought to the forefront here is, for the best chance of success, change efforts must involve team members not just as a *part* of the process, but as fully adopting, fully engaged participants in the change effort. The less this is the case during a change effort, the more likely the change effort will not succeed. As discussed earlier in this chapter, this was a truth found by many CM writers and researchers (McClellan, 2013; Raelin and Cataldo, 2013; Schlosser, 2013).

Summarizing the major themes from this review; at a minimum, lasting transformational change requires the following elements:

1. Committed leadership
2. Involvement of multiple organizational elements
3. Full organizational member buy-in and engagement

Utilizing these concepts leads to a whole-system way of thinking not unlike that spoken of by Senge (2005). Change management efforts that draw upon all three of these elements together in both the planning and performance of the work will have the best chance at achieving lasting transformational change; in other words, change that sticks.

A Whole-System Approach to Change Management

Teaching a Whole-System Change Management Approach

A first step in teaching anyone anything is to provide a foundation for the knowledge they are to learn. In the present context, this means presenting information provided in the previous section. Those intending to lead organizational change must recognize that no change has a chance at long-term success unless the three necessities that were identified in the literature are addressed. The three necessities in order for change to stick are (1) leadership that is committed to the change, (2) change-related activities that are "embedded" in the organization, and (3) full team member buy-in and engagement. Given the frequency of case study review in the CM literature, a teaching methodology that employs case studies seems natural for the profession.

According to Nilson (2010), the case study method of instruction is a valuable and proven tool for educational purposes. In an earlier work, Dunne and Brooks (2004) wrote extensively about the use of case studies for instruction. They found that one of the greatest advantages to using this method is that it allows learners to use low-risk situations to gain experience with high-potential principles and methods. Dunne and Brooks further find that through case study exercises, learners develop skills in the specific areas:

- Problem solving
- Analytical tools, quantitative and/or qualitative, depending on the case
- Decision making in complex situations
- Coping with ambiguities

149

This set of skills closely aligns with the people skills Levasseur (2005) speaks of that will be developed as CM leaders involve team members in change efforts. This is another reason case study method is recommended as a strategy for teaching how to create lasting transformational change in organizations. According to Nilson (2010), there are many types of case studies. One type of case study is the open-ended, "complete the picture" type exercise. Another form of case study is "review what happened." Here, the former type of case study is exemplified. Consider the following case with its accompanying questions:

> Marshall Academy Prep School opened in 1980 initially intended for 500 students. It now has an enrollment of 1,500. The original school building is now surrounded by temporary structures. Some teachers have room assignments everywhere on the grounds, and many of the rooms are either too small or too old to appropriately accommodate students. The supervising counsel has decided it is time to build a new school. To save money, they have decided to build the new school on the existing school grounds. Though there are a number of less-experienced teachers, many teachers have worked there for over twenty years.

- Considering the five organizational components listed in Schermerhorn (2010) and the six forms of team member engagement listed earlier in this chapter, develop for each organizational component a set of strategies and actions to take in the preparation of a successful building fund drive and building changeover.
- Consider resistance that might be encountered in this effort and how to address this.

Applying a Whole-System Change-Management Approach

Multiple experiences in practicing the whole-system approach as outlined above will prepare CM leaders for applying this approach in the field. Change management leaders may consider the following format as one possible approach to their planning:

Components to Alter/Address and Actions for Leaders and Team Members

Note: Set components include Organizational Purpose, Short-Term Objectives, Existing Technology

Actions for Leaders and Team Members	Strategy *Operational plans*	Structures *Organizational design*	Culture *Core beliefs and values*	Tasks *Job designs for people and teams*	People *Recruit and selection steps*
Education					
Communication					
Participation					
Involvement					
Facilitation					
Support					

After each of these areas has been sufficiently addressed, CM leaders can then put together a plan to carry out the identified actions within each area. CM leaders who employ a well-thought-out plan that address all of the components of an organization given in the above table and involve leaders and team members in at least the six ways, also listed in the table, will have the best chance at realizing lasting transformational change – organizational change that sticks.

References

Bamford, D., & Daniel, S. (2005). A case study of change management effectiveness within the NHS. *Journal of Change Management, 5*(4), 391–406.

Boga, I., & Ensari, N. (2009). The role of transformational leadership and organizational change on perceived organizational success. *The Psychologist Manager Journal, 12*, 235–251.

Church, A. H., & Rotolo, C. T. (2013). Leading diversity and inclusion efforts in organizations: Should we be standing behind our data or our values (or both)? *Industrial and Organizational Psychology, 6*(3), 245–248.

Cilliers, P. (2000). What can we learn from a theory of complexity? *Emergence, 3*(1), 5–23.

Cruickshank, A., & Collins, D. (2012). Change management: The case of the elite sport performance team. *Journal of Change Management, 12*(2), 209–229.

Driscoll, A., & Morris, J. (2001). Stepping out: Rhetorical devices and culture change management in the UK civil service, *Public Administration,79*(4), 803–824.

Dunne, D., & Brooks, K. (2004). *Teaching with cases*. Halifax, NS: Society for Teaching and Learning in Higher Education.

Fickenscher, K., Bakerman, M. (2011). Change management in health care IT. *Physician Executive, 37*(2), 64–67.

Graetz, F., & Smith, A. T. C. (2010). Managing organisational change: A philosophies of change approach. *Journal of Change Management, 10*(2), 135–154.

Harris, P. (2010, October). Crises management. *Training and Development*, 68–70.

Jones, R. L., & Wallace, M. (2005). Another bad day at the training ground: Coping with ambiguity in the coaching context. *Sport, Education and Society, 10*(1), 119–134.

Levasseur, R. E. (2005). People skills: Change management tools—leading teams. *Interfaces, 35*(2), 179–180.

McClellan, J. G. (2011). Reconsidering communication and discursive politics of organizational change. *Journal of Change Management, 11*(4), 465–480.

Nilson, L. (2010). *Teaching at its best: A research-based resource for college instructors* (3rd ed.). New York, NY: Jossey-Bass.

Raelin, J. D., & Catoldo, C. G. (2011). Whither middle management? Empowering interface and the failure of organizational change. *Journal of Change Management, 11*(4), 481–507.

Ruta, C. D., (2005). The application of change management theory to the HR portal implementation in subsidiaries of multinational corporations. *Human Resource Management, 44*(1), 35–53.

Schermerhorn, J., Osborn, R., Uhl-Bien, M., & Hunt, J. (2012). *Organizational behavior* (12th ed.). New York, NY: John Wiley & Sons.

Schlosser, M. (2013). OSUL2013: Fostering organizational change through a grassroots planning process. *College and Research Libraries, 72*(2), 152–165.

Thatchenkery, T. (2013). Leveraging appreciative intelligence for innovation in Indian organizations. *AI Practitioner, 15*(1), 29–33.

Voordijk, H. (2013). Facilities change management. *Construction Management & Economics, 31*(7), 789–791.

10

"Feminist" Is Not a Dirty Word in Leadership: How Feminist Principles Inform Transformational Leadership

Stephanie J. Brommer, PhD
School of Applied Leadership

Abstract

A feminist perspective illustrates valuable principles in the study of leadership. Discussing the negative stereotypes associated with the label and recognizing that the qualities of feminist principles can apply to the practice of women and men leaders offer key insights into inclusive, intersectional, and community-based leadership.

Introduction

Feminist perspectives are cloaked around inclusivity, human and equal rights, and empowerment of women individually and collectively. Activism to uproot structural inequalities underlies feminist values, as the ideology of feminism is fundamentally transformational. Leadership based on feminist values is collaborative, consultative, and caring—all behaviors that support empowerment and relationships.

These qualities of feminist principles apply to the practice of women and men leaders, offering key insights into inclusive, intersectional, and community-based leadership that seeks to empower and support. Yet, in numerous studies, women whose behavior is caring and consulting have been considered weak, incompetent, or indecisive leaders (Bongiomo, Bain, and David, 2013; Bornstein, 2008; Catalyst, 2007; Madden, 2011). At the same time, discourses around women and leadership often center around terms like "bossy," and researchers have shown that women who are assertive as leaders are less respected than assertive men (Catalyst, 2007; Chin, 2004; Leanin.Org and Girl Scouts of the USA, 2014; Toegel and Barsoux, 2014).

In this chapter, I discuss how feminist principles enhance the current valued style of transformational leadership, while paradoxically women leaders in the United States face stigmas in their leadership behaviors.

Feminist leaders acknowledge differences, recognize bias and oppression, and are community based. Feminism supports political, social, and economic equality with a social justice framework. The goals of feminist leadership include egalitarianism, empowerment, and gender-equitable organizational cultures and environments.

However, in the news and around the table, the term "feminist" elicits negative connotations, often going along with the phrase, "I'm not a feminist, but . . ." Yahoo! CEO Marissa Mayer said in an interview:

> I don't think that I would consider myself a feminist. I think that, I certainly believe in equal rights. I believe that women are just as capable, if not more so, in a lot of different dimensions. But I don't, I think, have sort of the militant drive and sort of the chip on the shoulder that sometimes comes with that. And I think it's too bad, but I do think feminism has become, in many ways, a more negative word. There are amazing opportunities all over the world

for women, and I think that there's more good that comes out of positive energy around that than negative energy. (PBS and AOL, 2013)

When former U.S. Supreme Court Justice Sandra Day O'Connor, a moderate conservative with a mixed record on issues involving women's rights, was asked by a newspaper reporter if she considered herself a feminist, she responded:

> I never did. I care very much about women and their progress. I didn't go march in the streets, but when I was in the Arizona Legislature, one of the things that I did was to examine every single statute in the state of Arizona to pick out the ones that discriminated against women and get them changed. (Solomon, 2009)

And women in the public eye have often discussed the idea of feminism, such as actress Susan Sarandon, who has spoken out for reproductive rights and human rights, calling the term "feminist" an "old-fashioned" word that is "used more in a way to minimize you" (Day, 2013).

The term "feminist" has been used to demean, dismiss, or silence conversations about sexual harassment, violence against women, pay structures, equal opportunities, and stereotypes. Feminist and feminine characteristics are interpreted through this socially constructed frame and accorded value or disvalue. As noted throughout this chapter, leadership qualities are socially constructed, validated, and perpetuated, and many currently valued leader characteristics are feminist principles as well and apply to women and men. In this chapter, I made a conscious decision to use the term "woman leader" instead of "female leader," although these terms are used interchangeably in the literature. "Woman" conveys characteristics and behaviors socially constructed as feminine or masculine, while "female" denotes biological sex.

Feminist Leadership Principles and Practices

The practice of feminism revolves around collaboration, mentoring, and social change, supporting the notion that leadership is a social process (Chin, 2004; Suyomoto and Ballou, 2007). Regarding leadership as a process moves away from looking at strategies used by leaders to looking at the underlying values demonstrated by leaders. Narratives of women leaders described leadership as making positive contributions, communicating, collaborating, caring, and giving back (Fine, 2007). "A commitment to social change through collaboration that is grounded in a feminist ethic of care provides a new vision of leadership for women and men" (Fine, 2007, p. 188).

Bringing in community and care through inclusiveness of diverse experiences, feminist principles also adhere to intersectionality, which acknowledges the interactions and intersections of race and gender, as well as ethnicity, class, sexual orientation, disability, and profession. "[I]ntersectionality might be more broadly useful as a way of mediating the tension between assertions of multiple identity and the ongoing necessity of group politics" (Crenshaw, 1991, p. 1296).

These identities inform experiences, meanings, choice, and opportunities. Scholars undertaking a feminist leadership initiative in the American Psychological Association (APA) in 2002–2003 emphasized that feminist leadership theory must conceptualize multiple perspectives and diversity in experiences and privilege (Suyomoto and Ballou, 2007). Contexts, biases, perceptions, and values inform and define ideas and behavioral expectations about leadership among women and men (Chin, 2007).

Gendered experiences and ideologies shape understandings of leadership. Men's experiences have informed the dominant representations and ideologies of leadership. According to communications scholar Marlene G. Fine (2009), "The male ideology of leadership is visible in two critical ways: (1) the lack of representation of women in leadership positions in the U.S., and (2) the construction of leadership as comprising masculine characteristics" (p. 181).

Confidence, masculinity, and dominance are among the characteristics that have defined leaders (Chin, 2004). Organizational structure and practice has often been skewed toward masculine-defined qualities, including power and assertiveness (Fine, 2007).

Business psychology professor Tomas Chamorro-Premuzic (2013) posited that the gendered numbers in management result from stereotypical notions of desired leadership traits that confuse confidence with competence.

> That is, because we (people in general) commonly misinterpret displays of confidence as a sign of competence, we are fooled

into believing that men are better leaders than women. In other words, when it comes to leadership, the only advantage that men have over women (e.g., from Argentina to Norway and the USA to Japan) is the fact that manifestations of hubris—often masked as charisma or charm—are commonly mistaken for leadership potential, and that these occur much more frequently in men than in women. (Chamorro-Premuzic, 2013)

Looking at women's experiences and feminist ideologies shifts these male-dominated understandings of leadership. Sharing power and helping others to develop their leadership skills are aspects of feminist leadership (Williams, 2008). A feminist leader values members' contributions and participation, seeking inclusion, community building, and egalitarian environments.

Feminist approaches to leadership interact with and contribute to the transformational leadership framework. The 2003 APA initiative on feminist leadership concluded that transformational leadership style is effective for many women leaders (Chin, 2007). Feminist principles apply to the concept of transformational leadership, which is values based and involves collaboration and inclusion, both feminist principles (Chin, 2007; Madden, 2007; Porter and Daniel, 2007). Transformational leadership is future oriented and processual, with often charismatic leaders who motivate employees or followers to reach their potential, inspire change, and are concerned with social and individual needs (Northouse, 2013). Transformational leaders help their employees see the value of their contributions to the organization, as well as look to the future, valuing change. The five practices of transformational leaders are (1) model the way through defining their values; (2) inspire a shared vision through listening and supporting; (3) challenge the process through changing the status quo, innovating, and learning from mistakes; (4) enable others to act through collaboration and fostering trust; and (5) encourage the heart through appreciation and encouragement (Northouse, 2013).

Transformational leadership is an androgynous style of leadership, encompassing inspirational role modeling, mentoring, motivating beyond expectations, and developing positive human relationships with followers, according to Alice Eagly (2013), a social psychology professor at Northwestern University who has studied gender and leadership since the 1980s. The charismatic features of transformational leadership are culturally ascribed to men, while the mentoring and relational aspects are culturally ascribed to women (Eagly, 2013). In her meta-analysis of leadership studies, Eagly concluded that:

> There is considerable evidence that female leaders have a somewhat more participative, androgynous, and transformational leadership style than their male counterparts. There are also multiple indications that women, compared with men, enact their leader roles with a view to producing outcomes that can be described as more compassionate, benevolent, universalistic, and ethical, thus promoting the public good. (2013, p. 8)

When African activist Mary Wandia discussed feminist transformative leadership, she emphasized that it is not "women's leadership" (2011, p. 50), but rather this form of leadership stems from the feminist mission of political, economic, and social equality of the sexes. According to Wandia (2011), feminist transformative leadership is a social process of change to support equality and social justice. In higher education, researcher Tracy Barton (2006a) found that women leaders were ambivalent about power yet saw themselves as promoting social justice and equity. Diversity, fairness, justice, equity, inclusivity, and community building were found to be central to female academic leadership (Barton, 2006b). And in higher education leadership in general, interaction, collaboration, and consensus building are essential. "[University] presidents in this era, both women and men, must be resilient, adaptable, and creative leaders, able to inspire trust and collaboration while juggling a myriad of external as well as internal responsibilities" (Bornstein, 2008, p. 175).

Perceptions of Women Leaders

Gender stereotypes influence perceptions of women leaders, as well as advancement in the pipeline to upper management and beyond. In studies by Catalyst, a global nonprofit research organization that centers on women and business, and McKinsey & Company, a global management consulting firm, stereotypes have significantly affected corporate and individual mindsets, thus stymying women's leadership opportunities (Barsh and Yee, 2011; Catalyst, 2007; McKinsey & Company, 2013).

Taking care versus taking charge underlies these stereotypes. When leadership is defined as assertive and taking charge, these stereotypical masculine behaviors become the "natural" leadership style (Catalyst, 2007). Women seeking consensus appear tentative and thus not as effective as leaders (Bongiomo, Bain, & David, 2013; Bornstein, 2008). Women leaders face the dilemma of conforming to feminine stereotypes and not being seen as leadership material or behaving with masculine characteristics and being labeled or judged harshly. They are either too soft and weak or too tough and aggressive. Regarding gender-stereotypic expectations, women leaders are "damned if they do and doomed if they don't," concluded Catalyst researchers (Catalyst, 2007).

According to leadership scholars Ginka Toegel and Jean-Louis Barsoux (2014):

> If women's behavior confirms the gender stereotype, it lacks credibility and is deemed incongruous with the leader prototype; and if it matches the leader prototype, it lacks authenticity and they are not thought to be acting as proper women. It is a lose-lose situation.

Studies on gender stereotypes have shown that "women can be feminine, warm, and incompetent *or* masculine, cold, and competent" (Madden, 2011). Women leaders are rarely seen as both competent and liked. Women leaders who act authoritatively are more disliked than men, while women and men leaders are equally liked when acting participatory through inclusive leadership (Catalyst, 2007; Cooper, 2013; LeanIn.Org and Girl Scouts of the USA, 2014). Success does not affect likability, but violating gender stereotypes can result in penalties, such as not being promoted (Cooper, 2013). In numerous contexts, women leaders are defined as "overbearing and angry" when the same behaviors displayed by a male leader would be described as "aggressive and direct" (Chin, 2004, p. 7).

In her analysis of women as leaders, Eagly (2013) found that "women often face a double standard in attaining leadership roles" and that "people usually react more favorably to women when they lead with an androgynous style [transformational] rather than one that is either very feminine or very masculine" (p. 5).

A 2013 Gallup poll found that Americans preferred male bosses over female bosses by 35 percent to 23 percent, although four in ten Americans indicated no preference (Newport and Wilke, 2013).

In 2013, 4 percent of CEOs in Fortune 500 companies were women, while 16.9 percent of Fortune 500 board seats were held by women (Catalyst, 2013). Of the 51.5 percent of women in U.S. management, professional, and related occupations, only 14.6 percent of women were represented in Fortune 500 executive officer positions (Catalyst, 2013). Women have not been sponsored as often as men to rise up the corporate ranks, nor have women been given as many large, high-profile assignments as men (Green, 2013).

The 2014 Grant Thornton International Business Report looked at business leadership worldwide, finding that region and gender affected leadership differences. Globally, 24 percent of senior management positions were held by women, with the United States ranking of 22 percent in the bottom ten of forty-five countries, while Russia led with 43 percent and Japan trailed at 9 percent (Grant Thornton International Ltd., 2014).

The context of leadership and power, as reflected in these studies, must be acknowledged, as they show that the pipeline feeding upper management narrows for women. Women, who comprise slightly more than half of U.S. management and professional positions, are dropping out of the pipeline leading to higher positions. In a survey of 4,143 MBA graduates, men started at higher positions than women after graduation, and men moved up the career ladder more quickly than women (Carter and Silva, 2010). Women tended to enter leadership development programs earlier and spend more time in them, but men, after participating in development programs, received more high-profile or mission-critical projects or roles, which often predict advancement (Silva, Carter, & Beninger, 2012). While 51 percent of men who participated in leadership development programs received promotions within a year, only 37 percent of women did (Silva, Carter, & Beninger, 2012). The odds of advancement of men from executive committee to CEO were five times higher than for women (McKinsey & Company, 2013). Yet women are equally as ambitious as men (Carter & Silva, 2010; McKinsey & Company, 2013). A study by McKinsey & Company for the *Wall Street Journal* in 2011 found that women, desiring to advance, remained at their current level due to lack of role models, not having mentors, or being unable to access informal good-old-boy networks (Barsh and Yee, 2011).

The Woman Leader Paradox

Feminist leadership traits rank high in studies of leader characteristics. The woman leader paradox is that feminist and feminine qualities—both chiefly collaboration and relational—are valued in modern business practice, yet stereotypical expectations hold women back. Women perceived that the current corporate environment hinders their chances of promotion to higher management levels, according to a survey of more than 1,400 managers worldwide (McKinsey & Company, 2013). Almost 40 percent of women and 30 percent of men in this survey believed that women's leadership and communications styles were incompatible with leadership styles in the top management of their companies (McKinsey & Company, 2013).

However, in a survey of more than sixty-four thousand people worldwide, researchers John Gerzema and Michael D'Antonio found that traits considered feminine were desired in the modern leader.

> [A]cross the globe, society wants those in power to connect more personally—an understandable response to the hidden agendas and tightly wound power circles often associated with men. . . . In a highly interconnected and interdependent economy, masculine traits like aggression and control (which are largely seen as "independent") are considered less effective than the feminine values of collaboration and sharing credit. (Gerzema & D'Antonio, 2013, p. 11)

Masculine characteristics were identified in the study as decisive, independent, analytical, proud, aggressive, and resilient. Feminine characteristics were named as expressive, loyal, flexible, patient, intuitive, passionate, empathetic, selfless, reasonable, and collaborative (Gerzema & D'Antonio, 2013).

In a survey of 7,280 leaders worldwide, women leaders ranked higher than male leaders in integrity, driving for results, developing others, motivating others, building relationships, collaboration, championing change, solving problems, communication, and innovation (Zenger & Folkman, 2012). Yet women leaders pointed out that they had to work harder to prove themselves and felt pressure to not make mistakes and prove value to the organization (Zenger & Folkman, 2012). Catalyst's analysis of data from more than 1,200

163

leaders worldwide concluded that "women leaders have to choose between working doubly hard for the same level of recognition and getting half the rewards for the same level of competence" (2007, p. 16).

Former U.S. Secretary of State Madeleine Albright, former First Lady and former U.S. Secretary of State Hillary Clinton, current president and chief executive officer of Yahoo! Marissa Mayer, former vice president of General Motors Susan Docherty, and current chief operating officer of Facebook Sheryl Sandberg are all leaders who have been defined against the masculine norm of leadership. Albright wrote in her memoir:

> As I began to climb the ladder, I had to cope with the different vocabularies used to describe similar qualities in men (confident, take-charge, committed) and women (bossy, aggressive, emotional). It took years, but over time I developed enough faith in my judgment to do my job in my own way and style, worrying at least a little less about what others thought. (2013, p. xii)

Clinton has been criticized as being powerful, outspoken, and aggressive, as these break the gender stereotypes. Articles have been written about her when she appeared without makeup and when she cried. Fashion, appearance, and motherhood have been the foci of media stories about Mayer. Sandberg and Docherty have been called bossy.

Docherty, a former vice president of General Motors and president of Chevrolet and Cadillac Europe prior to resigning in 2013 to spend time with her family, displayed a feminist leadership style, building diverse teams and collaborating and soliciting input and perspectives from others. Labeled "bossy," Docherty said:

> And there's a big difference between being a boss and being bossy. And I think it's even more negative when you're a female, because I think that there's a cultural bias. When a man is bossy, he comes across as assertive and in command. When a woman is bossy, she comes off as aggressive and power-hungry. . . . I knew that as a leader, the best way to counteract coming across as being bossy would be to ask others what they thought. (Bryant, 2010)

In early 2014, the "Ban Bossy" campaign, sponsored by Sandberg, LeanIn.Org, and the Girl Scouts of the USA, was launched. As documented by numerous studies and anecdotes by women leaders, the term "bossy" is a sexist, applying to women and implying negative behavior since direct and authoritative behavior by women is called heavy-handed and bossy. Yet that same behavior is labeled in positive tones for men, using words like authoritative, assertive, and commanding. The key message of this campaign is to understand how words and messages perpetuate stereotypes or become weapons of dominance.

"This is a word that is symbolic of systemic discouragement of girls to lead. We are not just talking about getting rid of a word, even though we want to get rid of a word," Sandberg said. "We're talking about getting rid of the negative messages that hold our daughters back" (McFadden & Whitman, 2014).

Conclusion

Words are powerful, describing and controlling meaning. Banning "bossy" would eliminate a term that has become defined as negative and misogynistic. While "feminist" has a negative connotation, this word should not be banned but embraced by women, as well as by men. While the historical foundations and standards of leadership are rooted in masculine-defined attributes, twenty-first-century best practices in leadership rely on historically feminine-defined attributes such as relationship building and collaboration. Feminist principles pervade the transformational leadership style favored by many twenty-first-century leaders, both women and men. Key feminist principles include collaboration, inclusion of diverse experiences and perspectives, acknowledgment of social context, mentoring, and attention to power and social construction of identities.

> For women leaders and feminist leaders, the objectives of leadership include empowering others through (a) one's stewardship of an organization's resources; (b) creating the vision; (c) social advocacy and change; (d) promoting feminist policy and a feminist agenda (i.e., family-oriented work environments, wage gap between men and women); and (e) changing organizational cultures to create gender-equitable environments. For many women, an effective leadership style is transformational. (Chin, 2007, p. 15)

A definition of feminist leadership proposed in the APA initiative is the following:

> Feminist leadership is transformational in nature, seeking to empower and enhance the effectiveness of one's team members while striving to improve the lives and social conditions of all stakeholders including those indirectly affected, such as consumers and other members of society. (Porter & Daniel, 2007, p. 249)

Leadership is a different experience for women and men. However, feminist leadership includes principles that enhance the effectiveness of leaders, regardless of gender. The feminine characteristics of relational practice enhance leadership models for leaders regardless of gender and can contribute to the transformative approach (Bornstein, 2008). Understandings of collaboration and diverse experiences, through the notion of intersectionality and through organizational structures and contexts within which leaders work, turn transformational leadership into feminist transformative leadership.

References

Albright, M. (2013). *Madam Secretary*. New York, NY: HarperCollins.

Barsh, J., & Yee, L. (2011). *Unlocking the full potential of women in the U.S. economy* [special report produced by McKinsey & Company for the *Wall Street Journal* Executive Task Force for Women in the Economy 2011]. Retrieved from the *Wall Street Journal* website: http://online.wsj.com/public/resources/documents/WSJExecutiveSummary.pdf

Barton, T. R. (2006a). Feminist academic leadership: Parallels to President MacKenzie Allen, in Commander in Chief. *Women in Higher Education, 15*(8), 7–9.

Barton, T. R. (2006b). Feminist leadership: Building nurturing academic communities. *Advancing Women in Leadership Online Journal, 21.*

Retrieved from http://www.advancingwomen.com/awl/fall2006/barton.htm

Bongiomo, R., Bain, P. G., & David, B. (2013). If you're going to be a leader, at least act like it! Prejudice towards women who are tentative in leader roles. *British Journal of Social Psychology*. Advance online publication. doi:10.1111/bjso.12032

Bornstein, R. (2008). Women and the college presidency. In J. Glazer-Raymo (Ed.), *Unfinished agendas: New and continuing gender challenges in higher education* (pp. 162–184). Baltimore, MD: The Johns Hopkins University Press.

Bryant, A. (2010, February 6). Now, put yourself in my shoes. *New York Times*. Retrieved from http://www.nytimes.com/2010/02/07/business/07corner.html?pagewanted=all&_r=1&

Carter, N. M., & Silva, C. (2010). *Pipeline's broken promise*. New York, NY: Catalyst.

Catalyst. (2007). *The double-bind dilemma for women in leadership: Damned if you do, doomed if you don't*. New York, NY: Catalyst.

Catalyst. (2013). *Catalyst quick take: Women in U.S. management and labor force*. New York, NY: Catalyst.

Chamorro-Premuzic, T. (2013, August 22). Why do so many incompetent men become leaders? [Web log post]. Retrieved from http://blogs.hbr.org/2013/08/why-do-so-many-incompetent-men/

Chin, J. L. (2004). 2003 Division 35 Presidential address: Feminist Leadership: Feminist visions and diverse voices. *Psychology of Women Quarterly, 28*, 1–8.

Chin, J. L. (2007). Overview: Women and leadership: Transforming visions and diverse voices. In J. L. Chin, B. Lott, J. K. Rice, & J. Sanchez-Hucles (Eds.), *Women and leadership: Transforming visions and diverse voices* (pp. 1–17). Malden, MA: Blackwell Publishing.

Cooper, M. (2013). For women leaders, likability and success hardly go hand-in-hand. [Web log post]. Retrieved from http://blogs.hbr.org/2013/04/for-women-leaders-likability-a/

Crenshaw, K. (1991). Mapping the margins: Intersectionality, identity politics, and violence against women of color. *Stanford Law Review, 43*, 1241–1299.

Day, E. (2013, June 29). Susan Sarandon: "Feminism is a bit of an old-fashioned word." *Guardian*. Retrieved from http://www.theguardian.com/theobserver/2013/jun/30/susan-sarandon-q-and-a

Eagly, A. H. (2013, February). *Women as leaders: Leadership style versus leaders' values and attitudes*. Paper presented at Gender & Work Research Symposium, Harvard Business School, Harvard University, Cambridge, MA.

Fine, M. G. (2007). Women, collaboration, and social change: An ethics-based model of leadership. In J. L. Chin, B. Lott, J. K. Rice, & J. Sanchez-Hucles (Eds.), *Women and leadership: Transforming visions and diverse voices* (pp. 177–191). Malden, MA: Blackwell Publishing.

Fine, M. G. (2009). Women leaders' discursive constructions of leadership. *Women's Studies in Communications, 32*(2), 180–202.

Gerzema, J., & D'Antonio, M. (2013). *The Athena doctrine: How women (and the men who think like them) will rule the future*. San Francisco, CA: Jossey-Bass.

Grant Thornton International Ltd. (2014). *Women in business: From classroom to boardroom* (Grant Thornton International Business Report 2014). Retrieved from http://www.internationalbusinessreport.com/files/IBR2014_WiB_report_FINAL.pdf

Green, S. (2013, September 5). Ambitious women face more obstacles than just work-life balance [Web log post]. Retrieved from http://blogs.hbr.org/2013/09/ambitious-women-face-more-obst/

LeanIn.Org and Girl Scouts of the USA (2014). *Ban bossy: Leadership tips for managers*. Retrieved from http://banbossy.com/manager-tips/

Madden, M. E. (2007). Strategic planning: Gender, collaborative leadership, and organizational change. In J. L. Chin, B. Lott, J. K. Rice, & J. Sanchez-Hucles (Eds.), *Women and leadership: Transforming visions and diverse voices* (pp. 192–208). Malden, MA: Blackwell Publishing.

Madden, M. (2011). Gender stereotypes of leaders: Do they influence leadership in higher education? *Wagadu*, 9. Retrieved from http://appweb.cortland.edu/ojs/index.php/Wagadu/article/viewArticle/638/872

McFadden, C., & Whitman, J. (2014, March 10). Sheryl Sandberg launches "Ban Bossy" campaign to empower girls to lead. Retrieved from http://abcnews.go.com/US/sheryl-sandberg-launches-ban-bossy-campaign-empower-girls/story?id=22819181

McKinsey & Company. (2013). *Gender diversity in top management: Moving corporate culture, moving boundaries* (Women Matter 2013). Paris, France: McKinsey & Company.

Newport, F., & Wilke, J. (2013). *Americans still prefer a male boss: A plurality report that a boss' gender would make no difference* (Gallup Poll). Retrieved from http://www.gallup.com/poll/165791/american-prefer-male-boss.aspx

Northouse, P. G. (2013). *Leadership: Theory and practice* (6th ed.). Thousand Oaks, CA: Sage Publications.

PBS & AOL. (2013). *Makers: Marissa Mayer* [video recording]. Retrieved from http://www.makers.com/marissa-mayer

Porter, N., & Daniel, J. H. (2007). Developing transformational leaders: Theory to practice. In J. L. Chin, B. Lott, J. K. Rice, & J. Sanchez-Hucles (Eds.), *Women and leadership: Transforming visions and diverse voices* (pp. 245–263). Malden, MA: Blackwell Publishing.

Silva, C., Carter, N. M., & Beninger, A. (2012). *Good intentions, imperfect execution? Women get fewer of the "hot jobs" needed to advance.* New York, NY: Catalyst.

Solomon, D. (2009, March 16). Case closed: Questions for Sandra Day O'Connor. *New York Times.* Retrieved from http://www.nytimes.com/2009/03/22/magazine/22wwln-q4-t.html?_r=1&

Suyemoto, K. L., & Ballou, M. B. (2007). Conducted monotones of coacted harmonies: A feminist (re)conceptualization of leadership addressing race, class, and gender. In J. L. Chin, B. Lott, J. K. Rice, & J. Sanchez-Hucles (Eds.), *Women and leadership: Transforming visions and diverse voices* (pp. 35–54). Malden, MA: Blackwell Publishing.

Toegel, G., & Barsoux, J. (2012, July 17). Women leaders: The gender trap. *European Business Review.* Retrieved from http://www.european-businessreview.com/?p=2482

Wandia, M. (2011, July). Challenging structural inequalities: The vision of feminist transformative leadership. *BUWA!—A Journal on African Women's Experiences, 1,* 47–52.

Williams, M. (2008, October). Principles for feminist leadership: Struggling to share power. *PeaceWork: Global Thought and Local Action for Nonviolent Social Change, 389.* Retrieved from http://www.peaceworkmagazine.org/principles-feminist-leadership-struggling-share-power

Zenger, J., & Folkman, J. (2012). Are women better leaders than men? [Web log post]. Retrieved from http://blogs.hbr.org/2012/03/a-study-in-leadership-women-do/

Developing Twenty-First-Century Leaders Through Transformational Leadership

Mary Mara, Matt Lechner, Tammy Salman, and Jennifer Bodley
Library and Learning Resource Center

Abstract

Creativity, collaboration, communication, and critical thinking are skills in demand by twenty-first-century employers to meet the needs of rapidly changing industries. Successful leaders will master these skills and effectively apply them to solve industry and organizational challenges. Librarians and academic technology staff at City University of Seattle apply creativity, collaboration, communication, and critical thinking skills to navigate today's changing digital information landscape and to transform the nature of the resources and services they provide. They serve as transformational leaders, collaborating with faculty to develop twenty-first-century skills in CityU graduates through an innovative information literacy and academic technology program that is integrated within the context of specific disciplines.

Description

Information science leaders and professionals working in libraries and learning resource centers are keenly aware of the rapid pace of change in the publishing and content aggregation industries, as well as the impact it has on the delivery of resources and services. Users increasingly expect that all information will be accessible online at no cost, contradicting the simultaneous drive by the publishers to maintain profitability in their role as information owners and producers. The rate of change and the needs of users and publishers create complexities which include:

- Vendor-specific discovery and delivery platforms, each with unique navigation and capabilities;
- Varied pricing and access models that limit length of access or users' ability to make print copies;
- Nonstandard formats that limit users' ability to access information on their device of choice; and
- An exponentially increasing amount of open access and self-published information and data of varying quality.

Librarians are all too familiar with the gap between users' expectations for free and easy online access to the exact information they need and the real challenges of facilitating access to valuable information via proprietary platforms. The complexities of the digital publishing industry and information landscape significantly affect the ability of librarians to meet the needs and expectations of the stakeholders they serve.

Evidence that librarians are wrestling with these issues and future models for resource and service delivery is evident in recent publications such as *Library 2020,* edited by Joseph Janes of the University of

Washington's iSchool; *Planning Our Future Libraries: Blueprints for 2025,* by Leeder and Frierson; and *Futures Thinking for Academic Libraries: Higher Education in 2025* prepared by Staley and Malenfant on behalf of the Association of College and Research Libraries division of the American Library Association. Academic and public libraries are responding to rapid change in a variety of ways, with each approach reflective of the unique population of stakeholders and their needs. As Molly Raphael (2013), 2011 president of the American Library Association, states:

> The pace of change is accelerating so rapidly that we have to be willing to take risks not only when developing and transforming our services but also in redefining our roles. We cannot just hold on to the things we like to do or the things that we studied in library school years ago. We must adapt to so many changes around us in our global, digital world—demographic, economic, social, and so forth—and take the opportunity to lead our communities. (p. 79)

Librarians are significantly challenged to meet their mission of acquiring, managing, and facilitating access to quality information that meets their stakeholders' needs when the entire information environment, particularly the model for digital information access, is in its current high state of flux. Not only must librarians possess the skills necessary to navigate a rapidly changing industry, they must provide leadership within their profession and for their stakeholders as they look to the future and transform their services and the role they fill within their organizations.

The pace of change experienced by librarians is not unique to their discipline. It mirrors changes found across such disciplines as communication, globally connected commerce, P–12 education, higher education, and many other professions. The futurist Thomas Frey (n.d.) is aware of the pace of change employers and employees are facing, with the demand for new skills changing quickly. As Frey states: "As a rule of thumb, 60 percent of the jobs 10 years from now haven't been invented yet" (section 8 para. 4). Preparing for the jobs of the future requires a new set of skills that goes beyond mere content knowledge. Harvard education specialist Tony Wagner further suggests that "because knowledge is available on every Internet-connected device, what you know matters far less than what you can do with what you know. The capacity to innovate—the ability to solve problems creatively or bring new possibilities to life—and skills like critical thinking, communication and collaboration are far more important than academic knowledge" (Friedman, 2013). Employers can teach workers the content they need for their job, but it is much harder to quickly teach an employee big-picture, future-oriented skills.

The skills needed to effectively adapt to changes within information science and other professions are commonly referred to as twenty-first-century skills.

> Twenty-first-century skills, crucial to learning success, are characterized by the "four Cs": creativity, collaboration, communication, and critical thinking. These skills are needed to succeed today and will remain in high demand in 2020. They are not based on knowledge of specific content; they are the abilities needed to analyze and solve problems regardless of the content area. Content knowledge remains important, but critical thinking skills are essential for success in a world where content is constantly changing and evolving (Hildreth, 2013, p. 100).

Within higher education, twenty-first century skills have been articulated and defined as "essential learning outcomes" by the Association of American Colleges & Universities (AAC&U) through the VALUE Rubrics. The VALUE Rubrics organize these skills into three groups: intellectual and practical skills, personal and social responsibility, and integrative and applied learning (AAC&U, 2014). Librarians must demonstrate twenty-first-century skills and master essential learning outcomes to maintain currency in their field and stay abreast of changes in the information and technology sectors that influence the resources and services they provide to their stakeholders.

In addition to applying twenty-first-century skills to navigate changes in the digital information landscape, librarians must be effective leaders as they assume new roles within their organizations and transform the nature of the resources and services they provide through libraries and learning resource centers to meet their users' needs and expectations. Librarians in academic settings must apply creativity, collaboration, communication, and critical thinking to transform from a traditional role as the keeper of materials to a contemporary role in which they facilitate access to digital information and support the development of these same twenty-first-century skills within their users. They must also adopt a culturally relevant leadership model that enables the evolution of their role within their institution. City University of Seattle's library and learning resource center staff apply twenty-first-century skills and transformational leadership to continually evolve to meet the needs of academic programs, while simultaneously supporting and instructing faculty and students in these critical skills that will enable graduates to become leaders within their future professions.

Application

Building Twenty-First-Century Skills at City University of Seattle

City University of Seattle (CityU) is a private, non-profit university with faculty and students distributed at thirty-three locations in eleven countries. Over the past seven years, the CityU Library and Learning Resource Center has transformed from a traditional print-based, in-person model of resource and service delivery to a non-traditional model facilitating access to a collection that is 97 percent digital and delivering instruction and support services through the application of constantly evolving technologies. Given the high percentage of digital resources in the CityU Library, faculty, students, and staff are particularly affected by industry changes in the models for proprietary digital information delivery. As CityU develops more courses with electronic textbooks, for example, it is increasingly important for the library to select materials on robust platforms that allow unlimited simultaneous users. Librarians must also watch for publishers pulling content, such as journal articles, from aggregated databases. Librarians work to ensure uninterrupted access to these resources by finding them elsewhere or finding suitable alternatives that meet the needs of students and faculty. It is also important to keep up with the multiplying access models being offered by content vendors. E-books can now be purchased individually, in subject sets, through short-term-loan and patron-driven acquisitions where purchases are triggered by users themselves, or even "all-you-can-eat" subscription models (Martin, 2014). To maximize return on investment and access to high-quality information in a predominantly digital collection, all options must be considered.

At CityU, librarians and academic technology (AT) staff are responsible for the development and delivery of a course-embedded instruction program that supports the university's learning goal of information literacy and critical thinking. These twenty-first-century learning skills set the standard that:

> City University of Seattle graduates are able to think critically and to reflect upon their own work and the larger context in which it takes place. They are able to find, access, evaluate, and use information in order to solve problems. They consider the complex implications of actions they take and decisions they make. (City University of Seattle, 2014)

In recent years, the CityU Library has broadened its role to provide support for academic technologies such as Tegrity Lecture Capture and Blackboard Collaborate web conferencing, which allow for increased faculty-student collaboration online. CityU librarians are creative in seeking affordable, relevant solutions for resource and service delivery that meet the needs of students and faculty distributed worldwide, mirroring the types of technology that graduates will encounter in their professions. CityU librarians effectively communicate their vision for equal access to resources and services wherever and whenever students and faculty are learning and teaching. CityU librarians collaborate with faculty to develop the university's innovative online and discipline-specific information literacy instruction and academic technology support program. They think critically about the resources and services they offer and take informed risks in the evolution of their role within the university.

Transformational Leadership: A Model for Achieving the Academic Library Vision

Applying and teaching twenty-first-century skills are important, but these skills alone are not sufficient for successfully achieving the library's vision. In order to help develop students who meet employers' needs for graduates with essential skills, library staff must serve as leaders who model these skills within the university, internalize the department's and university's vision, and engage in supportive methods for teaching students and collaborating with faculty. As leaders, CityU Library staff exhibit traits expressed by the transformational model of leadership: "Transformational leadership fits the needs of today's work groups, who want to be inspired and empowered to succeed in times of uncertainty" (Northouse, 2010, p. 171).

Given the state of flux in the library and information industry, CityU Library has adapted its practices based on changes in its external environment as well as within the higher education landscape and at the university itself. For example, librarians have led the charge to change the library's instruction model based on literature from the library science field indicating a need for instructional methods beyond the traditional one-shot, in-person delivery model, which typically comes at the beginning of a course and is not tied to any assignments. The literature confirms the personal experiences of CityU librarians, instructors, and students alike that this traditional model is not always the most effective. A recent study by Van Epps and Nelson (2013) indicated a correlation between just-in-time library instruction and an increase in students' use of high-quality resources. The researchers found that students in one-shot instruction sessions did not locate and use as many quality resources in their assignments. At CityU, librarians partner with faculty to move the library's legacy one-shot instruction program toward one that is discipline specific, integrated at students' point of need, and accessible to students worldwide online. CityU librarians, in collaboration with academic technology (AT) staff, use technology to deliver instruction, experimenting with emerging tools and resources to create engaging experiences.

From 2011 to 2014, the library has expanded its role at the university to include training and support for faculty and students on the effective use of academic technologies in the classroom and in online courses. Librarians and AT staff model use of these technologies and test them prior to recommending them for faculty and student use. The technologies that prove most effective are often adopted by faculty and students to develop engaging online interactions and are relevant for CityU graduates as they move into their professions.

Applying the Transformational Leadership Model

Avolio and Bass (2001) define transformational leadership through four factors: idealized influence, inspirational motivation, intellectual stimulation, and individualized consideration. Transformational leaders employ one or more of the four factors to serve as coaches and mentors who inspire and motivate followers and promote innovation (p. 2). Application of all four factors is evident in the work of CityU's librarians and AT staff and, while all factors contribute to the library's ability to evolve and effectively meet the university's goal to develop graduates who are information and technology literate, the factor of individualized consideration is most prominent.

Idealized influence. Through idealized influence, leaders provide a mission and vision for what they wish to accomplish and act as role models for their followers. They demonstrate high standards and are respected by those they work with.

In 2007, CityU librarians began the shift to an online instruction program, developed in collaboration with faculty, to ensure that graduates of CityU at locations worldwide achieve information and technology literacy relevant to their disciplines and professions. The instruction program incorporates methods for supporting and training faculty and students on the skills necessary to find, evaluate, and use information and on effective use of technology for teaching and learning. Specifically, librarians partner with faculty to ensure that students achieve the City University Learning Goals, aligned with AAC&U VALUE Rubrics, on the achievement of information and technology literacy.

CityU librarians understand and share with faculty their vision that all graduates will leave their programs with the ability to find, critically evaluate, and appropriately use information and data to make evidence-based decisions. The instruction program supports development of information literacy and technology skills from introductory to mastery levels across academic programs. Students begin by learning to access the information and resources they need to complete authentic assessments within their courses, developing into graduates with the skills necessary to continue using relevant, high-quality information through professional organizations and public libraries. Throughout student and faculty interactions with librarians, librarians model finding, evaluating, and using relevant information via instruction that is delivered using technology such as Blackboard Collaborate for webinars, Blackboard discussion boards, and media developed with tools such as Tegrity.

Respect for the program developed at CityU is evident in its growth over time, the ongoing commitment of faculty to collaborating with CityU librarians, and commendations received for the program from the university's accrediting agency, the Northwest Commission on Colleges and Universities.

Inspirational motivation. Through inspirational motivation leaders consistently communicate a vision, emphasize shared responsibility for and commitment to achieving the vision, and motivate those around them to contribute toward achievement of the vision (Avolio & Bass, 2001, p. 2).

CityU Library's instruction program supports student achievement of university and program learning outcomes on information literacy through an integrated, discipline-specific approach to developing essential skills and abilities graduates need to find, evaluate, access, and use information. The program aims to prepare information-competent students who can define the type of information needed for specific situations and effectively apply strategies to use information and technology for the purpose of academic achievement and lifelong learning. The library instruction program's success depends upon consistent communication of the vision for the program and collaboration between faculty and librarians to embed information literacy competencies and instruction in all programs at the introductory, practice, and mastery levels.

Through shared responsibilities with faculty for developing the information literacy and technology skills in graduates, instruction librarians collaborate with and support faculty and curriculum development in the following ways:

- developing institutional-, program-, and course-level rubrics with language specific to information literacy skills, such as finding, evaluating, and using information effectively;
- engaging faculty in discussions about information resources, technology, and instructional support available through the library;
- partnering with faculty in specific courses to teach twenty-first century skills;
- promoting and modeling the use of academic technology in face-to-face and online courses; and

- participating on school curriculum councils and university-level committees.

Successes achieved in programs are celebrated and shared between faculty and librarians to promote the continuing expansion and improvement of CityU's integrated information literacy and technology instruction and support programs.

Intellectual stimulation. Through intellectual stimulation leaders encourage followers to be creative and innovative in their approach to developing new ways to address organizational issues (Northouse, 2010, p. 179). Followers are encouraged to question assumptions and to approach persistent issues in new ways (Avolio & Bass, 2001, p. 2).

Librarians at CityU are encouraged to be creative and innovative in their approach to supporting the development of information and technology literacy in faculty and students. They are encouraged to read outside traditional library literature and across disciplines to stay current on best practices for learning and teaching, and to keep up with relevant trends within the disciplines they support. With faculty, they adapt instructional practices and create professional development opportunities that emphasize emerging best practices for teaching in-person or online in higher education.

The Association of College and Research Libraries (ACRL), for example, provides intense weeklong sessions on reflective teaching, teaching with technology, programmatic assessment, and leading from within to effect change (Association of College and Research Libraries, 2014). CityU instruction librarians and AT staff embrace such professional development opportunities and apply new pedagogical strategies to meet shifting higher education and technology trends. They also pursue opportunities to expand their view of trends through participation in online programs and publications from academic library organizations, as well as the e-Learning Guild, Educause, Blackboard's Exemplary Course Program, the Global Education Conference, and other higher education and technology-related organizations. CityU librarians follow developments in the professional organizations for the programs they support such as the Project Management Institute, Association for Supervision and Curriculum Development, and the Center for Creative Leadership.

Opportunities to share what they have learned and to mentor faculty on the adoption of proven strategies arise through librarian participation on academic committees, program and course design teams, and through the university's faculty learning community.

Individualized consideration. Through individualized consideration, leaders act as coaches or mentors, developing colleagues to successively higher levels of potential. Leaders listen effectively to the needs of followers and colleagues, recognizing different needs (Avolio & Bass, 2001, p. 3).

There are many ways in which the CityU Library's instruction and academic technology teams serve as coaches and mentors who model and share best practices for faculty and students navigating modern information systems. One way librarians share learning with others is in an online learning community for staff and faculty where they post and discuss new ideas and methods of teaching and learning. Another way is by featuring exemplary practices by CityU instructors in faculty vignettes. A standout instructor is interviewed about his or her particular practice of using technology to improve course delivery, and this is condensed and published as a one-page vignette to spread the innovative instruction technique to other instructors.

Just as CityU Library's instruction program exemplifies collaboration and teaches critical thinking, the academic technology team promotes communication along with creativity—addressing all four twenty-first-century skills as embodied by the Four Cs. Many CityU students do not ever visit the main campus in person, and when they graduate, they may very well work in fields in which key constituents are not physically present. AT staff administer and teach tools and techniques, to facilitate communication with remote users, which are similar to those that CityU graduates may use in their professions. For example, CityU uses Blackboard Collaborate for web conferencing, and AT staff train faculty and staff in its use, but the skills they learn—from hardware setup to online etiquette—apply to all web conferencing platforms. Web conferencing allows groups of students to work collaboratively on projects, share their desktops with one another for demonstrations, or even meet with their instructor for virtual office hours. In the business world, web conferencing is a vital method of connecting with both colleagues and clients; CityU graduates will be primed to participate and communicate online as a result of their academic experiences.

An added effect of online communication tools supported by the CityU Library is to increase the connection between faculty and student in the online environment. This improves students' sense of the instructor as a person, and builds a sense of community in the online course. Effective participation in online communities benefits students who may find themselves working in distributed organizations after graduating, whether they are businesspeople working with remote colleagues or teachers developing rapport online with parents unable to visit in person. Another tool employed for this purpose is Tegrity Lecture Capture software, which allows students to view video content posted by their instructor and ask follow-up questions about difficult concepts in the presentation. Students can chat in real time with each other and/or their instructor if they want to view lectures together online (or even watch lectures in real time if the instructor so chooses). Finally, instructors can enable students to create their own recordings to submit for a graded presentation or simply to share a project with their classmates.

In addition to promoting tools that support critical thinking and collaboration, academic technology staff in the library and LRC empowers faculty and students to create their own rich media content—addressing the twenty-first skill of creativity. Users are assisted with video creation and editing in dedicated Recording Rooms on both PC and Apple computers. As part of the content creation process, users also learn the best ways to stream media content as well as store content with an understanding of the associated privacy concerns. The AT staff recommends tools and techniques as well as guides users through the steps to create and manage content, from self-recordings for job applications to video mash-ups for class assignments to webinars for reaching a wider audience with an educational presentation. For remote users, AT staff create screencast tutorials to introduce new tools and technologies. They help users create their own screencasts using free online tools. In a world increasingly focused on visual communication through the effective use of media, the ability to condense and creatively present instructions for a complex task is an important twenty-first-century skill that will serve graduates well in their chosen fields.

Case Study: Applying Transformational Leadership to an Academic Program

The following case study provides an example of how CityU librarians have applied transformational leadership to move its Bachelor of Arts in Education (BAEd) program from the model of traditional one-shot, in-person information literacy instruction sessions to an innovative information literacy and academic technology program, developed in collaboration with faculty and integrated within the context of specific disciplines. The BAEd program supports development of twenty-first-century skills (creativity, collaboration, communication, and critical thinking) in CityU graduates through EDU 350, Introduction to Field Experience.

About EDU 350. EDU 350 is typically the first course in the Bachelor of Arts in Education (BAEd) program where students encounter professional, education-related resources and engage with peers in collaborative work. Throughout the BAEd program, students need to access the type of professional education resources introduced in EDU 350 to enhance learning and for use in assignments. In this course, the librarian works with instructors and students to establish student confidence and success in performing research and collaboration online.

Librarian support of EDU 350 includes a range of activities such as creating learning units, posting announcements, presenting research strategies via Blackboard Collaborate web conferencing, hosting weekly discussion boards, and providing individual reference and instruction to students. Learning units specific to writing in a professional style and finding professional resources are developed in collaboration with faculty and embedded in Blackboard, CityU's online learning management system. Announcements, posted throughout the quarter, initiate a relationship between the librarian and students and extend instruction that supports the development of information literacy skills. Announcements may include the librarian's welcome and introduction, research and professional writing tips, and instructional session recaps.

Blackboard Collaborate sessions focus on database search skills, modeling research and information literacy skills for students such as how to articulate an issue and develop effective keywords to find relevant information. Discussion boards focus on finding professional associations and education-related websites, extending the scope of resources consulted and connecting students early in the program to the organizations that drive research agendas and discuss industry standards and best practices within the discipline. Individual reference and instruction on various topics is initiated by student contact.

Idealized influence: Articulate vision of skill acquisition. Librarians exhibit idealized influence through work with faculty in academic programs by articulating why students at all levels should know how to find, use, and evaluate information critically; by modeling best practices in the use of technology and research strategies; and by supporting students and instructors equally in face-to-face and online classes. Librarians target key courses for instruction based on curriculum matrices that show course and program alignment with university learning goals, including the goal for information literacy. The matrices also highlight specific assignments across each program that meet introductory, practice, and mastery levels for each learning goal.

At the course level in EDU 350, idealized influence is demonstrated through librarian-led course activities which model the use of technology in a class setting, guide students to relevant resources, and coach students in all course sections in effective library research methods. Activities include learning units, regular announcements, research strategy exercises, synchronous Blackboard Collaborate web conferencing, librarian-led discussion boards, and individual instruction for students.

For example, the librarian for EDU 350 hosts a synchronous Blackboard Collaborate session with face-to-face class sections that convene at locations across western Washington. The librarian leads the session from her computer with the help of the students' instructor, who helps engage the class in a variety of activities. This instructional session covers multiple information literacy topics, such as keyword searching and locating resources through professional teaching organizations. For online class sections, the librarian provides equivalent instruction via announcements, short tutorial videos, and learning activities that cover the same topics.

Inspirational motivation: Facilitate shared responsibility for teaching. At the program and course level, librarians exhibit inspirational motivation by emphasizing a commitment to CityU's vision of achieving information- and technology-literate students. This is accomplished through shared responsibility with faculty for developing instructional support. Throughout EDU 350, the librarian maintains contact with instructors for all sections, asking them how they and the students are doing and adjusting instructional content based on faculty feedback. Specifically, the librarian asks whether students understand library research and whether they need further help learning how to provide proper attribution in their assignments. If many students are struggling, the librarian responds immediately with announcements, tips, and strategies for writing and citing.

Intellectual stimulation: Stay informed about trends and model technology use. Through intellectual stimulation, librarians monitor trends in higher education and instructional technology, and they test and apply a variety of strategies and academic technology to enhance instructional content. As part of course preparation for ECU 350, the librarian encourages instructors to set up and participate in synchronous online sessions. The librarian collaborates with academic technology staff to ensure instructors have prior training and feel comfortable using it in their courses. During synchronous sessions, students and faculty can see the librarian, ask and respond to questions, and view real-time library search strategies.

Individualized consideration: Coach students toward future professions. In EDU 350, the librarian exhibits individualized consideration by coaching students as a group and one-on-one, addressing each student's unique needs and assessing their library research comfort level. Additionally, the librarian hosts a weeklong online discussion on finding and exploring professional associations within the context of the teacher candidates' future subject specialty. While some students are interested in literacy, others want to focus on special education, and others may want to become math teachers. Through online discussions, the librarian has a conversation with each student about his or her particular research interest.

With every online or in-person encounter with students, the librarian's message is always that her job is to support and guide the students. In this way, the librarian works as a coach and mentor to the students. The series of encounters provides scaffolding opportunities through which students are coached to successively higher skill levels of finding, evaluating, and using information to solve an issue. The librarian is able to give individualized feedback in both discussion boards and in student-initiated reference contacts.

Analysis

All CityU Library staff are passionate about helping people find and use information and helping students get the most from their education, whether they take classes in-person or online. To this end, the Four Cs of creativity, collaboration, communication, and critical thinking are important skills for the library staff both to model and to promote. Librarians aid students' development of these twenty-first-century skills through application of transformational leadership, which offers a model for positive, visionary change within an organization.

This model fits with the work librarians do to carry out the library's instruction program, but it may not be the best model for students moving into the workforce or into new careers. While graduates will be able to carry twenty-first-century skills into their future workplace, they may adopt different leadership models or develop specific leadership skills relevant to effecting change in their organizations.

The library's course-integrated instruction program has been generally successful, taking longer to develop and implement than anticipated since its inception in 2005. A variety of factors contributed to this: faculty buy-in to a shift in academic library pedagogy from the one-shot orientation, which attempts to fit the whole of library research into one session and does not correlate to any assignments, to instruction focused on specific information skills; librarians' buy-in to a new instructional model; and librarians' understanding and internalizing of the library's vision for student learning. Librarians needed to feel confident in articulating this vision in order to build trust with faculty, test tools and methods for online instruction delivery, and partner with faculty willing to integrate the revised instruction model.

CityU librarians understand anecdotally from colleagues at other institutions what works and what does not in terms of information and digital literacy instruction, but librarians often struggle to balance an orientation toward service with wanting to provide meaningful, lasting instruction that elevates students' skills beyond just knowing that there is a library available. The pervasive understanding that libraries are accommodating and simply fill requests—for resources or orientations or anything related to finding information—can be a hurdle to overcome when faculty and staff outside the library do not understand the depth of assistance librarians can provide. Librarians may adopt this way of thinking and may consider that not fulfilling the wishes of students and faculty could be seen as a weakness or lack of service (Meulemans & Carr, 2013).

In order to overcome this hurdle and build trust with faculty, CityU librarians focused on collaboration and engaged in "small conversations" with faculty about common themes related to finding, evaluating, and using the types of information sources faculty deemed important for student success (Jacobs & Jacobs, 2009, p. 79). From these conversations, the integrated instruction program began with primarily non-required activities related to information and digital literacy. Gradually, from 2011 to 2014, librarians' confidence in the vision grew, and librarians began to consider themselves teachers and partners with a stake in meeting essential learning outcomes. This shift in thinking has led to librarians feeling ownership over the university's information literacy learning goal and building twenty-first-century skills into the curriculum and into specific courses. From small-scale work in a few online or in-person courses, librarians moved to developing instructional modules and required course activities. Since the librarians began tracking required course activities, the number of required activities created by and/or delivered by librarians has increased from fifty-seven in the 2012–13 academic year to sixty-seven from summer through winter quarters of 2013–14. Addition of the academic technology team hastened the adoption of tools for delivering instruction in a variety of ways and helped to increase collaboration between faculty and the library.

Looking at the library's instruction efforts through the lens of transformational leadership, empowering instruction librarians and the academic technology team at CityU to view themselves as teachers and leaders who are responsible for carrying out the CityU information literacy learning goal has elevated the teams' work within the department and across the university.

The instruction team's next phase of leadership will include a coordinated and robust assessment of student attainment of information literacy as part of the university's comprehensive assessment plan. Librarians will use this assessment to make revisions to the instruction program, which will further enhance faculty-librarian relationships and increase students' attainment of essential learning outcomes.

Value

The rapidly changing digital information environment within which librarians work mirrors the pace of change experienced across higher education and other professions. The rate of change is not slowing, but increasing, and academic libraries are well positioned to develop information and technology literacy among graduates. Librarians can accomplish this by adopting a leadership model such as transformational leadership, which emphasizes inspirational motivation to facilitate team achievements, development of innovative approaches to solve issues, and responsiveness to individual needs through coaching and mentoring.

Transformational leadership is a flexible model for positive, visionary change within an organization that has value for many professions beyond the library and higher education. Transformational leaders initiating or responding to changes in the workplace may adopt any one or more of the four factors identified by Avolio & Bass (2001), which include idealized influence, inspirational motivation, intellectual stimulation, and individualized consideration. Initial efforts may focus on a single factor and build on its success over time. This encompassing approach can be adopted by staff at any level of an organization to effect change; it "can be used to describe a wide range of leadership, from very specific attempts to influence followers on a one-to-one level, to very broad attempts to influence whole organizations" (Northouse, 2010, pp. 171–172).

References

Association of American Colleges and Universities. (2014). *VALUE: Valid Assessment of Learning in Undergraduate Education*. Retrieved from http://www.aacu.org/value/rubrics/index_p.cfm

Association of College and Research Libraries. (2014). *ACRL information literacy immersion program*. Retrieved from http://www.ala.org/acrl/immersionprogram

Avolio, B. J., & Bass, B. M. (2001). *Developing potential across a full range of leaderships: Cases on transactional and transformational leadership*. Mahwah, NJ: Lawrence Erlbaum.

City University of Seattle. (2014). *Academic model*. Retrieved from http://www.cityu.edu/about/profile/academic_model.aspx

Frey, T. (2014, March 21). *162 future jobs: Preparing for jobs that don't yet exist*. Retrieved from http://www.futuristspeaker.com

Friedman, T. L. (2013, March 31). Need a job? Invent it. *New York Times.*

Hildreth, S. (2013). Chapter 15. In J. Janes (Ed.), *Library 2020: Today's leading visionaries describe tomorrow's library* (pp. 99–103). Lanham, MD: Scarecrow Press.

Jacobs, H. M., & Jacobs, D. (2009). Transforming the one-shot library session into pedagogical collaboration: Information literacy and the English composition class. *Reference & User Services Quarterly*, *49*(1), 72–82.

Martin, E. J. (2014, January 2). Unconventional ebook pricing: Digital publishers thinking outside the a la carte box. *Econtent*. Retrieved from http://www.econtentmag.com/Articles/News/News-Feature/Unconventional-Ebook-Pricing-Digital-Publishers-Thinking-Outside-the-a-la-Carte-Box-94013.htm

Meulemans, Y., & Carr, A. (2013). Not at your service: Building genuine faculty-librarian partnerships. *Reference Services Review*, *41*(1), 80–90. doi:10.1108/00907321311300893

Northouse, P. G. (2010). *Leadership: Theory and practice* (5th ed.). Los Angeles, CA: Sage Publications.

Raphael, M. (2013). Chapter 11. In J. Janes (Ed.), *Library 2020: Today's leading visionaries describe tomorrow's library* (pp. 77–82). Lanham, MD: Scarecrow Press.

Van Epps, A., & Nelson, M. (2013). One-shot or embedded? Assessing different delivery timing for information resources relevant to assignments. *Evidence Based Library & Information Practice*, 8(1), 4–18.

Institutional Leadership for Multicultural Integration in Higher Education

Laura Carrillo de Anda
CETYS University System: International Relations

Abstract

In order to be able to conduct an effective multicultural analysis, many features need to be evaluated to find strengths and weaknesses, to determine where change is needed, to define new strategic measures, and to take strategic decisions with the purpose of improving the multicultural setting of the organization. CETYS University is at a stage where leadership is aware of the multicultural trend in higher education, and it is taking a proactive role by engaging its people—the human talent—in assessing global risks to build its knowledge of customs, norms, languages, legal systems, and other cultural capabilities. This paper describes as a case example a multicultural analysis of CETYS University with a clear depiction of its cross-cultural challenges and commitment to multicultural leadership. A diversity of strategic actions is being embraced by leadership for helping and supporting a new direction in the improvement of the institution's global performance.

Introduction

The common practice of internationalization in higher education brings along a valuable strength represented in academic mobility that contributes to the development of science, technology, and innovation in teaching and learning. Multicultural learning happens when mobile students and scholars bring cultures, languages, curricula, organizations, and traditions with them when they choose to live an international experience in higher education (Fletcher, 2012). Understanding diversity is no longer optional for students, it is a must-have ability for developing a global mindset; leadership understands that embracing the necessity of diversity will create a competitive advantage (Uhlig, Quentin, Chang, & Dominguez, 2007). As an example of one institution that has recognized the need to embrace multiculturalism into its future, CETYS University is highlighted as a case study example.

An appropriate and realistic organizational transition analysis of CETYS University starts with the long history of transition events in the life of the institution. Since 1961 when CETYS was born in the city of Mexicali, Mexico, leadership has faced many challenges, has explored new approaches for a renewed decision-making process, and has established new strategies for institutional assessment and for institutional planning where the workforce is connected to a core mission and vision. The management of diverse resources at CETYS University is a strategic action with different levels of complexity depending upon the organizational framework. Leadership at CETYS University is facing multicultural challenges mainly due to an innovative decision-making process by leadership seeking broader international activity in the global context of higher education; this includes international mobility of students and faculty, and collaborative academic projects with foreign institutions. Ultimately, the organization depends on its professional workforce to make it increasingly more competitive in the global economy (Caligiuri, 2012). Leadership has embraced the responsibility of providing international awareness, international knowledge, international experiences, and international development for students and faculty as one of the main streams of the institutional strategic plan.

The 2020 Strategic Development Plan of CETYS defines this institution's raison d'être for the following years; it poses strategic trends and clearly expresses the challenges and implications it faces. The purpose is the opportunity for students (high school, undergraduate, and graduate) and faculty of developing a global mindset in terms of multicultural environments, global business frameworks, and international collaborative efforts. Many institutions in higher education throughout the world have been attracting students to study abroad because it is important to establish the linkage between "knowledge-producing countries" and "knowledge-seeking students" (Fletcher, 2012). Leadership must be willing to take more risks, to understand and learn from experiences of institutions of higher education around the world, to face undetermined issues, to place the image of the institution at high national and international level, and to create a change in international attitude inside and outside of the institution, if they want to increase international attraction.

International Exposure and Its Effects on the Development of Students as Future Global Leaders

The new vision of CETYS University is set as follows: "CETYS University will be a high-quality educational institution, competitive worldwide, functioning as a learning community, and recognized by its actions and results in favor of sustainable development." The focus of this vision is that it defines the type of university CETYS intends to be by its humanist education parameters, global competitiveness, viability, and sustainability for the following ten years. Leadership defines and operates a high-quality education strategy that guarantees measurable results in the key processes of the institutional life (student learning, the role of faculty, academic programs, and finance management, among others). Additional emphasis of this new vision is the strengthening of strategies that consolidate CETYS in the international field, and its positioning as a competitive university in this context (2020 CETYS University Strategic Development Plan).

Institutional leadership has decided that the first strategy for enhancing international development opportunities for students and faculty is the transformation of the institutional vision into a new vision with an international approach. A new strategic line of direction in this vision is sustainability in higher education, and leadership has gone through the process of identifying and defining leadership capabilities and challenges in the context of sustainability. Some of the strategic actions are offering students the opportunity to acquire an international dimension, by adding value to people, and by contributing with ideas and principles that lead to the solution of local and global problems while fostering a global mindset. This is supported by an immersion in multicultural experiences with the understanding and sensitivity toward other cultures, by achieving the mastery level in an additional language, and by acquiring the required skills that will allow them to excel in their professional lives. One learning strategy with strong presence in current higher education is distance education (e-learning) by structuring academic programs in a diversity of disciplines, and it does not necessarily require the physical movement of the educational consumer or provider (Linhan, 2012).

Thomas and Inkson (2004) defined that cultural intelligence enables people to recognize cultural differences through knowledge and mindfulness, and it gives a propensity and ability to act appropriately across cultures and the many strategic actions that CETYS has embraced. This explains how the institution has taken the stepping stone in each of the stages of global development using a set of values embedded in the institutional education model, the mission, and a newly designed international vision. Leadership has been increasing the level of awareness of the importance of social, cultural, and contextual factors of an organization's creativity (Paulus, 2003). From the academic program's perspective, leadership expects that academic staff participate in the design of programs ready to undertake new multicultural experiences with institutions from other countries.

The Board of Trustees of CETYS University represents the main strength for the decision- making process geared toward the growth and development of the institution. The board of the three campuses is very committed and aware of the many challenges that the institution is currently facing in all three locations (Tijuana, Mexicali, and Ensenada, Mexico); as entrepreneurs, they understand and get involved in a well-planned decision-making process. Sustainability on the board is continuing on a natural pathway. The second-generation board members are coming on board with an innovative attitude, and they are ready to undertake the challenges and carry out strategic changes.

Efforts to become a sustainable institution of higher education are being implemented by leadership at CETYS based on a transformational leadership direction with emphasis on: (a) faculty development, (b) investments in information technology, (c) renewal of library resources, (d) new infrastructure, and (e) a more aggressive globalization strategy creating more international relations around the world. Additionally, new strategic actions are in place: improved academic exchange agreements, foreign languages for students, the search for more funds for scholarships with the main goal of recruiting talented students, a stronger linkage with industry, increase knowledge of environmental issues, and more community presence. Authors Ter Horst and Pearce (2010) stated that integrating environmental issues with foreign language study provides important opportunities for students to increase their language proficiency, develop their understanding of concepts related to the environment, and become more involved in a global community through virtual learning projects. CETYS' students have been associated with environmental international projects in the United States with partner institutions, and by students participating in international conferences and research projects.

A competitive advantage for CETYS in the region is its reputation as a top-ranked university, which includes a recognized longevity of more than fifty years in higher education at the regional and national level, an MBA program ranked among the best in the nation, and a recently granted U.S. accreditation from the Western Association of Schools and Colleges (WASC). All the previous features are strategic instruments to display the capability of the institution to grow beyond borders, and to become a leader in innovation and transformation of quality in higher education. Additionally, leadership promotes accomplishments of students, faculty, and the institution; with no doubt, these outcomes support the image of a sustainable institution in the minds of the public. Since the current president took office back in 2010, international promotion and communication efforts have been focused on heavily covering the Southern California market. This has helped the institution to remain financially healthy through very harsh economic conditions. Currently, the institution has more than two hundred students from this region enrolled in the Tijuana and in the Mexicali campuses.

The benefit of international exposure that the leadership at CETYS is looking for within an innovative international dimension includes the following strategic actions:

1. Developing a global mindset in students and faculty by applying a value proposition by being flexible, innovative, and competitive.
2. All the students have an international exposure to multicultural settings.
3. Students learn about international standards in higher education.
4. Achieving the mastery level of the English language (bilingual graduates).
5. Students seeking certificate programs in foreign universities are aligned with institutional academic programs.
6. Enhancing students' mobility via new international agreements in other countries.
7. Enhancing global perspective and global experiences for students via double-degree programs with foreign institutions.
8. More faculty with doctoral degrees.
9. Active faculty participation in research, academic, and cultural projects with partner institutions.
10. Distinguished Chair program.

The current purpose of leadership is that students starting at high school level embrace an international perspective and develop a global mindset. This is going to be a major challenge due to the fact that internationalization at this level in all three high schools has been limited to the International Baccalaureate program (IB). Although this is a recognized international program for high schools, high school students at CETYS are also starting to engage in international mobility. Last year, high school students participated in a program in India, and this year in one program in the United States. Additional international experiences for high school students are being planned in Prague, the States, and in Canada by the end of this year or early next year. These early international experiences for high school students are giving students the ability to appreciate a teaching-learning process where innovation and creativity from cultural diversity is inspiring. Acquiring generic skills like teamwork, presentation, writing skills, and communication skills is emphasized and integrated by visiting organizations (Svanström, Palme, Maria, Carlson, Nyström, & Eden, 2012).

In regards to supporting undergraduate students' global leadership mindset, CETYS needs to deal with a big challenge, which is recruiting talented bilingual faculty with doctoral degrees. The state of Baja California is in the northwestern part of Mexico and too far from the other states, and in particular from the nation's capital. Thus, a very important advantage is being close to the States, but hiring faculty from there is very costly; therefore, a special fund to hire this type of faculty has been established according to the stages of the new 2020 Strategic Plan. This action will also address a requirement from the U.S. accrediting agency, to which the institution is committed. One critical way for organizations to achieve a competitive advantage is for them to create an approach of recruiting and retaining high-quality managerial talent that includes a focus on developing the kinds of skills and behavior that tie directly to the needs of the business (Berke, Kossler, & Wakefield, 2008).

Analysis of International Leadership Strategies

Living multicultural experiences is the key factor for all students when trying to link the institutional educational model and internationalization. In addition, the teaching-learning process has to reinforce this mind-set, which is embedded in the curriculum and the co-curriculum requirements of each academic program. The key questions that leadership has structured to approach this analysis based on the American Council of Education (ACE) International Laboratory conducted at CETYS University in 2010 are:

1. What is the level of alignment of internationalization and the institutional educational model?
2. Are there institutional learning outcomes related to internationalization and global learning?
3. How is internationalization embedded and implemented within the academic programs and co-curricular activities?
4. Is institutional leadership setting up goals for students to learn additional languages? In addition, how are they going to make sure that these requirements are fulfilled?
5. Has the institution implemented an assessment process regarding internationalization and global learning outcomes?

The top priority is to reach the level of alignment necessary for the educational model and internationalization goals. The purpose is to meet the effectiveness goal while seeking a comprehensive alignment with the global learning outcomes. In addition, it is to know how these outcomes have been embedded in each academic program and co-curricular activity. A benefit to this learning experience is the students' life within internal and external communities as part of their academic development. Students are being prepared to act as promoters of internationalization by learning global leadership strategies through international programs, visits to international organizations, international internships, and participating in academic exchange programs in other countries. By doing so, students are helping to enhance and produce innovative international projects at CETYS in their role as future leaders with a global mind-set. There are now international outcomes in each of the academic programs, so each student needs to live an international experience during his/her academic life at CETYS. All undergraduate students need to fulfill a graduation requirement of passing the English as a foreign language (TOEFL) exam with a minimum of 550 points.

The focus of this requirement is in the commitment that students need to demonstrate by passing the TOEFL exam (the official version or an institutional one). This learning outcome represents an international standard requirement within the global context of higher education. It is recommended that all undergraduate students pass the TOEFL exam prior to graduation date, so this does not become a hindrance for graduating or for obtaining the degree. This way, students and the institution will have a quantitative measure of the English level of their graduating students in regards to an international standard (ACE International Lab, 2010). Students with English fluency are privileged to interact with international students; the knowledge of this language opens the door for collaborative academic projects and effective communication and understanding (Jon, 2012).

The institution fosters the learning of the English language by offering a series of free English courses to all students so that they can get a passing grade in the TOEFL exam. This is carried out through a so-called College English program, which is offered at all three campuses. The starting point is the placement exam that tells the English Language Center where each student should be placed. There are five modules and the content is grammar, writing, conversation, and cultural aspects of the English language.

As part of students' international profile regarding the English language, their English level is assessed for oral, writing, and reading skills by using a simple scale that identifies three levels per aspect: Basic, Intermediate, and Advanced, in addition to asking whether they have taken the TOEFL, and if so, the points scored. It cannot be denied that English knowledge empowers international students to establish relationships with other students (Jon, 2012).

American Council of Education Engagement

The American Council of Education (ACE) is considered one of the top academic organizations. One of the most important international strategies that leadership has taken is the decision of seeking an international self-study approach established by ACE. This self-study was conducted in the year 2010, which was guided by an institutional international committee and a coordinating group. The scope of this self-study is directed toward the institutional community by focusing on CETYS University as a learning community. CETYS University assists participating institutions in the development of a comprehensive internationalization strategy, in addition to the assessment and follow-up of each institution's advances toward achieving its internationalization goals (ACE International Lab, 2010). The content of this self-study contains topics related to the international initiatives, opportunities for development, and the opinions from students and faculty for approaching new geographical areas for international development. The results of this self-study showed that students and faculty would like to have more opportunities in the international arena, and participate in international projects. This feedback recommended the inclusion of international learning outcomes in each academic program. The institutional vision was changed mainly because of this reason.

In addition, preparing faculty members within the international context to understand the trend of higher education is another of the top priorities of leadership. Every year since 2010, faculty members have been participating in the ACE international program. There are more than ten people at the institution (including the president) who have had ACE Fellowships. This fellowship has brought many international opportunities to the institution; from the individual point of view, it represents international exposure to faculty members from the United States and their academic culture for one year, and the opportunity to exchange experiences among members from different countries. They all participate in collaborative activities with leaders at the host institution, and the strengths of this international effort are the continuing relationships among peers and the continuous improvement of the fellows (ACE International Laboratory, 2010). At the institutional level, CETYS University is getting more recognition for its emphasis in academic development by supporting faculty professional development.

Another international strategy is the Distinguished Chair program. In the context of continuous improvement in pursuing global competitiveness, three centers of excellence (Competitiveness; Innovation and Design and Innovation; and Social and Human Development) were established, with each being supported by the recurring visits from experienced foreign faculty, and in particular from the CETYS' global network of partner universities. This global network includes prestigious universities in Europe, Asia, and the States. Linhan (2012) noted that image, resources, and coalition are the most important factors for a successful international relationship in the global market of higher education. These visitors serve as mentors and distinguished lecturers when they are on campus. CETYS University is finding new strategic ways of operating and getting support from partner universities in offering a variety of academic alternatives, which emerged from a collaborative effort that helps the teaching-learning process when the universities send their own faculty to assure and enhance the quality of the programs (Linhan, 2012).

Some people at the institution are not convinced that CETYS needs to seek a more extensive globalization strategy; they strongly believe that the priority is the continuous improvement of the institution within the internal context, mainly the improvement of academic programs and faculty development However, changes in societies, markets, customers, competition, and technology around the globe are forcing organizations to clarify their values, develop new strategies, and learn new ways of operating. Leadership at CETYS University has undertaken major challenges in competition and in organizational changes. The customers (parents and students) go through the selection process for higher education in a more detailed way, and they are looking for important benefits that include image, accreditations, scholarships, international activity linkage with the business community, and job opportunities, among others. With the demanding new profile of customers, the institution is ready to continue making investments in learning resources, more qualified faculty, computer labs, library, classroom technology, Internet, videoconference, etc.

Institutional Cultural Diversity Awareness

The institution's cultural awareness and perspectives are integrated in a set of institutional capabilities emerged from the institutional mission and vision to enhance the competitiveness, image, growth, and international development of CETYS University. The multicultural awareness of CETYS was born in the early 1990s when the first exchange agreements were signed with universities in the United States, one of them being San Diego State University (SDSU). This agreement was an innovative student exchange program called MEXUS, where students from both institutions would attend two years at their home institution and two at the foreign institution. Furthermore, in the 1990s CETYS began to establish international relations with several Canadian universities; a couple of years later, student mobility became a central means for multicultural awareness. Nowadays, the institution has advanced to multi-collaborative agreements with universities in many countries (the U.S., China, Spain, Finland, India, Japan, Korea, Canada, Chile, France, and Italy, among others).

Learning communities are growing, networking among students and faculty is increasing, and the pattern of communication is improving; these strategic actions have been in continuous transformation with the support of technology using Skype, videoconferences, e-mail, etc. The ability of the institution to improve global competitiveness is a customer/community partnership perspective that Hubbard (2004) explained as the understanding to perceive demographic changes in the global marketplace. By having an U.S. regional accreditation from the Western Association of Schools and Colleges (WASC), and the accreditation for the business programs with the Accreditation Council for Business Schools and Programs (ACBSP), leadership is seeking a third one for the engineering programs with the Accreditation Board for Engineering and Technology (ABET). CETYS is reinforcing its global awareness in academic quality and the global trend in higher education of student learning accountability and institutional quality assurance. Cultural diversity awareness is one of the main concerns of current leadership at CETYS University. In Table 1, data is presented regarding student mobility in different programs across the world as a demonstration of this initiative.

Table 1. *Student Mobility: National and International Exchange Programs*

Institution	2009	2010	2011	2012	2013	Total
Foreign Exchange	44	50	47	32	66	239
National Exchange	17	27	17	21	23	105
CityU Double Degree	42	69	72	106	93	382
SDSU Double Degree	13	17	8	7	2	47
DG Hogeschool Zeeland	1	1	7	7	0	16
Summer/Winter Programs	22	2	36	33	41	134
Linguistic Programs	1	1	9	10	5	28
Total	140	169	196	220	230	955

Source: Office of International Programs

The Value of International Development

Developing a global mindset involves a fundamental transformation, and the only way to achieve it is through an extended assignment requiring real work in another country (Mobley & McCall, 2001). The cultural awareness at CETYS is being enhanced by valuable proven international strategies. Leaders of the institution are capable of designing double-degree programs, bringing distinguished lecturers from different countries, providing the opportunity for faculty to continue their doctoral studies, supporting faculty to do international internships, promoting international stays for graduate students around the world, and the probability of participating in a higher education consortium. All the previous actions show the level of importance that leadership assumes for learning innovative strategies for improvement of its capabilities for international development.

The knowledge acquired from international partners is the turning point to leverage the competencies gained from the international assignees' experiences upon their return (Caligiuri, 2012). Proving that when people are focused and clear about their decision-making criteria, they can begin to achieve what they may previously have thought impossible (Wheeler, 2009). Every faculty member who has the opportunity to experience an international venture brings the knowledge back to the institution via improved teaching abilities, and students get to enjoy active learning within multicultural settings. Shaules (2010) stated that what deep culture empathy requires is more than adopting an intellectual stance of tolerance for diversity.

The value of a very intense strategy embraced by the president of CETYS is the structure of an International Educational Committee and the integration of a group of international advisors. Members of the International Educational Committee have been engaging in group conversations that are critical during the analysis of potential international opportunities for the institution. Schamber and Mahoney (2006) described group critical thinking as a "purposeful, collective judgment produced by a task-oriented small group of four to six members that combines interpretation, analysis, evaluation and inference, or contextual considerations upon which the judgment is based regarding the specific task at hand." Each advisor has been assigned a geographical area for international exploration for future international opportunities for the institutions. These opportunities are the student exchange programs, short academic programs, certificate programs, faculty exchange, and research projects, among others. In an internal collaborative effort, the president and the group of international advisors have created a very important networking of international peers for exchanging knowledge, expertise, and for planning mutual strategic projects.

Students and faculty have travelled for academic and cultural purposes from Central America (Costa Rica) to South America (Argentina, Chile, Brazil), to Europe (the United Kingdom, France, Germany, Portugal, Czech

Republic, Ireland, Spain, Finland, Austria, Switzerland, Italy), to Asia (Japan, China, India), Australia, as well as the United States and Canada. As part of the students' international profile regarding interests in their future international development, there are three main reasons, which have to do with culture, technological development, or an area related to their major. One of the most popular means of international experience preferred by students is the double-degree program with City University in Seattle, WA, where almost three hundred students from multidisciplinary academic programs have lived this valuable experience since 2005.

Institutional learning outcomes and program learning outcomes are expected as part of any accreditation process. Four institutional learning outcomes were developed by CETYS, and one of them focuses on cultural diversity ("Embracement of cultural diversity"), defined as follows:

> *Upon concluding the academic programs, students will show knowledge and tolerance towards other cultures, and will apply these skills to establish human relations, thus manifesting respect towards diversity.*

Another institutional learning outcome applies only to college programs where the English language is required; this outcome is "Clear and effective communication in English," and it is structured as follows:

> *Upon concluding the academic programs, students will be able to express ideas clearly and using the appropriate language in English in an oral, written, and visual way.*

These two learning outcomes related to internationalization include assessment tools and observations about the evidence required for achieving the level of learning expected in each outcome. In another institutional learning outcome, assessment tools are an institutional rubric to assess attitude toward cultural diversity, and upon the end of the academic program,

> *It is expected that students will show knowledge and tolerance towards other cultures, evidence of this outcome is the skill demonstrated by students in case studies and papers related to cultural diversity.*

In another institutional learning outcome, upon concluding the academic program, students will be able to express their ideas clearly using appropriate English language skills in oral, visual, and written modes. The assessment tool for this outcome is the application of the standardized English language test with a minimum passing grade.

Conclusion

The current global environment is placing organizations under new challenges, and CETYS University is not the exception. Leadership models that new leaders follow will play a critical role in the success of their organizations. Innovation, technology, collaboration, and effective communication are some of the best features an effective leader must engage in. Higher education is a field where transformational leaders are visionaries, role models, and facilitators who prepare their employees to work in a dynamic environment. Therefore, transformational leaders are at the forefront, guiding people to work toward the mission and sustainability of the institution (Hawkins, 2009). Perhaps what is lacking in many leadership practices is transformational leadership, which is based on personal values, beliefs, and qualities in combination with the ability to elevate the interests, awareness, and acceptance of the group, and to stir followers to look beyond their own interests (Berendt, Christofi, Kasibhatla, Malindretos, & Maruffi, 2012). Leadership at CETYS is trying to achieve the goal of integrating high schools, undergraduate, and graduate programs in one big international community. The reason for this is with the purpose of: (a) creating international awareness for global leadership issues among students; (b) enhancing faculty development; and (c) taking to a higher level the image and prestige of the institution as an international role model for institutions in its own country (Mexico).

To sustain long-term performance with current public scrutiny and transparency with coherent, aligned actions with the strategic plan of the organization, universities must develop an analytical strategy based on a sustainable operation seeking global development. This strategy at CETYS includes a set of actions, where its complexity would be to continue the practice of self-analysis and describing how meaningful every feature involved in sustainability is. Transformation, innovation, effective communication, employee commitment, and a new culture of globalization are part of an effective decision-making process of institutional leadership. Other issues related to strategic international development at the institution are the understanding of technology innovation, rapid competitive moves, peer-related international work, and work ethics aligned with the institutional ethics framework based on the institutional mission. The pathway for reaching global competitiveness is by applying these strategic actions to internal and external sustainability planning, and by extending leadership decision making beyond the organization into the community.

References

Berendt, C. J., Christofi, A., Kasibhatla, K. M., Malindretos, J., & Maruffi, B. (2012). Transformational leadership: Lessons in management for today. *International Business Research, 5*(10), 227–232. doi:10.5539/ibr.v5n10p227

Berke, D., Kossler, M., & Wakefield, M. (2008). *Developing leadership talent*. New York, NY: Wiley Publishers. Retrieved from

Caligiuri, P. (2012). *Cultural agility: Building a pipeline of successful global professionals*. San Francisco, CA: Jossey-Bass. Retrieved from http://proxy.cityu.edu/login?url=http://library.books24x7.com.proxy.cityu.edu/library.asp?^B&bookid=49583&refid=GFV5U

Fletcher, D. (2012). Higher education and international student mobility in the global knowledge economy. *Journal of International Students, 2*(1), 128. Retrieved from http://search.proquest.com/docview/1355246929?accountid=1230

Hawkins, C. (2009). Leadership theories: Managing practices, challenges, suggestions. *Community College Enterprise, 15*(2), 39–62.

Hubbard, E. E. (2004). The diversity scorecard: Evaluating the impact of diversity on organizational performance. Taylor and Francis. Retrieved from http://proxy.cityu.edu/login?url=http://library.books24x7.com.proxy.cityu.edu/library.asp?^B&bookid=28171

Jon, J. (2012). Power dynamics with international students: From the perspective of domestic students in Korean higher education. *Higher Education, 64*(4), 441–454. doi:http://dx.doi.org/10.1007/s10734-011-9503-2

Linhan, C. (2012). Internationalization of higher education and its market—taking international college as an example. *Higher Education Studies, 2*(1), 65–69. Retrieved from http://search.proquest.com/docview/1059517120?accountid=1230

Mobley, W., & McCall, M., (2001). *Advances in global leadership,* Volume 2. Bradford, West Yorkshire, GBR: Emerald Group Publishing Ltd. Retrieved from http://web.a.ebscohost.com.proxy.cityu.edu/ehost/pdfviewer/pdfviewer?vid=9&sid=32371056-71e8-4fa0-a4c5-c20f0ad2685e%40sessionmgr4005&hid=4112

Paulus, P. B., & Nijstad, B. A. (2003). *Group creativity: Innovation through collaboration.* New York, NY: Oxford University Press. Retrieved from http://proxy.cityu.edu/login?url=http://library.books24x7.com.proxy.cityu.edu/library.asp?^B&bookid=13726&refid=GFV5U

Schamber, J. F., & Mahoney, S. L. (2006). Assessing and improving the quality of group critical thinking exhibited in the final projects of collaborative learning groups. *JGE: The Journal of General Education, 55*(2), 103–137.

Shaules, J. (2010). *A beginner's guide to the deep culture experience: Beneath the surface.* Boston, MA: Intercultural Press. Retrieved from http://proxy.cityu.edu/login?url=http://library.books24x7.com.proxy.cityu.edu/library.asp?^B&bookid=36606

Svanström, M., Palme, U., Maria, K. W., Carlson, O., Nyström, T., & Edén, M. (2012). Embedding of ESD in engineering education. *International Journal of Sustainability in Higher Education, 13*(3), 279–292. doi:http://dx.doi.org/10.1108/14676371211242580

Ter Horst, E. E., & Pearce, J. M. (2010). Foreign languages and sustainability: Addressing the connections, communities, and comparisons standards in higher education. *Foreign Language Annals, 43*(3), 365–383. Retrieved from http://search.proquest.com/docview/87 2088077?accountid=1230

Thomas, C., & Inkson, K. (2004). *Cultural intelligence: People skills for global business*. San Francisco, CA: Berrett-Koehler Publishers.

Uhlig, K., Quinten, B., Chang, L., & Dominguez, A. (2007). *Making diversity work in your organization: Training strategies.* Portland, OR: AK Learning

Wheeler, C. (2009). *You've gotta have heart: Achieving purpose beyond profit in the social sector.* New York, NY:AMACOM.

Part III

Specialized Leadership Strategies

Entrepreneurial Leadership Theory Supported in Business Accelerator Programs

Gregory Price, MBA
School of Applied Leadership

Abstract

Entrepreneurs start businesses that provide many benefits to the community, such as a strong tax base, lowered unemployment, and a higher standard of living. What often occurs, though, is that many business ventures fail in their first years. There is much data to support this reality, but there is little research to explain why many entrepreneurs are unable to sustain their business through start-up and into the organizational phase. Often this failure is commonly thought of as a regular occurrence in start-up development. There are organized support mechanisms available to entrepreneurs, but failure rates continue to be high. Business incubators have supported entrepreneurial start-ups for the past fifty years, but business today has become more complex. This complexity has produced another form of support for entrepreneurs following the start-up phase; they are identified as business accelerator programs. These are three- to four-month, high-intensity, concentrated learning programs that can quickly transform an entrepreneurial start-up into a sustainable organization. This research will focus on these business accelerator programs to learn and understand the applied leadership strategies used in the program and their effect on entrepreneurs. This will support the literature on entrepreneurial leadership theory and help develop curriculum in higher education designed to support entrepreneurial education.

Support for Entrepreneurs Makes Economic Sense

Entrepreneurs are known risk takers and start businesses out of passion, energy, and perseverance. They also assume all "financial, psychological and social" risk. These individuals are considered "explorers" and follow paths often not followed by others, operating under a different set of rules and relying on their own understanding of the world around them (Cook & Yamamoto, 2011). For nearly forty years, entrepreneurial research has grown significantly (Kuratoko, 2007), and though literature continues to expand our understanding, there are still many questions. With much of today's research focused on the economic effects of entrepreneurial success, or lack thereof, new research is beginning to explore the following areas: (1) entrepreneurship as a personal choice, (2) an entrepreneur's personal traits, and (3) entrepreneurial psychology (Antonakis, & Autio, 2007).

The cumulative economic effects entrepreneurs have on society are enormous as business development is considered the engine of economic expansion (Kobe, 2012). Business, industry, and government all place a premium to encourage it, and entrepreneurs make up this risk-taking segment by advancing their ideas into the shape of a business entity. Entrepreneurs take advantage of their personal characteristics to find market segments that are not being served or are underserved. They identify a business process that can be performed better or more efficiently, and they work to exploit these opportunities. They do this as much for personal satisfaction as they do for monetary rewards, and the rewards reach into the local community through job expansion, a higher standard of living, and economic vitality (Hisrich & Peers, 1992).

The fact is, though, entrepreneurial ventures often fail. There is much data to support the failure rates of small business. The Small Business Administration (SBA) presented data published in 2012 showing that 40 percent of all newly formed organizations do not survive more than three years. Looking further out, the study (United States Census Bureau, 2011) showed business failure rates were a dismal 67 percent of all business start-ups after ten years (Figure 1).

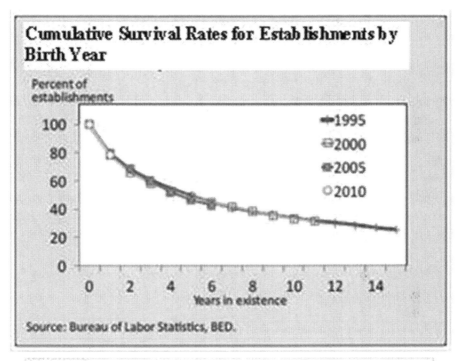

Figure 1

In 2011, newly started enterprises with less than twenty employees made up 90 percent of all operating firms in the United States. In Washington State, this number was slightly less at 88 percent (U.S. Census Bureau, 2011). Stated another way, firms in Washington State with twenty employees or less employed approximately one of every five working adults (Table 1). It is evident that small business plays a major role in the labor markets.

Analoui and Karami (2003) stated that success in business is probably most related to an individual's leadership capacity. But there is still limited research regarding the process of entrepreneurship and how this translates into starting and growing a sustainable business, especially one that becomes high performing (Rae & Carswell, 2000). The link between leadership and entrepreneurship can be made by examining an individual's historical and internal personal leadership experiences (Byrd, 2010). These experiences are subjective in nature and are influenced by the individual's "conditioning, socialization and acculturation" (Byrd, 2010, p. 1). The behavioral traits exhibited are the tools the individual brings to the entrepreneurial platform.

As stated, entrepreneurs start their business out of passion, and successfully guiding the business into a sustainable organization delivers economic utility for the community. This utility generates revenue, a strong tax base, employment, and an improved quality of living. Yet, starting a business has never been the problem for entrepreneurs; it is the continuing of the business that presents the issue. Entrepreneurship, at its core, is experiential learning; learning while doing, learning from mistakes, and learning to do it all over again (He, 2013). This learning helps the entrepreneur grow as an individual, adding experiential development that helps the individual grow into a balanced leader. This accumulated know-how helps to develop a high level of leadership agility and competency. He (2013) noted that some entrepreneurs have the capacity to develop highly successful businesses, while others do not.

Table 1 (United States Census Bureau, 2011).

Employment in Categorized Sized Firms (%)	Percentage of Firms Operating Nationally	Employees against total U.S. Employment (%)
62%	1 – 4 employees	5%
89%	< 20 employees	18%
98%	< 100 employees	35%
Employment in Categorized Sized Firms (%)	Percentage of firms operating in Washington State	Employees against total Washington State employment

1 – 4 employees	61%	6%
< 20 employees	88%	21%
< 100 employees	96%	38%

History of Entrepreneurial Incubators

The early years for support centers, otherwise known as incubators, looked to develop their base of support. It was in 1953 that the U.S. Small Business Administration was formed, which helped to create a solid foundation and framework from which further work could be accomplished (Shepard, 2013). This was accomplished, albeit slowly.

Jumping ahead thirty years, the economic environment in the 1980s saw severe layoffs in the corporate sector, causing a spike in the unemployment rate. It was during this period of time that incubators ramped up their service offerings and government and industry began increasing the number of incubators to help revitalize economically suppressed regions of the country (Shepard, 2013). Congress enacted the Small Business Innovation Research Program in 1992, which was to help assist small business to develop technological advances. This one act provided enough economic support to increase the nation's gross domestic product (GDP) and provided the structure to support the critical advances necessary for business to integrate these innovative technologies. This period was important as it helped solidify the recognized need for innovative advances in business and technology brought on by the entrepreneur (Shepard, 2013). Today, researchers are finding that incubators are supporting two definitive population groups: one that follows a path conducive to business coaching, which has a more growth emphasis structure, and the other has developed its infrastructure to support more cost minimization strategies (Todorovic & Moenter, 2010).

The idea behind incubators are many including a place where the entrepreneur can bring up a question, find low-cost services, gain another's expertise, share rental space and technological necessities, network with other entrepreneurs, and find opportunities for funding (Shepard, 2013). All of these activities and services make up many of the aggregate needs an entrepreneur requires to run and manage a start-up business while also reducing their operating costs. Since 1980, the National Business Incubator Association (NBIA) has estimated that of the thirty-five thousand start-up ventures that have left incubator support, these businesses have created eighty-two thousand full-time jobs and generated annual revenues of more than $7 billion (Scillitoe & Chakrabarti, 2010). Shepard (2013) has added that as of 2007, there existed 1,115 incubators across the United States and about 20 percent supported a business-academic partnership.

The Next Phase of Entrepreneurial Support

Once past the start-up phase though, entrepreneurs find they may not have the needed skills to develop the organization into an ongoing, sustainable business platform. According to Jones (2011), leadership skills may be the most important skill set to support the growth of a successful business venture. Entrepreneurs come to find that passion, energy, and perseverance may not be enough to sustain an organization; they realize that leadership strategies are necessary skills to develop their business through the organizational development phase (Shafer, 2012). Though leadership skills may not be a necessary part of the entrepreneur's capacity through the start-up phase, they are needed in the organizational development phase, and they are skills that can be learned.

One of the many challenges for incubator phases is to understand which services support the start-up venture. The varied services and inconsistent delivery that incubators offer require an understanding to identify which of these services drive entrepreneurial success (Yusuf, 2014; Scillitoe & Chakrabarti, 2010; Todorovic & Moenter, 2010). Additionally, because incubators do not incorporate a selection process as to who is accepted into their incubator, it is unknown what effect the self-selection process has on an entrepreneur's start-up success (Yusuf, 2014; Shepard, 2013).

Communication and engagement between entrepreneurs and incubator management can be as frequent as necessary, yet understanding what constitutes successful knowledge transfer and what works and what does not has become an area of great interest to social scientists (Scillitoe & Chakrabarti, 2010). Researchers are looking at the many different variables associated with the incubator services, such as the needs of the entrepreneur, and the links and correlations between them and incubator personnel. To an entrepreneur client, the incubator management comprises the incubator's social capital and expertise, knowledge, and contacts (Scillitoe & Chakrabarti, 2010).

This transfer of knowledge is taking center stage in today's research and the business community has noticed that filling a gap in consumer demand supports this entrepreneurial need. Consequently, the next phase of entrepreneurial support comes in the form of a business accelerator program. Business accelerators are the next iteration of an incubator. They are a relatively new business idea starting as recently as 2007 (Carr, 2012), and the number of accelerator facilities has grown quickly (Andruss, 2013). Since their inception, they have focused heavily on technology and health-care companies, but more recently, they have started to open up access to other industry segments such as fashion and food, and there is significant interest in those businesses that focus on socially conscious endeavors (Andruss, 2013). Millennial entrepreneurs tend to incorporate social consciousness into their business as an intrinsic value, and though they may think that investors will shy away from their start-up due to higher initial costs, entrepreneurs quickly realize this value supports investor interest.

There is a big difference between an incubator and an accelerator. Incubators support a start-up business by laying a foundation of support for entrepreneurs that can last anywhere from a few months to a few years. Accelerators, on the other hand, take the start-up and move the business into an intense training program. Accelerators support entrepreneurial development through a structured curriculum designed to help with marketing, team development, funding and financing, and leadership functions. The training is like turning on a fire hose to get a drink of water with the idea of moving the business into quick and sustainable profitability. Most accelerator programs charge client businesses anywhere from 5 to 8 percent of the equity in their business, and in return the client business receives a stipend range of $15,000 to $100,000 along with the training. The average is about a 5 percent stake in equity for a cash stipend of $20,000. Though the cash is a helpful boost, an accelerator's real benefit for the client business comes from the knowledge and expertise, as well as the networking and fund-raising opportunities (Andruss, 2013); upon graduation, the business success rate from these client businesses is quite good. In the end, the high failure rate experienced following the start-up phase of a business idea may have found a solution through these supportive accelerator programs.

From this success, expansion is occurring and today's business accelerator programs are becoming increasingly complex. It has been learned that the personnel needed to run these programs must be entrepreneurs themselves as well as highly skilled individuals (Shepard, 2013). Accelerators have also learned from their incubator predecessors what Shepard (2013) identified as indirect services. Indirect services are becoming more necessary and would include applied educational services. These services would help the entrepreneur better understand how to innovate and organize strategic plans, develop organizational leadership competencies, as well as decision making and critical thinking agility (Shepard, 2013).

Experiential learning is a key component to entrepreneurial success, but why not learn necessary strategies from others who have previously followed the same path? Why not learn from those who have already been down the path of trial and tribulation? By moving through the accelerator process, entrepreneurs learn from executives and the learning is focused on just these things—leadership and agility development.

From the Start-Up to Organizational Phase

To bring the problem back into focus, it is the frequent failure of small business, which may be caused from a lack of entrepreneurial leadership agility to carry the business into the organizational development phase. It is understood that the start-up phase supports an entrepreneur's core competency, yet the start-up phase has limited opportunity to develop the necessary leadership skills to move it forward. The organizational development phase is where these leadership skills play an important role, and business accelerator programs target this phase of the entrepreneur's development. The importance of supporting small business at becoming successful is clarified in Table 2 where businesses of under five hundred employees generate just over 30 percent of total government receipts and employ just under half of total U.S. employment (Kobe, 2012). Developing improved methods of supporting entrepreneurs through leadership education at critical points of the entrepreneurs' business may help support a higher sustainable business success rate.

Table 2 (Kobe, 2012).

Nonfarm Corporate and Non-corporate Shares of Receipts and Employment 2007					
	Revenue			Employment	
	Small Business	Large Business		Small Business	Large Business
Total	30%	70%		49%	51%
Source: *Statistics of U.S. Businesses, 2007 and Non-employer Statistics. U.S. Census Bureau*					

Theories for Further Study

The literature supports the belief that entrepreneurs learn by doing, which is simply known as experiential theory. This same belief is found in leadership theory (Kempster & Cope, 2010). Experiential theory can be broadly defined as learning that is developed through knowledge, skills, and values that are not directly accrued through an academic setting. It is learning through a variety of activities experienced through real-world experiences. Another theoretical framework that is incorporated into this research is entrepreneurial leadership theory. This is a relatively new theory where, independently, the two words have been well established in the research, but together they are not often combined as one theory (Roomi & Harrison, 2011). Defining each term briefly, *entrepreneurship* is generally the creation of opportunity beyond the resources the individual controls, whereas *leadership* combines strategic vision and influence with the goal of motivating others through a cultural process in the organization (Roomi & Harrison, 2011).

It is common thought to consider an entrepreneur and a leader as two individuals moving down different career paths, yet when looking at the job function for each, they have many common qualities. It can be observed that a leader performs duties within an established organization with organizational structure firmly established while an entrepreneur engages in more complex solo roles where organizational structure is not so developed. Additionally, it would also appear that the personality traits and skills needed to create and develop a new entrepreneurial venture support the idea that entrepreneurial character traits could be far more complex (Vecchio, 2003; Mattare, 2008). Thus, because the functions of each can be somewhat similar, both theories can be used to support the newer theoretical approach of entrepreneurial leadership theory (Cogliser & Brigham, 2004).

There is little evidence in current literature that supports entrepreneurial leadership theory. Because little research supports any understanding of the contribution that business accelerator programs provide to the literary community, further research to convey both "what" and "how" type questions is necessary to advance these theoretical foundations. "What" questions can be answered by way of explanatory study, while "how" type questions can be answered through the use of a descriptive study format. Both descriptive and explanatory study questions postulate an element supported by the case study approach (Creswell, 2014).

Significance and Contributions for Further Research

Business accelerator programs are fairly new business operations; they support the entrepreneur's world of getting a business into quick profitability. The learning experiences offered within the program are short, delivered quickly, and provide the entrepreneur a highly structured environment wherein to take risks while decision making is supported with expertise. The premise of the business accelerator program is to generate income for the program investors, and because of this stake in an entrepreneur's business, the stakeholders will want to ensure that the business is successful.

Though research has only begun to understand how business accelerators can develop the entrepreneurial community, further literary contributions can add significantly to the field of entrepreneurship. Because entrepreneurs add value to the general population through economic variables, further research is encouraged in this field to develop an accessible entrepreneurial culture to the general population. The second area of emphasis is to further research business accelerator programs so that they may continue to learn and develop their specific brand of business development.

Finally, the third area of significance is to support university initiatives to further develop entrepreneurial leadership education that would help "teach students to cultivate their entrepreneurial capability in leadership roles and their leadership capability in entrepreneurial contexts" (Roomi & Harrison, 2011, p. 31).

References

Andruss, P. (2013). Rev up your startup. *Entrepreneur, 41*, 77–83.

Antonakis, J., & Autio, E. (2007). *Entrepreneurship and leadership: The psychology of entrepreneurship* (pp. 189–208). Mahwah, NJ: Lawrence Erlbaum Associates, Inc.

Byrd, W. C. (2010). *The personal leadership practices of successful entrepreneurs*. Pepperdine University. Retrieved from http://search.proquest.com/docview/649391178?accountid=1230 (Order No. 3412018)

Carr, A. (2012). Are accelerators losing speed?, *Fast Company, 168*, 51–56.

Cogliser, C. C., & K. H. Brigham. (2004). The intersection of leadership and entrepreneurship: Mutual lessons to be learned. *The Leadership Quarterly, 15*, 771–799.

Cook, P., & Yamamoto, R. (2011). Inside the mind of the expert entrepreneur: The explorer's view of strategy. *Journal of Management & Strategy, 2*(3), 77–85. doi:10.5430/jms.v2n3p77

Creswell, J. W. (2014). *Research design: Qualitative, quantitative, and mixed methods approaches* (4th ed.). Thousand Oaks, CA: Sage Publications.

He, F. (2013). *Learning from failure: The making of entrepreneurial leaders*. The George Washington University, Ann Arbor, MI. Retrieved from http://proxy.cityu.edu/login?url=http://search.proquest.com.proxy.cityu.edu/docview/1314799274?accountid=1230 (3553304)

Jones, K. (2011). *A biographical approach to researching leadership and entrepreneurship development processes in a small business context* (proceedings of the European conference on management, leadership, and governance), 199–205.

Kempster, S. J., & Cope, J. (2010). Learning to lead in the entrepreneurial context. *International Journal of Entrepreneurial Behaviour and Research, 16*(6), 5–34.

Kobe, K. (2012). *Small-business GDP: Update 2002–2010.* Retrieved from http://www.sba.gov/sites/default/files/rs390tot_0.pdf

Mattare, M. (2008). *Teaching entrepreneurship: The case for an entrepreneurial leadership course* (USASBE proceedings), 78–93.

Rae, D., & Carswell, M. (2000) Using a life-story approach in researching entrepreneurial learning: The development of a conceptual model and its implications in the design of learning experiences, *Education and Training, 42*(4/5), 220–227.

Roomi, M. A., & Harrison, P. (2011). Entrepreneurial leadership: What is it and how should it be taught? *International Review of Entrepreneurship, 9*(3).

Scillitoe, J. L., & Chakrabarti, A. K. (2010). The role of incubator interactions in assisting new ventures. *Technovation, 30*(3), 155–167. doi:10.1016/j.technovation.2009.12.002

Shepard, J. M. (2013). Small business incubators in the U.S.: A historical review and preliminary research findings. *Journal of Knowledge-Based Innovation in China, 5*(3), 213–233. doi: 10.1108/JKIC-07-2013-0013

Todorovic, Z., & Moenter (Meyer), K. (2010). Tenant firm progression within an incubator: Progression toward an optimal point of resource utilization. *Academy of Entrepreneurship Journal, 16*(1), 23–40.

U.S. Census Bureau. 2007. *Statistics about business size (including small business).* Retrieved from http://www.census.gov/econ/smallbus.html

Vecchio, R. P. (2003). Entrepreneurship and leadership: Common trends and common threads. *Human Resource Management Review, 13,* 303–327.

Yusuf, J.-E. W. (2014). Impact of start-up support through guided preparation. *Journal of Entrepreneurship and Public Policy, 3*(1), 72–95. doi: http://dx.doi.org/10.1108/JEPP-01-2012-0004

14

Building Capacity in the Not-for-Profit Sector: Executive Leadership Education

Arden Henley, EdD
Canada School of Education

Abstract

This chapter describes the development, delivery, and evolution of an Executive Leadership certificate program and proposes a set of promising practices based on this experience. It traces the origins of this program in the university's commitment to lifelong learning and the connections of this commitment to continuing education and community capacity building. It considers issues such as relevance, immediacy, and quality of instruction. Several innovative features of the program including the use of follow-up mentorship and seminars in specific topic areas such as social media are examined. The chapter also explores the significance and value of corporate sponsorship in the context of continuing education for the not-for-profit sector and speculates about the ongoing relationship of graduates and the university.

Continuing Education: Why Bother?

Many universities regard Continuing Education as an academically inferior, low margin sideline. More recently in Canada, universities have experimented with turning Continuing Education departments into travel agencies offering trips to the far reaches of the globe mixed with a range of structured learning experiences. Some universities have also seen Continuing Education as a way to engage seniors in learning often with emeritus professors providing the teaching. This is not to suggest that these and other experiments are without merit, but that this more limited view overlooks the power and vitality of Continuing Education in engaging alumni, enhancing the university's profile in the community and building capacity in various communities of practice, all of which are elements in the Executive Leadership program. A vibrant School of Continuing Education and Community Engagement can also assist universities in rethinking who and what they are.

Engaging Alumni

In previous eras and with universities at which residency was a major feature of the student experience, alumni programs focused on the kind of loyalty that was related to the memories of youth, nostalgia, and the lasting connections resulting from sharing those formative years. Increasingly, and especially for institutions with a history of low or no residency requirements and student populations of adult learners, these emotional factors are less influential. CityU and similar institutions specializing in adult learning historically paid little or no attention to alumni. However, shifts in the complexity and rate of change in society, and the associated demands for lifelong learning open up a new set of possibilities for universities.

The possibilities foreseen at CityU in Canada entail continued engagement with alumni in the service of lifelong learning. For example, the graduates of our unique practitioner-focused and practitioner/scholar-instructed counseling programs are very successful in obtaining employment and advancing as professionals. Many become program directors and, ultimately, executive directors and board members. Though they have little formal preparation for responsibilities as administrators, managers, and leaders, they quickly become aware of what they need to know. This is a juncture at which education in administration, management, and leadership can be most helpful (Mintzberg, 2004).

Enhancing the University's Profile

Universities in the private, as opposed to public, sector often depend heavily on enrollments for revenue, and CityU in Canada is no exception. Private universities that are nonprofit as is the case with CityU are frequently under-resourced in the areas of marketing and advertising, and therefore have difficulty competing with both private, well-capitalized-for-profit institutions and government-subsidized public institutions. On this tightrope recognition, reputation and word of mouth are critical success factors and community engagement crucial. Our evolving Executive Leadership program has currently engaged over fifty leaders from the nonprofit sector. Many of their organizations hire or could hire graduates of the degree-based programs. Continuing Education provides a means of introducing participants to the values, ethos, and pedagogical approach of CityU in Canada.

Building Capacity in Communities of Practice

The vision, mission, and values of City University of Seattle as a whole and the Canadian programs in particular are consistent with the university's critical role in building the capacity of specific communities of practice. In Canada to date the focus to this point has been on the education of practitioners in Education and Counseling at the master's degree level, though our aspirations include the establishment of a School of Business and Management. Through its intellectual resources, experience in teaching, and practice of applied research, the university plays an important part in the currency and vitality of communities of practice. It introduces and reintroduces practitioners to the ongoing conversations and research of academics and programs in different places and cultures. Because of its greater capacity to be detached, the university serves a safe environment for debate and dialogue, as well as a reminder of integrity. At its best the university infuses communities of practice with a willingness to confront the most challenging and pressing issues faced by society.

Rethinking Universities

In some ways, because of its freedom from the academic constraints imposed by degree-granting status, Continuing Education provides educators with the opportunity to ask again what the university's role in society is. What is the public trust bestowed on us by society when it permits us to operate as "universities."

It is certainly the case that there are different kinds of universities. This has been broadly recognized by legislated distinctions between research, teaching, and technical universities. In our particular situation, the closest familiar approximation is probably to the "professional schools" that educate professions such as law and medicine.

The leading edge of our thinking has taken us to the proximal zone in which theory meets practice, and the creative tension and learning that is possible when neither is excessively privileged and each informs the other. Our thinking has also returned us to one of the originating sites of western education, the *agora*, or marketplace. We see the marketplace as alive and vibrant rather than crass and commercial, a vital meeting ground and a site at which educators should hawk their wares. Our aspiration as an "engaged university" is to create a robust intellectual commons for the professions and shape this commons in a way that consciously serves the community.

In re-visioning the role of the university along community development lines, curriculum becomes a contract between the university and a professional community; situated and project-based learning find natural homes; scholar/practitioners are supplied with a venue; and students truly become colleagues.

The increasing rate of change and escalating complexity create a growing need for lifelong learning and a continuing education home for the professions. There is also a growing need for dialogical forums in which theory and practice can be considered and ethical issues debated. New ideas and practices need to be circulated and evaluated, and thorny ethical issues wrestled with. Small urban, podlike communities of learning and applied research are ideal forms to achieve these ends. These communities of learning need to be embedded in the urban centers that are increasingly the vortex of change. They need to be flexible enough and on a small enough scale to be responsive to their changing environments. This is not the stuff of large institutions, layered bureaucracy, and procedural decision making. The CityU Canada vision is to create responsive, loosely affiliated centers of learning in urban environments. The purpose of affiliation is to realize economies of scale in intellectual resources and social capital and to provide a medium of exchange for the cultivation of ideas and practices. Think globally; act locally.

Rhizomatic Development of a Continuing Ed. Executive Leadership Program

The university historically offered a range of supplementary workshops mostly in the area of counseling, our largest program. Some workshops brought world-class presenters with whom members of the faculty were connected through the university while they were in Vancouver offering training in public workshops; others brought local experts in particular specialties. Some workshops were freestanding; others were incorporated in ongoing courses. Some involved a charge to participants; most were free of charge, particularly to CityU students, alumni, and faculty. This is an integral part of what universities do.

Over time a more systematic approach to developing Continuing Education was warranted to both extend the range of our offerings and make them more economically viable.

Employing Networks and Rhizomes

Over the past two decades sociologists, economists, and other social scientists have been interested in human society's propensity to organize itself in networks. Topographically these networks can in turn be understood to comprise interconnected clusters (Watts, 2004). The equivalent in the natural world is plants that employ an underground, interconnected root system to grow, regenerate, and persist, known as rhizomes. Bamboo is an example of a plant that employs such a root system, as are blackberries and Aspen trees. More recently, rhizomatic structuring has been seen as a useful analogy for the evolutions of communities (Kinman, 2014; Deleuze & Parnet, 1987).

From the perspective of organizations and communities and, in particular, the task of building capacity in the institutional world, understanding rhizomatic structure is very useful, and in our situation the application of an understanding of rhizomatic structure was consistent with our values and a primary means by which we developed an Executive Leadership program for the nonprofit sector.

To further clarify what is meant by rhizomatic structure, visualize for a moment the set of family, social, and collegial relationships in which you live your life, some with your family, some with colleagues, some with friends, some with various kinds of service providers; some influential, some transient; some formal, others informal. These relationships are integral in the unfolding of our individual lives, but they also affect the shape institutions take and influence the organization of society as a whole. This relational network is the nervous system of the social world. For example, information travels like wildfire across the synapses of this ever-changing set of human connections—trends emerge, new ideas spread, and epidemics rage.

Conversations Over Breakfast

The CityU in Canada Executive Leadership program emerged from a rhizomatic structure and, in turn, consciously made use of it in its development. But, how did it all begin? As conversations between two veterans of the nonprofit sector who had previously worked together in a number of contexts, one of whom is now a university administrator. One of the themes of these conversations was the changing landscape of the nonprofit sector and the challenges faced by the next generation of leaders in that sector. A second theme that had not changed—the degree to which leadership in that sector is often provided by graduates in social work, counseling, and community development who often have little previous education and training in administration, management, and leadership.

My breakfast colleague, now Director of Continuing Education and Community Engagement at CityU in Canada, is a gifted leader, with knowledge and skills highly evolved through a lifetime of rich experience, learning, and self-reflection. On my end as the university administrator conversationalist, I wanted our graduates, particularly those who are now assuming leadership positions to benefit from my colleague's formidable knowledge and impassioned approach. After several years of breakfast meetings, I prevailed. A new shoot emerged from the rhizome. The program structure then began to emerge in the context of further conversations between additional already-connected prominent practitioners and by asking the question, "What does the next generation of nonprofit leaders need to know?" The modus operandi is following the connections of a preexisting network of relationships in search of answers to this fundamental question while simultaneously evoking a willingness to contribute among prominent practitioners. Each module of this six-module certificate program reflects an outgrowth of the rhizome or social network and a visible manifestation of the invisible, that is a manifestation of relationships in which knowledge and skills are embedded, but have not previously been expressed in an educational context.

The effect of this approach is to create an educational program that emerges from a community of practice addressing the educational needs of that community, making use of the university's particular resources and expertise in delivering educational programs. Through the good offices of the university, a community, in this case the nonprofit sector in a large city, informs, inspires, and regenerates itself. At the same time, the academic and scholarly environment of the university is enriched by the presence of the proximal zone in which theory and practice meet. One of the many advantages of the "rhizomatic method" is that it takes the guesswork out of determining the educational needs of a particular community of practice. Rather than imposed from outside, education is experienced as emergent from inside.

Six Modules

The design of the certificate program Executive Leadership: Developing Sustainable Nonprofit Organizations in the 21st Century includes six half-day modules, offered from 9:00 a.m. to 2:00 p.m., including lunch. The first iteration included the following thematic workshops:

1. Urban Development, Sustainability, and Government Relations
2. Leading with Integrity
3. Fund Development and Building Strong Corporate/Nonprofit Relationships
4. Strategic Planning and Financial Management
5. Corporate Relations and Social Enterprise
6. Professional Development and Succession Planning

The second and third iterations substituted the following for Workshop #1: Communications and Media in the Nonprofit Sector.

Sponsorship

One of the ongoing challenges in delivering cost-effective Continuing Education programs, especially to the nonprofit sector, is the balance of financial viability and quality. Accordingly, one of the key strategies in implementing the CityU Executive Leadership program in Vancouver is the attraction of corporate sponsorship with the goal of offering the program at an affordable price.

Social Venture Partners Vancouver stepped up to sponsor the Executive Leadership program over the past one and a half years. Social Venture Partners is an international network of engaged philanthropists who invest time, money, and professional expertise in local nonprofits. Their mission is to build the capacity of local nonprofit organizations and strengthen their impact in creating sustainable outcomes and positive social change. Similar to the rhizomatic development of the modules and the engagement of presenters, SVP Vancouver sponsorship emerged from an initial discussion with a board member, followed by negotiations with the Executive Director and, finally, formal submissions for funding. SVP Vancouver sponsored an initial pilot and, subsequently, three iterations over the 2013/14 year.

Promising Practices and Lessons Learned

Though rhizomatic development contributes to thematic consistency across the program, modules having a convener present at all sessions provide further assurance. The convener hosts and facilitates all modules with a focus on building relationships with the participants and coaching faculty. The Executive Leadership program convener is the Director of Continuing Education and Community Engagement, who also is the presenter of one of the modules. The following two stories illustrate the value of this approach:

> *The second iteration of the program included an executive who had substantially more experience than most of the other participants. Her random assignment to team exercises during the first two modules that included several participants who were less experienced highlighted this imbalance and left her dissatisfied with the quality of the learning experience. She e-mailed the convener as she had been encouraged to do at the outset. His immediate follow-up and adjustment of the composition of team exercises and communication of her concerns to the presenters of subsequent modules resulted in her enthusiastic continuing engagement and positive evaluation at the end of the program.*

> *One of the presenters in the first iteration used a very didactic PowerPoint-dominated approach that resulted in subpar evaluations by the participants. Again, the convener intervened, providing two extended coaching sessions that resulted in a much more interactive and learner-friendly version of the module next time out that was much more highly rated by participants.*

Follow-Up Support

In addition to the six modules, the program provides one free-of-charge follow-up mentoring session delivered by module presenters and/or program convener. This has been a very attractive and well-used feature of the program. The following two accounts illustrate the significance of this feature:

> *One of the program participants is the inaugural Executive Director of a professional association. One of the challenges that he faced was the development of a first Board of Directors. Having used the*

mentoring feature for follow-up discussion about this challenge, he subsequently retained the services of one of the presenters to provide an orientation for the board.

The initial Professional Development and Succession module incorporated completion and interpretation of a 360 evaluation for participants. One of the participants found the results of her 360 quite shocking and used the mentorship feature to meet with the presenter to further examine the results. This conversation resulted in her deeper understanding of how she was being seen by others but eventually led to further dialogue about the viability of her position in her organization.

Immediate, Objectives-Driven Feedback to Presenters

Educational research has consistently demonstrated that the more immediate and specific the performance-related feedback, the more useful it is to the recipient (Hattie & Timperley, 2007). The Executive Leadership program design required that each module have specific objectives. For example, the objectives of the Professional Development and Succession Planning module are:

1. Explore the ways in which leaders learn to lead and the key factors in the development of successful leaders.
2. Map out ways in which leadership knowledge and skills can be consciously enhanced by leaders.
3. Identify organization strategies to recruit, educate, empower, and retain leaders.
4. Examine succession practices and develop a professional development and succession plan.

The participant evaluation form for this module is then framed in terms of the extent to which participants feel that each objective is addressed (results from the most recent iteration):

Table 1. Module-Specific Outcomes

Module-Specific Outcomes:	1	2	3	4	5	6	7	8	9	10	11	12	13	14	15	Average
1. To what extent did this module provide you with an opportunity to explore the ways in which leaders learn to lead and the key factors in the development of successful leaders?	5	5	5	5	4.5	4	4	5	4	4	5	4	4			4.5
2. To what extent did this module map out ways in which leadership knowledge and skills can be consciously enhanced by leaders?	5	5	5	4	4.5	4	4	4	4	4	5	4	4			4.3
3. To what extent did this module identify organization strategies to educate, empower, and retain leaders?	4	4	5	4	4.5	4	4	4	3	4	4	4	4			4.0
4. To what extent did this module assist you in examining succession practices and developing a professional development and succession plan?	4	5	5	5	4.5	4	4	4	4	5	5	4	5			4.5

The following table summarizes the evaluation results over the first three iterations of the program:

Table 2. Executive Leadership Evaluation Results Summarized

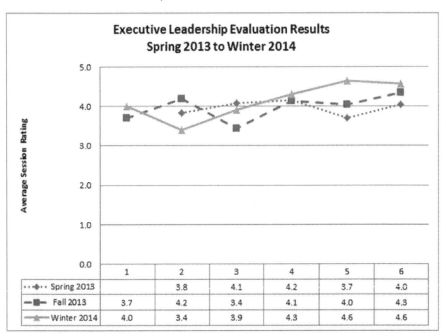

The delivery of this program continues to be refined. A continual question is the timing of delivery considering the extremely busy schedules of the participants. Our current format features biweekly module delivery from 9:00 a.m. to 2:00 p.m., with a working lunch. It is still the case that we often lose a participant at the lunch break. Currently under consideration is 8:00 a.m.–1:00 p.m. delivery, with lunch at noon sharp.

Through the comment section of the evaluations participants have the opportunity to share more narrative feedback with the presenters and also speak to the conditions they encountered in the environment in which the module was delivered. Milk instead of powdered milk; all these details matter.

Theory

With exception of the sixth module, Professional Development and Succession Planning, the Executive Leadership program does not explicitly espouse a theory of leadership. However, several themes of a theoretical nature are woven throughout the program and explicitly addressed in the sixth module:

- Leadership serves the organization in articulating its vision and mission and achieving its goals and objectives (Henley, 2011, pp. 46–51).
- Leadership is fundamentally relational; it entails building relationships and ongoing collaboration with others (Hornstrup et al., 2012; Zipursky, 2014).
- Organizations work best when they are *leaderful*, i.e., many leaders are empowered or, alternatively, all members of the organization are empowered to be leaders to the extent of their capacities and the scope of their positions (Realin, 2003).
- Leadership can be learned, and organizations can establish environments that intentionally attract and enhance leadership (Senge, 1990).
- Creating leading organizations, delegating and empowering, and intentional planning are the conditions that assure continuity of leadership or succession (Jackson, 2013).

The Participants Speak

The following are the comments of all participants at the conclusion of the third iteration:

- *Excellent information! Relevant on so very many fronts. Would highly recommend to others.*
- *Very valuable. Group size was perfect. Many ideas will be implemented in our organization.*
- *I really enjoyed the great discussions!*
- *Extremely valuable—I look forward to continuing the relationships and applying the lessons.*
- *What a fantastic series—practical, thought provoking—enjoyed the interaction with presenters and peers. Such value and insight! Thank you for the information and support. Please send this week and last week's PowerPoints. Please send the peer contact sheet. Thank you so very much!*

- *Really enjoyed it. Great to take the time to examine all sectors we covered and to meet like-minded individuals and organizations doing great work! Very professional!*
- *Overall very good. I learnt a lot and this workshop series has really helped me to stimulate my thinking and become enthusiastic and engaged in improving my skills and the strength of my organization.*
- *Very insightful and great materials. Hope not to put it on a shelf but implement it ... thanks!*
- *Really appreciated Gerry's focus on relationship building throughout.*

Conclusion

Additional discussions with participants have emphasized the extent to which they experience the CityU Executive Leadership program as different and preferable to similar programs taken from other universities and private training organizations. The differences center on two key issues:

1. The relevance and immediacy of the material because of its presentation by actively engaged prominent practitioners.
2. The felt sense of being invited by the university into a reflective community of leadership practitioners.

The intention is to further engage with the participants in the aims of serving their learning needs as leadership practitioners and learning from them more about how to serve the community of practice of nonprofit leadership as a whole. The theme is always one of developing ongoing community and never one of providing a "one-off" program.

References

Deleuze, G., & Parnet, C. (1987). *Dialogues*. New York, NY: Columbia University Press.

Hattie, J. & Timperley, H. (2007). The power of feedback. *Review of Educational Research. 77*(1), 81–112.

Henley, A. (2011). *Social Architecture: Notes & Essays*. Vancouver, BC: The Write Room Press.

Hornstrup, C., Loehr-Petersen, J., Madsen, J. G., Johansen, T. & Jensen, A. V. (2012). *Developing relational leadership: Resources for developing reflexive organization practices*. Chagrin Falls, OH: Taoist Institute Publications.

Kinman, C. J. (2014). *Two images: Rhizome and gift-exchange in life and service*. In H. Á. Marujo & L. M. Neto (Eds.), *Positive nations and communities: Collective, qualitative and cultural-sensitive processes in positive psychology*. New York, NY: Springer.

Jackson, D. J. (2013). Personal communication.

Mintzberg, H., (2004). Managers, not MBAs: a hard look at the soft practice of managing and management development. San Francisco, CA: Berrett-Koehler.

Raelin, J. A. (2003). *Creating leaderful organizations: How to bring out leadership in everyone*. San Francisco, CA: Berrett-Koehler.

Senge, P. (1990). *The fifth discipline: The art and practice of the learning organization*. New York, NY: Currency/Doubleday.

Watts, D. J. (2004). *Six degrees: The science of a connected age*. New York, NY: W. W. Norton

Zipurksky, G. (2014). Personal communication.

Socially and Environmentally Responsible Leadership

Kurt Kirstein, EdD
School of Management

Abstract

To address increasing calls from stakeholders of all types, companies need to infuse social and environmental responsibility into their missions and strategies. More commonly referred to as corporate social responsibility (CSR), these actions help an organization ensure a more balanced approach toward meeting the needs of all stakeholders. Higher education institutions have an important role to play when preparing future business leaders to face unprecedented challenges in a new global business environment. An effective approach for teaching CSR to business students consists of five parts: (a) examining ethical models to clarify the relationship between an organization and its stakeholders; (b) creating a sense of urgency regarding the impacts of business on society and the environment; (c) identifying and managing stakeholders; (d) implementing triple bottom-line (TBL) leadership; and (e) infusing CSR directly into an organization's strategy at the time that it is drafted to ensure that all operational and tactical actions are driven from a plan that has CSR at its core.

Corporate Social Responsibility

Sustainable development and corporate social responsibility remain important issues both in business and in the education of future business leaders. To address many of the pressing environmental and social problems attributed to a traditional singular focus on corporate profits, businesses today must consider the needs of their stakeholders. In the developed western world, this expanded focus is leading to an increasing number of programs at the corporate and governmental levels to foster environmentally and socially responsible leadership. It is also leading to an increasing number of business schools and, specifically, MBA programs that are teaching students the importance of integrating sustainability and corporate social responsibility directly into an organization's strategy. It is clear that, in western developed nations, the economic benefits of responsible business are driving a slow and steady change in perspectives and behavior among established and future leaders (Weybrecht, 2010). However, the rest of the world may be addressing the issue of CSR, from both a business and education perspective, at a pace that differs from the developed west. This chapter will present an approach for teaching CSR in business programs from a strategic perspective that also respects cultural differences in attitudes.

CSR in Business

The need for CSR in business is driven by many factors. Companies are recognizing that old ways of doing business, focused on profit maximization and shareholder value, are not sustainable given the changing nature of global business (Weybrecht, 2010). A singular focus on economic factors produces business leaders who maximize profits at the expense of the environment and society (Kirstein & Diamond, 2011). Extreme examples of this singular focus are seen in the news and have become case studies for how not to run businesses. But these examples do not represent the struggles that most business face when they decide to become more socially responsible.

Business leaders are pressured to become more environmentally and socially responsible from many fronts, including customers and investors. Customers often consider the social activities of companies when making purchasing decisions. Investors seek the financial benefits of good governance, a favorable reputation, good partnerships, lower financial costs, and minimized legal risks. Investors now recognize the potential impact to an organization's reputation if it fails to consider its social responsibilities (Weybrecht, 2010). To make CSR activities more visible, many companies are including sustainability or CSR assessments in their marketing and annual reports. CSR is considered standard strategic practice for many businesses because of its contribution to financial performance and to market value (Sharp & Zaidman, 2010).

The problem is that many companies do not know how to proceed from their current position to one that would be regarded as socially responsible by their stakeholders. The fact is that most business leaders were taught how to maximize profits and often don't embrace CSR, which can be perceived as running counter to the financial interests of the organization (Pies, Beckmann, & Heilscher, 2010). Many leaders are uncomfortable leading their businesses in a way that is not founded on the practice of maximizing value for the shareholders. This is where education on CSR can have its biggest impact. Educators can first dispel the myth that CSR will hurt corporate profits. Properly done, CSR will not only save companies money, it will help companies earn more money (Sharp & Zaidman, 2010). Once business leaders can embrace this paradigm shift, they are more open to learning how to implement CSR. Higher education institutions can affect social change by providing opportunities for leaders to learn how to implement CSR in their businesses (Angus-Leppman, Metcalf, & Benn, 2010).

CSR in Higher Education

Traditionally, most business schools have provided a nearly exclusive focus on the financial, economic, logistical, and strategic factors associated with a traditional business education (Webrecht, 2010). Many students expect this type of traditional focus in their business programs as, in many cases, the primary motivation for attending business school is to earn a degree that will teach students how to enhance their economic well-being. Given these factors, how can academic institutions work to expand the perspectives of their students and community leaders in regards to CSR? How can they get them to see the need to focus as much of their energy on social justice and environmental protection as they traditionally have dedicated to economic factors? Furthermore, how can business education evolve to link the environmental and social aspects, embedded in CSR, to economic drivers in a way that students can see a clear business case for all three?

Universities in the United States are recognizing this need. Werther and Chandler (2014) cited an Aspen Institute study that showed that 79 percent of business schools "required students to take a course dedicated to business and society issues" (p. 100). Werther and Chandler also cited growing membership in Net Impact, an organization of graduate students and professionals who focus on responsible business. Yet, despite this increased focus on CSR among U.S. universities, there remain some serious challenges to socially responsible education. There is still a great deal of debate in the academic literature as to how socially responsible business education can be achieved and whether it is desirable in the first place (Pies, Beckmann, & Heilscher, 2010). Some believe that CSR is poorly defined and therefore does not belong in business education. Still others feel that incorporating ethics and CSR in business education will undermine its capitalist foundations. Despite these challenges, CSR has gained a solid foothold in higher education institutions in the States as evidenced by the number of institutions that include topics related to social responsibility in their curriculum.

But what about the developing nations of the world? In today's global economy, geographical boundaries are becoming increasingly obsolete due to technology-enabled connections (Werther & Chandler, 2014). Companies are addressing a number of aspects of globalization and universities are educating increasing numbers of students who come from, or live in, regions that may not have the same awareness or attitudes toward responsible business as has materialized in many areas of developed nations in recent decades. Students in developing countries may not consider CSR important in an environment where the standard of living and availability of good jobs is not equal to that of the west; their nations' lower level of affluence forces them to focus on more immediate needs. Considering cultural and national differences in values, power distance, and attitudes toward the purpose of business, how can American and European institutions design education for social responsibility when they may be serving a highly diverse population of students with different interests and motivations?

The remainder of this chapter describes a method of teaching CSR to diverse populations of students. The process begins with a primer on ethical models, continues with an examination of the need for CSR, and concludes with specifics about how to integrate CSR directly into organizations' strategic plans.

Teaching Corporate Social Responsibility

For many business students, especially those in the developing world, CSR is seen as an add-on to their business education and, for many, one that runs counter to the business concepts they are learning. To give CSR its proper consideration as a business practice necessary for any high-performing organization, it needs to be seen as enhancing the competitive value that the organization provides. To do this, the fundamental tenets of CSR need to be reconsidered so that CSR is not seen as a deterrent to effective business, but rather a conduit to effective business. And this must be done in a way that accounts for differing cultural perspectives.

One effective way for an instructor to incorporate CSR into business education involves three phases. First, establish a universally understood model for responsible business behavior by connecting business vision and mission to common ethical models. Second, establish a sense of urgency for businesses to act responsibly by presenting the current impact that businesses are having on both the environmental and social aspects of global societies. Lastly, present a practical process of infusing CSR into an organization's strategy. Each of these three phases and their role in CSR education are described in more detail below.

Ethical Models

Given the likelihood of significant cultural differences on dimensions such as power distance, uncertainty avoidance, and long- versus short-term orientation among varying populations of international business students, it is important to establish a socially based norm for interpreting business behavior. One effective way to do this is to utilize some of the more common ethical models. Students need to be able to acknowledge the differences between what is accepted as universally ethical behavior as opposed to behavior that is relative to the norms of a culture. Thus, a conversation about universalist versus relativist ethical models can be an effective way to begin this discussion. It is also important to acknowledge both the Deontological and Consequentialist approaches, with the former being focused on ethical nature of the act itself without regards to the consequence and the latter being focused on the ethical nature of the outcomes of personal or business activity. From there, the real discussion of the impact of business actions, relative to society and the environment, can begin.

Perhaps the clearest ethical model that can be used to support CSR is utilitarianism, which pushes for the greatest good for the greatest number (Frederiksen, 2010). Using this model, an instructor can illustrate the shortcomings of the profit maximization motive, which tends to favor a small group of shareholders, often at the expense of a larger group of stakeholders. Utilitarianism is an effective way to introduce the concept of stakeholder management in regards to business strategy as it gets students thinking about the "greatest good" as being something separate from the highest profits. Once students' attention is focused on the impacts that a business is having on stakeholder groups, they can begin to consider the relative influence that each group has on the organization. This leads to a deeper level of consideration about the relationships between stakeholders and the business when students have to potentially exclude certain stakeholder groups with lower priority from the "greatest number." This process can help students to better focus corporate strategies.

To further the conversation about ethical models, both the rights- and justice-based models can be useful. The first focuses on the rights that are, or should be, allocated to every person simply by being a human. This model is useful to illustrate the ways in which a business can violate these rights. Second, the justice model can be useful in demonstrating how business can often deny justice to stakeholder groups through their environmental or social actions. Both models can be used to further explain the need for a utilitarian approach to stakeholder management.

Establishing Urgency

Conversations about ethical models can set the stage for discussions that center on some key questions. Those questions include the following:

- What is the purpose of being in business? Is it to make money or it is to fulfill a social need with a secondary outcome of profitability?
- How can a business meet the greatest need of its significant stakeholders while remaining profitable?
- How can a business strive for sustained competitive advantage through practices that respect the long-term needs of the business, the environment that it operates in, and the societies that are affected by its actions?
- And, perhaps most importantly, why do businesses need to worry about this?

To address this last question, it is important to establish a sense of urgency regarding the nature of the world relative to environmental and social problems. Many students are shielded from the irresponsible actions of many businesses and, therefore, do not understand why CSR is important. Raising awareness of the traditional impacts of business, which have originated from, and are sustained by, a purely profit-driven model, helps to establish the need for more responsible business practices.

An effective way to establish this sense of urgency is to cite statistics. Well-selected statistics can tell stories that connect students to the need for environmental and social responsibility. A sampling of these statistics is listed below:

- Solid waste—The world produces billions of tons of solid waste annually and most of this goes into landfills.
- Plastics—Plastic waste is being found in many locations on land and in the oceans. Plastics take hundreds of years to break down.
- Electronic waste—More than 90 percent of computers, TVs, video and audio recorders, PDAs, and other electronics end up in landfills.
- Automobiles—About 20–30 million cars are taken off the road each year and most of these, in developing countries, end up in landfills.

- Industrial pollution—Giant clouds of industrial pollution are covering entire regions of the world. This is causing health problems for thousands.
- In early 2014, residents of Beijing, China, were told to stay inside because their air quality was dangerous.
- Water and land pollution—70 percent of the developing world's untreated industrial waste is dumped into rivers, lakes, oceans, or just onto the soil.
- Oil and gas—World oil and gas reserves will be unable to keep up with demand in the next twenty-five years.
- Coal—The world has a good supply for coal, but it is the largest source of pollution. Much of the world uses coal to generate electricity.
- Drinking water—20 percent of the world's population does not have access to clean drinking water. Much of what was once available is now polluted with fertilizers and pesticides from industrial farms.
- Fisheries—Over 70 percent of the world's fisheries are chronically overfished. Many species are not likely to recover.
- Forests—More than one-third of the world's forests have disappeared, and one-third is in danger. Forests are important in the absorption of greenhouse gasses.

But many of the world's scientists agree that the biggest environmental problem that we face is from carbon dioxide. The Intergovernmental Panel on Climate Change (IPCC, 2013) stated in their most recent report that human-caused increases in carbon emissions are a direct cause of global climate change. According to the Earth System Research Laboratory (2014) at Mauna Loa, Hawaii, the current level of carbon dioxide in the atmosphere is about four hundred parts per million which represents a 43 percent increase since the start of the industrial revolution. As more carbon dioxide holds more heat in the atmosphere, a number of events are likely to occur. Both the air and water on the planet will increase in temperature, affecting the global climate and making significant weather events more common and increasingly severe. The large ice sheets on Greenland and Antarctica will melt, raising ocean levels anywhere from ten to one hundred meters. Snow in the mountains, which generates seasonal runoff for irrigation, will, in a warmer future, fall as rain and run through the water system long before it is needed, and eventually, areas where it is already warm may become too warm and dry to support life or agriculture (Senge et al., 2008).

In addition to the large number of environmental problems, business students need to be aware of a number of social problems that companies can influence as they choose how to conduct business. Following is a sampling of these social problems, cited by the United Nations:

- Poverty—Great progress has been made in reducing poverty. However, as of 2008, 1.29 billion people still lived on less than $1.25 per day.
- Health—Significant efforts are under way to eliminate disease around the world. More work needs to be done especially to ensure the health of women and children.
- Education—Despite being guaranteed by the Universal Declaration of Human Rights, many global citizens do not have access to basic education.
- Development—Too often, the benefits of economic development are not shared with all members of the communities in which it occurs.
- Income disparity—In the past thirty years, there has been a significant increase in the difference in income between top earners and the middle class. This acts as a significant impairment to economic growth for an entire society.
- Peace and security—A good number of the world's citizens face threats both from inside and outside of the communities.

Combining these environmental and social snapshots underscores the need for leadership to help resolve these many issues. And, as has been clearly described by many, it is business that can have the biggest impact (Werther & Chanler, 2014). But to effect real change, each business must assess its place in and impact on the community and must ask itself to examine its mission, its reason for being in business, and the relationship that it has with its stakeholders. In short, it is to a business's great benefit to be seen as making a conscious choice to be part of the solution to the many social and environmental problems that have been created by business of the past. To do so, a business must make an intentional decision to structure its strategy so that a socially responsible position is a key part of its identity. This is an important lesson for current and future business leaders to learn.

Teaching Leadership for Corporate Social Responsibility

Business leaders who want to establish a strategic position with CSR need to learn how to design and implement CSR strategies. They also need to learn what CSR's proper place is in the organization and how to fulfill the organization's obligation to its stakeholders. A clear understanding of the needs of each stakeholder group, their relative importance, and the impact that the organization has on them, are all key in formulating a position on social responsibility that places the organization in a positive light. All of these topics can be covered in well-designed business education as a natural part of a student's process. It is important to integrate CSR into business education so that the two are understood as interwoven parts of the same whole. CSR is not an add-on to business education; it is the way that business should be conducted.

Three important parts of CSR that can be infused into a standard business education are stakeholder identification and management, TBL leadership, and socially responsible strategy development. Each of these three topics is reviewed in the sections to follow.

Stakeholder Identification and Management

Business students should be able to identify various stakeholder groups and their relative importance to the organization. Most students can easily identify customers and shareholders as key groups given their importance to the profitability and financial security of an organization. However, students should be encouraged to look beyond short-term profits in identifying those groups who can and will have a significant impact on the organization. Activities supporting the identification of stakeholders can be distributed throughout the business curriculum. These topics can first be introduced in a course on ethics, and can be further covered in courses on marketing, economics, entrepreneurship, organizational dynamics, operations and strategy. The goal is to underscore the importance of the increasingly symbiotic relationship between an organization and all of its stakeholders as business students learn to create strategies that provide the organization with a sustained competitive advantage.

Questions that business students should examine, relative to an organization's relationship with its stakeholders, include the following:

- What is an organization's obligation to the many stakeholder groups with which it interacts?
- How can an organization create a corporate identity and position that includes considerations of social responsibility? How can the organization become known for responsible business to its stakeholders?
- Are there business opportunities linked to CSR that an organization can pursue that will resonate with key stakeholder groups?
- How should the business be organized to better respect the needs of its stakeholders?
- Are there changes that the organization could make to its operations to reduce any negative impacts it might be having?
- How can the organization incorporate stakeholder management into its forward-looking strategy?

Stakeholder management can be a part of all courses in a business program; there are ample opportunities to demonstrate the importance of this relationship throughout the business curriculum.

Triple Bottom-Line Leadership

Running counter to traditional business education, students should be taught to lead an organization from three key perspectives: people, profit, and the planet. Triple bottom-line leadership is a different approach to the goal of profitability. Both the traditional and TBL approaches are concerned with profit maximization; they just use different methods to accomplish this goal. Traditional business approaches maximize profit at the expense of everything else and are focused on the short term. Triple bottom-line leadership maximizes profits but adopts a respectful perspective toward social and environmental limits. It also includes the understanding that these profits may be realized at a slower rate.

The business program topics that are most likely to be affected by TBL leadership are those focused on accounting and finance. Such a focus may encourage students and instructors to ask the following questions:

- Is there a way to quantify the expenses and risks that are associated with a traditional approach to business?
- What will be the positive impacts of conservation-related actions intended to cut the organization's consumption of increasingly expensive key resources, such as energy and materials?
- In what ways can an organization capitalize on its socially responsible position to enhance its financial bottom line?
- To what extent will employees be attracted to and retained by an organization because of its socially responsible business practices?
- To what extent will investors be attracted to an organization because of its socially responsible business practices?
- Can a business depart from short-term financial thinking and, instead, embrace longer-term financial plans that could, in the long run, help it realize a larger return?

Triple bottom-line leadership can be integrated into nearly all aspects of business education including leadership, organizational dynamics, economics, operations, and strategy.

Applying a CSR Filter to Strategy Development

Understanding the needs and influence of stakeholders along with a triple bottom-line approach to leadership is a good place to start. But every organization needs a strategy, and this is where CSR can have the largest and most sustained impact. Teaching CSR as a core part of a business program's focus on strategy will ensure that CSR is an integral part of students' understanding of how businesses should be run.

There are a number of ways that business graduates have been taught how to design corporate strategy, but one of the most common is to conduct a SWOT analysis and utilize the findings to determine a course of action that uses a company's strengths to capitalize on opportunities in the marketplace by creating a sustained competitive advantage. Such lessons are taught in all levels of business education where the vision, mission, strategy, and operational tactics continuum are used to help business students understand an effective way of devising strategy. Students are taught that an organization's vision is the reason it is in business; the mission is how the organization expects to realize its vision; the strategy is what the organization will plan to do to enact the mission that supports the vision; and the operational tactics are the daily actions that managers and employees will take to make everything come together.

So, where does CSR fit in? In most organizations, there is an effort to add CSR to the operational tactics, once they are defined. Organizations often attempt to alter their annual plans to try to make them more socially responsible, but this approach is often an afterthought since both the strategy and the tactics have already been defined. Attempting to make an organization's actions more socially responsible is often a departure from the original plan and it can be seen as a distraction from the initial strategy.

A better way is to consider socially and environmentally responsible business practices at the point in the process where the strategy is first being considered and drafted. As each strategic initiative is considered, it can be run through a CSR filter to determine the extent to which it (a) considers the needs of the stakeholders and the impact the organization is likely to have on key groups if it pursues a particular course of action and (b) whether the initiative being considered follows TBL leadership practices to ensure that it will lead to profits without a negative impact on people and the planet. Subjecting each initiative in a strategic plan to this filtering process will create both a strategy and a list of operational tactics that have CSR infused directly into them. CSR is not an afterthought if it is an integral part of the strategy that is driving the organization. This is the way that business school students can be taught to incorporate social and environmental responsibility directly into strategy.

Another way to consider strategic CSR is to view it using the SWOT tool. Students can be taught to identify corporate strengths that will allow the organization to capitalize on external opportunities in a way that is socially and environmentally responsible to create sustained competitive advantage. Again, social responsibility is inserted into the process, as a filter, to ensure the key strategic initiatives that are intended to drive corporate action for the next one, three, or five years have corporate social responsibility built into their core.

Conclusion

The process of educating future business leaders in regards to CSR can be broken down into five steps. The first is to begin the conversation about CSR within the context of commonly taught ethical models and to use these to show how current and future business leaders have an ethical obligation to strive for the greatest good for the greatest number while, at the same time, respecting the rights of key stakeholders in all of their business practices. The second part of the process is to show, through statistics and examples supported by science, the impacts of irresponsible business practices which, in many cases have been encouraged by a traditional, profit-driven approach to business education. Students need to see the link between a short-term emphasis on profitability and the many environmental and social programs that this can cause. Understanding this relationship helps students see the need for socially responsible business practices.

The process of infusing CSR into business education makes up steps three, four, and five. In step three, students are encouraged to consider who an organization's stakeholders are and how influential each will be on how the organization should be run. Examining stakeholders and their importance helps business students better understand just who CSR is for. Using the ethical models introduced earlier helps clarify what the relationship between the organization and its stakeholders should be. In step four, students are asked to consider a different way to consider how an organization earns it profits. While the end point of profit maximization is the same, a triple bottom-line approach helps to ensure that those profits are not earned as a result of unnecessary exploitation of people or the environment. This approach also asks students to consider a longer-term approach to profits with the trade-off being that, over the long run, profits may be greater than those that were earned quickly using a traditional and irresponsible approach to business. Finally, in step five, students are taught to develop a corporate strategy for sustained competitive advantage by applying a CSR filter early in the strategic development process to ensure that all long-term strategic initiatives, and the operational tactics that will be used to implement them, are grounded in socially responsible approaches to business.

References

Angus-Leppman, T., Metcalf, L., & Benn, S. (2010). Leadership styles and CSR practice: An examination of sensemaking, institutional drivers and CSR leadership. *Journal of Business Ethics, 93*, 189–213.

Earth System Research Laboratory. (n.d.). Global Greenhouse Gas Reference Network. Retrieved from http://www.esrl.noaa.gov/gmd/trends

Frederiksen, C. S. (2010). The relationship between policies concerning corporate social responsibility (CSR) and philosophical moral theories—an empirical approach. *Journal of Business Ethics, 93*, 357–371.

Intergovernmental Panel on Climate Change (IPCC). (2014). Fifth Assessment Report (AR5). Retrieved from http://www.ipcc.ch/report/ar5

Kirstein, K. D., & Diamond, J. (2011). Inspiring action for sustainable business: A five-phase approach. In K. Kirstein, J. Hinrichs, & S. Olswang (Eds.), *Authentic instruction and online delivery: Proven practices in higher education* (pp. 115–132). Charleston, SC: CreateSpace Publishing.

Pies, I., Beckmann, M., & Hielscher, S. (2010). Value creation, global competencies, and global corporate citizenship: An ordonomic approach to business ethics in the age of globalization. *International Journal of Business Ethics, 94*, 265–278.

Senge, P., Smith, B., Kurschwitz, N., Laur, J., & Schley, S. (2008). *The necessary revolution: How individuals and organizations are working together to create a sustainable world*. New York, NY: Doubleday.

Sharp, Z., & Zaidman, N. (2010). Strategization of CSR. *Journal of Business Ethics, 93*, 51–71.

United Nations (n.d.). *Global issues*. Retrieved from www.un.org/en/globalissues

Werther, W. B., & Chandler, D. B. (2014). *Strategic corporate social responsibility: Stakeholders in a global environment* (3rd ed.). Los Angeles, CA: Sage Publications.

Weybrecht, G. (2010). *The sustainable MBA: The manager's guide to green business.* West Sussex, England: John Wiley & Sons.

Part IV

The Behavior Aspects of Leadership

The Dark Side of Leadership: Combating Negative Dimensions of Leadership

Kelly A. Flores, EdD
School of Applied Leadership

Abstract

This chapter includes a discussion of dark side tendencies in the classroom, an analysis of basic needs, and the behaviors that are exhibited when these needs aren't met. A series of proven practices educators can implement to minimize these behaviors in the classroom is discussed.

The Dark Side of Leadership: How It Shows Up in the Classroom

Anyone who has watched *Star Wars* remembers Yoda's persistent warnings: "But, beware. Anger, fear, aggression. The dark side are they." Young kids—and adults, too—are intrigued by this "dark side" phenomenon. Yet, as we become more self-aware, we also begin to recognize that we all have dark side tendencies. In his seminal work on human motivation, Maslow (1943) theorized that for people to achieve higher levels of motivation (self-esteem and self-actualization), they must first get their basic needs (such as physiological, safety, and belonging needs) met. In academic settings, students will have difficulty achieving goals, mastering skills, and exhibiting creativity if they don't first feel safe and a sense of belonging (McLeod, 2007).

To develop leaders who exhibit strong character, personal capability, initiative, interpersonal skills, and strategic perspective (Zenger & Folkman, 2009), instructors need to recognize when behaviors stem from unmet needs and nurture higher levels of motivation (Maslow, 1943) and emotional intelligence (Goleman, 1997). Students come from diverse backgrounds and social environments that have shaped their values, behaviors, and norms. While these environments can nurture strengths in character and leadership abilities, they can also cultivate dark side tendencies, including compulsiveness, narcissism, paranoia, codependence, and passive-aggressive behavior.

Compulsive students constantly look for reassurance and approval; need to maintain absolute order, often following highly regimented routines; often see the classroom as an extension and reflection of themselves; are excessively moralistic and judgmental; are status conscious (often sharing their position or titles); and exhibit workaholic tendencies (McIntosh & Rima, 2007). Since compulsiveness can stem from angry and rebellious attitudes, these students often feel they cannot express true feelings, and will repress anger and resentment (though their feelings can surface in end-of-course evaluations or in classroom activities).

Narcissistic students are driven to succeed by a need for admiration and acclaim; have an overinflated sense of importance; have great ambitions, grandiose fantasies; have difficulty with criticism, often responding in anger; are often dissatisfied with achievements; and are self-absorbed (McIntosh & Rima, 2007). They display an inability to learn from others or experiences and are unwilling to take responsibility for their actions (Kakabadse & Kakabadse, 2013). Since self-absorption and uncertainty often stems from deep feelings of inferiority, these students may not enjoy their success and may feel dissatisfied with their lives.

Paranoid students often exhibit suspicious, hostile, fearful, and jealous behaviors; are worried that someone will undermine their leadership; are hypersensitive to actions of others, attaching subjective meaning to motives; often create rigid structures for control; and take lighthearted jokes seriously (McIntosh & Rima, 2007). Paranoid students can become argumentative, belligerent, and stubborn (Kakabadse & Kakabadse, 2013). Since paranoia can stem from strong feelings of insecurity and a lack of confidence, these students may interpret otherwise innocuous behaviors as threatening or condescending.

Codependent students are often peacemakers who cover up problems; are benevolent with a high tolerance for deviant behavior; are often willing to take on more work so that they don't have to say no; react rather than act; and take responsibility for problems (McIntosh & Rima, 2007). Since codependent students often feel repressed and frustrated, they often have trouble giving full, honest expression to emotions or problems.

Passive-aggressive students are often stubborn, forgetful, and intentionally inefficient; they tend to complain, resist demands, procrastinate, and dawdle as a means of controlling those around them; and on occasion, can exert control by short outbursts of sadness or anger (McIntosh & Rima, 2007). Since passive-aggressiveness can stem from anger and bitterness, many passive-aggressive students are afraid of success, since it leads to higher expectations.

Combatting Negative Dimensions of Leadership

Educators have the responsibility to address inappropriate behaviors in the classroom. Once the roots of these behaviors are understood, instructors can structure their learning environments to nurture higher levels of motivation (Maslow, 1943) and emotional intelligence (Goleman, 1997), which will, in turn, help students develop into strong leaders, respected employees, and active, contributing members of the community (McLeod, 2007). The following eight basic needs (Miller, 2004) provide a framework for understanding the needs of students, and to meet these needs in the classroom.

Belonging

Students need to feel a sense of belonging where they feel like they add value and have a role to play in the classroom (Miller, 2004). When students do not feel like they belong, they can feel like an outsider, isolated and insecure. This feeling can manifest itself in shyness, fear in group settings, separation anxiety, or identity confusion. Students who don't feel like they belong often withdraw, contribute only the bare minimum, act out in group settings, and create tension in the classroom.

Instructors can help students overcome these tendencies by:

- Creating a space that students can call their own
- Being hospitable—acknowledging special dates, welcoming students, exchanging contact info, and meeting with them
- Building trust and being trustworthy
- Developing a desire to know people
- Being aware of learning preferences, needs, health issues, allergies
- Calling people by name
- Sharing personal stories and allowing others to share their stories (according to level of comfort)

Nurturance

Students need to feel like instructors care about them as individuals. They need to know that faculty value their contributions, and that they will be supported in meaningful ways to help them be successful. Many students long for opportunities to grow and pursue their passions, but often need someone to help nurture these talents and draw them out. Students who do not feel cared for can feel burned-out, depressed, and bored (Miller, 2004). Many who go long periods of time without nurturance can question an instructor's motives when attempts are made to show them support.

Instructors can help students overcome nurturance issues by:

- Actively listening, demonstrating genuine curiosity and interest
- Acknowledging effort
- Giving second chances

- Connecting with those who might feel lonely
- Reaching out through cards and words
- Seeing the good in others
- Considering how others best receive nurturance—through words? Time together? Acts of service? (Chapman & White, 2012)
- Giving public positive feedback, so others know you appreciate their work
- Being hospitable—bringing treats, eating meals together
- Providing resources needed
- Discovering needs through inquiry or surveys
- Focusing on strengths and drawing them out

Support

Students need to feel supported in problem solving and risk taking (Miller, 2004). They need to know that instructors are here for them, and that they will receive help to figure things out when they are struggling. Students need to feel like they will be supported and encouraged as needed. They need to know that they will be taught what they need to know to be successful. Students who don't feel supported can exhibit helplessness and dependency, panic about new experiences, and fear of or resistance to change. They may have difficulty solving problems, asking for help, and taking risks. They might become either overly dependent or overly independent. They may lack innovation and creativity.

Instructors can help students feel supported by:

- Providing role and assignment clarity
- Having regular check-ins (one-on-ones)
- Providing team-building exercises
- Creating a positive atmosphere using peers' positive reinforcement
- Creating confidence by giving them 90 percent of what they already know how to do and then pushing them another 10 percent out of their comfort zone
- Backing them up and encouraging them
- Acting consistently
- Communicating that you'll be there during the journey
- Doing what you say you're going to do

- Not being judgmental, displaying both empathy and sympathy
- Asking them what they need
- Anticipating needs
- Giving of your time during office hours and before or after class
- Using written communication (including the syllabus and announcements) to show support

Protection

Going back to school can be scary for many adults, especially if they have been out of school for a long period of time. Providing a safe environment for them to learn can include acknowledging this fear, helping them to navigate unknown pitfalls, and giving them a safe place to be themselves and discover their new scholarly voice (Miller, 2004). Students who don't feel protected can feel anxious, fearful, timid, and skeptical. They can be afraid to take risks, and if there are too many risks without a safe place to try new things, some will choose to leave.

Instructors can provide a safe environment by:

- Providing a safe place to be
- Co-creating norms of safety in the classroom
- Responding without judgment
- Refraining from gossiping
- Being open/vulnerable about struggles
- Listening actively
- Asking questions without interrogating
- Providing positive responses to questions
- Being warm, cheerful, and helpful
- Reaching out to new students personally to understand their fears

Structure

Students need clear boundaries so that they know what to expect and how to be successful. They need limits on time and behavior so that they can feel free to focus on their work within these limits (Miller, 2004).

Without this structure, students can be prone to lateness, procrastination, and non-assertiveness. They can be obsessive and compulsive about their work, fixating on small details, and asking many questions to be sure they have things just right.

Instructors can provide structure by:

- Managing through expectations
- Teaching, correcting, and training
- Helping establish good habits
- Following through on commitments
- Modeling desired behaviors
- Setting balanced personal boundaries
- Not having unannounced expectations
- Communicating clearly (don't expect others to read your mind)
- Providing clear guidelines in the syllabus, announcements, and other communications

Emotional Containment

Students also need support and safety in emotional expression and learning to focus emotions (Miller, 2004). The classroom can provide a safe place to express emotions (yes, even strong emotions). Students need to know that their emotions aren't too intense for instructors to respond to and help them express those feelings safely. Without limits of emotional containment, students can exhibit unbounded physical expression of feelings, numbness or repressed emotions, or fear of expressing emotions. They can also have difficulty getting in touch with their emotions.

Instructors can provide emotional containment by:

- Remaining calm and clear when someone else is emotionally distressed
- Showing compassion
- Listening actively and being in tune to others
- Not being defensive or offended by emotions
- Identifying emotions
- Being a good listener
- Validating others

- Asking for time to process before responding
- Not trying to problem solve, just listen

Respect

Respecting students conveys valuing them as individuals (Miller, 2004). Respect communicates recognition that they have their own strengths and ways of experiencing, and these are valued. Respect gives them the freedom to be who they are, and communicates stability. It also gives them the space to evolve and grow even beyond what the classroom alone can offer. When students don't feel respected, they can have difficulty functioning autonomously. Creativity and innovation can be stifled, and they can exhibit absenteeism. They can also develop inappropriately close attachments to others.

Instructors can demonstrate respect to students by:

- Allowing for individuation and separation
- Valuing thoughts, feelings, and differences
- Asking questions
- Speaking the truth—after drawing them out
- Seeking to understand their perspective
- Seeking to understand their experiences in the context of their upbringing and life
- Exhibiting genuine curiosity
- Embracing differences
- Exhibiting cultural competence
- Providing constructive feedback mixed with encouragement for the things they do well
- Encouraging creativity and innovation
- Drawing out their strengths and individuality

Bonding

Students need to observe healthy, appropriate, and positive relationships (Miller, 2004). This might be in our interactions with other students, faculty, and administrators. They need to know that faculty are connected in these relationships. They need to know that our relationship with them is different than with others. And students need to know that collectively, instructors will share information to help them be successful. Without bonding, students can feel uncertain about forming and maintaining relationships. It can hinder collaboration, and students can have difficulty working with others to solve problems. Cliques can be formed, and students can feel like those around them are playing favorites.

Instructors can nurture bonding by:

- Acting respectfully toward other students, faculty, and administrators
- Modeling healthy bonding
- Maintaining relationships over time
- Creating memories together
- Sharing meals together
- Reminiscing together
- Sharing verbal expressions of recognition and encouragement
- Being present at celebrations, such as commencement ceremonies and retirement parties

Conclusion

Most educators will recognize these basic needs and how unmet needs can manifest dark side tendencies. These proven practices can be implemented in classrooms both proactively (to prevent these behaviors), and reactively (when we recognize these behaviors). To best help students, educators can exhibit genuine curiosity and caring, evaluate the expectations that are placed on students, and provide safe places for growth and overcoming behaviors.

References

Chapman, G. D., & White, P. E. (2012). *The 5 languages of appreciation in the workplace: Empowering organizations by encouraging people.* Chicago, IL: Northfield Publishing.

Goleman, D. (1995). *Emotional intelligence: Why it can matter more than IQ.* New York, NY: Bantam Books.

Kakabadse, A., & Kakabadse, N. (2013). How to spot a destructive leader. *Management Services, 57*(3), 16–17.

Maslow, A. H. (1943). A theory of human motivation. *Psychological Review, 50*(4), 370–396.

McIntosh, G. L., & Rima, S. D. (2007). *Overcoming the dark side of leadership: How to become an effective leader by confronting potential failures.* Grand Rapids, MI: Baker Books.

McLeod, S. A. (2007). *Maslow's hierarchy of needs.* Retrieved from http://www.simplypsychology.org/maslow.html

Miller, J. (2004). *Meeting the needs of the child within us.* Retrieved from http://www.mindspring.com/~joanmiller/download-files/all%20pdfs/Meeting-Needs-Child.pdf

Zenger, J. H., & Folkman, J. R. (2009). *The extraordinary leader: Turning good managers into great leaders.* New York, NY: McGraw-Hill.

Managing Boundaries in the Multiple Relationships Created by Mentorship

Pressley R. Rankin IV, PhD
School of Applied Leadership

Abstract

Boundaries define the spaces or domains in which one lives her or his life. They also define the roles that one enacts in each domain, e.g., being the boss at work or being a spouse at home. Leaders are most often responsible for creating some of the rules that define the boundaries within the work domain. Additionally, socially constructed ideas about a role (faculty) or a domain (the university) automatically suggest the boundaries that are in place and how one should behave. However, in a mentorship relationship, the ideas about what is appropriate are not as clearly defined (Barnett, 2008; Clark, Harden, & Johnson, 2000). This chapter will explore the nature of boundary setting in mentorships where there is a power differential and a strong chance of multiple relationships (PDSCMR), like program director to a faculty member. The specific example discussed here will be faculty/student mentorship, which best illustrates the complexity that can emerge in PDSCMR mentorships.

Introduction

Boundaries play an important role in the regulation of human relationships as well as the creation of the spaces, or *domains*, where people live, work, and play. Boundaries provide limits or rules that guide how one interacts with people. Leaders, whether in an educational setting or in an organization setting, are typically highly involved in boundary creation for their students or employees.

The domains that are created by boundaries typically have physical or mental borders. For example, a faculty member may consider the work domain as an assigned office on campus with four solid walls, a specific desk at home used to grade papers, a coffee shop with Wi-Fi access, or a combination of all three. That all depends on how that faculty member defines the borders of the space and the boundaries or rules set to enforce those borders, mental or physical.

When a person creates borders through boundary setting, those borders are crossed often during the course of the day. Checking Facebook at work is an example of border crossing. Leaders in the domain, such as faculty members in the school domain, are responsible for setting or maintaining the domain boundaries and thus the boundaries' borders. They are in charge of making sure boundary rules are followed. These domain leaders are sometimes referred to as border keepers, and it is they who regulate the ease at which a border between boundaries can be crossed (Clark, 2000).

Therefore, if faculty members or leaders become involved as a mentor to a student or junior colleague, they are creating another domain (the mentorship space) that they must define and border-keep. Plaut (2008) defined the management of boundaries in professional relationships in terms of the power differential that exists between two parties, e.g., physician-patient or faculty-student. Some power differentials are small, such as a peer mentorship between faculty. Some are larger, like the difference between a dean and faculty member.

Plaut (2008) saw boundaries as important in establishing healthy professional relationships. If the faculty member who is defining the mentorship boundaries is also someone who is a border keeper for the school domain, that mentor is now in a multiple relationship with the protégé (both as a mentor and as a grader). Managing the boundaries and borders in a multiple relationship is more difficult because each relationship or role one has with the other person may have a different set of boundaries. Being clear about those boundaries from the beginning sets up expectations for the mentorship and minimizes the misunderstandings that lead to ineffective mentorships.

While faculty/student mentorship or professional mentorship within an organization typically involves multiple relationships, professional development through an outside organization where the mentor has no other connection to the protégé other than through the organization would not typically involve multiple relationships and would not be considered in this chapter. The same is true for peer mentorships that don't often have strong power differentials. Instead, this chapter first presents a discussion of how boundaries create domains, borders, and roles. Then, in that context, the specifics of mentorship boundaries are discussed from the psychological perspective. The chapter ends with the final recommendations for mentors.

Domains, Roles, and Boundaries in Mentorship

Domains

Domains are spaces to which people subscribe specific categorical boundaries to such as work, home, and the gym. Categorical boundaries are socio-cognitive borders that individuals or cultures create and must continually maintain in order to exist (Nippert-Eng, 1996b). Other social scientists have defined categorical boundaries as "conceptual lines of demarcation that separate domains and domain-relevant behaviors" (Matthews & Barnes-Farrell, 2010, p. 330). Since individuals socially construct the characteristics of the boundaries between the domains, some domains may have less rigid boundaries and perhaps even overlap or exist within other domains (Ashforth, Kreiner, & Fugate, 2000; Nippert-Eng, 1996a, 1996b; Rankin, 2013). The domain of mentorship could, therefore, be constructed mentally and be entered into when the mentor and protégé get together in other spaces. The separation or overlap of these domains and the boundaries used to define them are based on individuals actively defining what those spaces are and who is a member of them (Clark, 2000; Kossek, Lautsch, & Eaton, 2006; Nippert-Eng, 1996a).

Boundary work. Nippert-Eng defines the act of maintaining categorical boundaries as *boundary work* and she asserts "each time we engage in the process, the actual practice of sorting out, assigning, and defending the inclusion/exclusion or categorical contents into specific mental and physical spaces and times, we show the collective, mental frameworks that guide our lives" (1996, p. 564). While each individual constructs and maintains these domain boundaries within his or her own cognitive borders, some domains, such as work and home, can be considered to be institutionalized in that most people share a consensus of what *home* and *work* mean (Ashforth et al., 2000). Mentorship literature suggests that the central concepts defining the role of mentor and what constitutes the domain of mentorship are less defined than domain concepts, such as *home* and *work*. (Barnett, 2008; Clark, Harden, & Johnson, 2000; Johnson, 1999; Lechuga, 2011; Straus, Johnson, Marquez, & Feldman, 2013). The lack of consistent cultural norms for the practice of mentorship means that each mentor must define the nature of the mentorship boundaries and must define the extent of the domain for themselves and the protégé.

Border power. Clark (2000) posits that while individuals have the power to negotiate and make changes to the domain borders, whether they choose to exercise this power is tied to their identification with domain responsibilities. Depending on the nature of the power relationship between the mentor and protégé, the protégé may place all the responsibility on the mentor for the establishment of the domain boundaries. However, protégés are likely to pay close attention to border keeping and management if their values and identity are embedded or closely tied with their role in a specific domain (Clark, 2000). A senior faculty member mentoring a junior faculty member would be an example of closely tied identity. Nevertheless, even an individual who is closer in power to their mentor does automatically have unlimited power to change domain borders since the setting of these borders is most often socially constructed by many actors within the domain, including border keepers (leaders).

Roles

Ashforth et al. (2000) expanded Nippert-Eng's (1996a, 1996b) ideas around domain boundaries to the idea of roles and summarized the concept of roles:

> Roles tend to be associated with specific individuals who are labeled accordingly (e.g., employee, parent, parishioner). Thus, a role boundary refers to whatever delimits the perimeter—and thereby the scope—of a role. Given the more or less institutionalized nature of work, home, and third-place domains, roles tend to be bounded in both space and time—that is, they are more relevant in certain physical locations and at certain times of the day and week. (p. 475)

This definition of role adds an important aspect to the discussion of boundaries since roles can be enacted within, between, and across the boundaries that are associated with domains. Roles can be domain-specific or carried into other domains, such as in the role of doctor, which is most often thought of as being associated with a hospital, but one could still be a doctor on a plane if called upon to exercise this role.

Bazalgette (2009) examined roles in relation to the system (domain) in which they are played. Using a group relations perspective, he divided role into two components: psychological and sociological. Bazalgette asserts that a "system" is a construct created within an individual's mind to organize persons, equipment, finances, buildings, and resources (2009). Using the system as a reference, individuals express their psychological roles in behaviors they believe are associated with their purpose in the system. Mentors may believe that their roles require them to act as an aloof professional or perhaps a kindly father figure depending on their internal thoughts and beliefs associated with their role.

While this psychological role is internal, the sociological role is contingent on an individual's perception of the expectations of others within the system: as to how he or she should behave within his or her role in the system (Bazalgette, 2009). The experiences mentors have with their previous mentors or the behaviors they are modeling from peer faculty members dictate the sociological role behaviors in their mentorship relationships. Therefore, the sociological expectations of the domain it is embedded in often flavor the type of mentorship a protégé receives.

Barnett (2008) asserts that faculty typically have multiple roles in a student's life, which often include grading, advising, recommending, and serving as the border keepers for the profession by monitoring each student's progress in their program. As a mentor, the faculty member is also serving as a role model to aid students in their professional development. For this environment to be safe, boundaries must be established for the role of mentor that help to differentiate the mentor role from the other roles.

Role transitions. As with domains, role boundaries can also be transitioned. Ashforth, Kreiner, and Fugate (2000) refer to the regular movement between roles as micro-transitions (e.g., moving from the role of father to the role of spouse). Role segmentation (how different one likes to keep the roles) and role integration (how similar one feels the roles are) influence micro role transitions (or, more simply, role transitions). To understand this process, one must first understand role identity, a concept that is a similar to Bazalgette's (2009) concepts of sociological and psychological roles.

Role identity. Ashforth (2001) defines role identity as including the goals, values, beliefs, norms, interaction styles, and time horizons associated with a particular role. He also asserts that role identities are socially constructed and can be either strongly associated with a person's sense of self-worth or weakly associated. Therefore, a mentor can believe she or he is an incredible mentor and thus have a strong role identity or he or she could feel unqualified to mentor someone and thus have a weak role identity as mentor. The relative strength of one's role identity affects role transitions in that weaker role identities are easier to transition from but may be harder to transition into from a stronger role identity. Following this reasoning, a mentor's role identity is strongly influenced by his or her self-in-role definition (self-worth) for the role in which he or she is mentoring the protégé to succeed (e.g., an engineering faculty mentoring an engineering student). It is therefore easier for a mentor with strong self-worth to create a mentor role with firm boundaries. Mentors with weaker self-worth will struggle with multiple roles overlapping.

Role identity also effects role transitions based on the contrast between roles. Low-contrast roles (e.g., mentor vs. faculty member) are easier to transition between, in comparison to high-contrast roles (e.g., faculty member vs. friend). The ease of transition is due to the similarity of the key features of the roles. This is irrespective of the domain. For example, a woman may have trouble transitioning between the role of mother to the role of wife within the domain of home if there is high contrast between the key features of each role. Roles or mentorships that have high power differentials are also high in contrast and vice versa. For example, if as a faculty member one is also the dean, the role of dean has more power than the role of faculty and thus more contrast. Switching then to a mentor role from that of a dean would be more challenging than that of faculty to mentor.

However, high contrast isn't always a bad thing; in faculty mentorship relationships, the ability to create a high contrast between the role of mentor and the role of faculty member can help the mentor manage the boundaries in multiple relationships. By firmly defining the boundaries and borders on the mentoring relationship, the mentor is less inclined to slide into another role and the protégé receives clear communication as to her or his expected role within the relationship. This is especially important since the roles of protégé and student are very low contrast. Ashforth et al. (2000) argued that high-contrast role identities are highly segmented with inflexible and impermeable boundaries, whereas low-contrast role identities are more likely to be highly integrated with flexible and permeable boundaries.

Role segmentation. The benefit of highly segmented roles is the reduction of role blurring (confusing role boundaries), but the cost is an increase in the magnitude of transition between roles (Ashforth et al., 2000; Bulger et al., 2007). Having a large magnitude of transition makes role exit more difficult. This difficulty means mentors need to put time and energy into transitioning from a faculty role into a mentoring role. This may include leaving the school domain in order to escape the sociocultural role expectations embedded in that domain. Transitioning role boundaries involves what Ashforth et al. (2000) refer to as role exit, which they described as psychologically and sometimes physically disengaging from the role. This can be accomplished as on the domain level through the use of rituals, external cues, or internal cues. Ashforth et al. (2000) provided an example of role exit:

> A commuter may begin to psychologically disengage from her home role and prepare for her work role by following her daily routine of showering, dressing in work attire, reading the business section of the newspaper over breakfast, and listening to traffic reports. (p. 478)

Role entry may also be marked with similar rituals or routines.

Role integration. Role integration in opposition to segmentation increases role blurring but decreases the difficulty of role transition. The lack of difficulty in the transition between roles inherently means "the role exit–movement–role entry sequence may occur rapidly with little or no conscious awareness" (Ashforth et al., 2000, p. 480). The lack of conscious awareness can result in role blurring that weakens boundaries between roles, and thus allows for more frequent role identity confusion and disruption of a role activity. Therefore, if a mentor believes that the role of mentor is part of the role of faculty, the boundaries between both domains are blurred. This means the protégé will have trouble seeing the mentor outside of the faculty role, which can cause conflicts of interest and minimize the establishment of a safe space.

The choice: Transition work or boundary work. A mentor who integrates his or her role may have issues with role overlap. One might think it is better to highly segment or separate the roles of mentor and faculty. Ashforth et al. (2000) posit that there is perhaps a greater concern for role identity being interrupted when there is high segmentation between roles, given that a boundary violation from another role will cause the segmented roles to compete in one's mind for supremacy in the moment. For example, if a faculty mentor highly segments his or her roles, having the protégé as a student in class could create a mental disruption if the student asks a mentorship question in that space. Ashforth et al. (2000) go on to suggest that:

> Because the cost of segmentation . . . [roles are very different] . . . is the benefit of integration . . . [roles are similar] . . . and the benefit of segmentation . . . [clear role borders] . . . is the cost of integration . . . [vaguely defined roles] . . . there is an ongoing tension between segmentation and integration that necessitates ongoing boundary and transition work. (p. 482)

This work takes the form of segmentors spending more energy on transitions work and intergraters spending more energy on boundary work. Nippert-Eng (1996a) would also agree that the boundary work associated with maintaining boundaries around domain transitions would also share the same qualities as with role transitions. Therefore, mentors who choose to see their roles as similar (professional/mentor, faculty/mentor) need to take extra care and be mindful of boundary creation and management.

Psychological Prospective on Mentorship Boundaries

The very nature of faculty mentorship creates a multiple relationship between the student and the faculty member. The faculty member is both a professor who can grade the student and a role model or professional mentor to the student. Barnett (2008) related the psychological concept of boundaries to mentorship and defined them as:

> Boundaries are the basic ground rules for the professional relationship. They add a structure to mentorships that provides guidance regarding appropriate actions and interactions for mentors and protégés . . . the boundaries construct is relevant to all professional relationships that involve a power differential. Thus, boundaries are relevant to the roles of psychotherapist, clinical and research supervisor, faculty advisor, mentor, and all other professional roles. . . . Boundaries in professional relationships include dimensions such as touch, location, self-disclosure, time, gifts, fees, and personal space. Boundaries may be rigidly enforced, crossed, or violated. (pp. 5–6)

Barnett's definition allows room for the mentor and protégé to decide how the boundaries in the relationship will be enforced and what the difference might be from boundary crossing, which may be necessary, and boundary violation, which is never acceptable.

Boundary crossing. While boundary crossings may or may not always be negative, they can lead to a slippery slope that may carry the professional into a boundary violation. The crossing of a professional boundary that is harmful for the client or protégé is a boundary violation (Barnett, 2008). Most commonly these boundary violations are of a sexual nature (Barnett, 2008; Smith & Fitzpatrick, 1995). Looking at boundary violations from a mentorship perspective, Barnett states:

> Effective mentors will have an emotional investment in their protégés' personal and professional development; a true caring. Yet, at the same time, this closeness and emotional investment must not lead the mentor to boundary violations and inappropriate multiple relationships. Similarly, protégés may easily come to idealize the mentor, feel special as a result of the commitment and caring evident in the mentor's behavior and the extra time spent together, and be vulnerable to boundary transgressions by the mentor which would violate students' dependency and trust. (2008, pp. 7–10)

While the violation of boundaries is never acceptable, the crossing of boundaries may be a necessary part of mentorship when one has multiple relationships with protégés. Yet as a border keeper, the mentor is responsible for the way in which these crossings occur. An important part of mentorship is the understanding that boundaries are necessary and engaging in serious consideration of the ethical implications involved when a boundary is crossed (Barnett, 2008).

Recommendations

Faculty/student mentorships offer the opportunity for students to develop their professional identity, learn important career tips, and practice strategies that will create success in their future careers (Clark et al, 2000; Noonan, Ballinger & Black, 2007; Lechuga, 2011). From the mentor's perspective, mentorships offer less tangible rewards like the development of future colleagues and the reward of seeing her or his students' success in the workplace (Barnett, 2008; Lechuga, 2011). The benefit of mentorship is skewed toward the protégé, while the power differential is skewed toward the mentor. Barnett (2008) asserts that effective mentorship involves the mentor emotionally investing in the protégé. At the same time, protégés "may easily come to idealize the mentor . . . [and] feel special as a result of the commitment and caring evident in the mentor's behavior and the extra time spent together . . . [thus becoming] vulnerable to boundary transgressions" (Barnett, 2008, p. 10). The following section lists this author's recommendations drawn from the literature on mentorship and discussed through the lens of PDSCMR faculty mentors who are considering starting a mentorship with a student.

Recommendation 1: Awareness. Clark et al. (2000) found training, instruction, role modeling, acceptance, support, and encouragement to be highly rated traits by protégés. Mentors have to balance the need for a personal and close relationship with their desire to create a relationship free of boundary violations. The mentor is the border keeper for the domain of the mentorship. He or she is in the power position and must not lose sight of his or her position even as the protégé grows in her or his professional development to the point of becoming closer to the mentor in professional status. Barnett (2008) suggests faculty mentors pay close attention to their motivations during the mentorship, being sure that all actions are in the best interest of the protégé. He also asserts that mentors remain aware of their "own emotional state, stresses, relationship history, and emotional vulnerabilities" (Barnett, 2008, p. 14).

Awareness also includes being aware of cultural, gender, and age differences between the mentor and the protégé. Understanding the power differences can help to minimize boundary crossings and boundary violations. Finally, self-awareness and self-worth in the faculty member's role as mentor allow for higher contrast between the mentorship role and the faculty role. The faculty mentors should be aware of their own feelings of competence within their role as mentor and as faculty member.

Recommendation 2: Communicate clear boundaries expectations. Barnett (2008) suggests having an open discussion at the start of a mentorship relationship to discuss role and domain boundaries. Mentors in their role as border keeper should discuss how their role as mentor is different from the other multiple roles they may have with the protégé: such as friend, faculty member, and/or professor. Defining the domain would also include a discussion about what is safe to do or say when in the mentorship space, what responsibilities the mentor and protégé have for confidentiality, and both parties' need for privacy. The mentor should discuss what boundary crossings are acceptable and what to do if a boundary violation occurs. Being clear about boundaries from the beginning sets up expectations for the mentorship and minimizes the misunderstandings that lead to ineffective mentorships.

Recommendation 3: Be a good boundary role model. The protégé is watching the mentor closely. This is the nature of mentorship. The mentor is a role model professionally, but she or he is also modeling relationship behaviors. Mentors must strive to create a mentorship domain, which is bounded and has rules, rituals, and mental or physical domain boundaries. By being clear in one's role, the mentor is modeling effective professional boundaries and minimizing role blurring. The mentor must also be careful to obey the rules and boundaries she or he creates. Even a small lapse could signal to the protégé that the space is not safe or that the mentor is not serious.

The mentor may want to designate a place for the mentorship to take place, such as an office or a coffee shop, and be strict about not allowing mentorship conversations outside of those boundaries. However, such a segmented approach may not work in situations where the mentee needs to observe behaviors and reflect on them. In such cases, the mentor may need to create flexible boundaries or integrate the mentorship domain into other domains. However, the decision to allow domains to overlap should be a conscious decision with open communication about how that overlap affects the boundaries. For example, a faculty member who has a student observe him or her teaching a class would need to clearly communicate boundaries and role expectations concerning how the student should behave in the classroom and what expectations the faculty member will have of him or her for participation and interaction with the other students. In turn, the faculty member would need to respect the role assigned to the student and not ask the student to do other tasks, such as run off copies or write on the board.

Recommendation 4: Policies and standards. Policies and standards are also forms of boundaries. Barnett (2008) recommends consulting with colleagues about professional standards and mentorship expectations. If the department or organization that a mentor is a part of does not have policies on the mentorship process, it is important that the mentor create a document that defines their role and the role they expect the mentee to take in the mentorship. Mentors need to create personal boundaries to address how much time he or she is willing to devote to the process and set expectations with protégés about what their expectations about the mentor's availability should be. Clark et al. (2000) found that 25 percent of their eight-hundred-student sample complained that the mentor was not as available as they would have preferred. Clear establishment of time boundaries and expectations would minimize that type of complaint. Finally, be sure that there is a formal policy to handle disputes and conflicts. That policy should designate a person or group to process and handle conflicts and disputes.

Summary

Mentors are the leaders and boundary creators in the mentorship relationship. Mentorship allows for the professional and social development of the protégé and can establish a collegial relationship that might last a lifetime. This author asserts that the need to communicate boundaries, overtly, is necessary due to the lack of strong socially constructed boundaries on the domain of mentorship and the role of mentor. There is also an added ethical need to be clear with boundaries whenever there is a power differential or multiple relationships between the mentor and protégé. The establishment of policies and procedures to address where and when the mentorship relationship will be enacted can defuse many of the common complaints protégés have with their mentor. The open discussion of boundaries is not a typical conversation faculty members are used to having with their students. However, some faculty may be familiar with the process from setting up rules to govern their classes. Therefore, all it takes is transferring that type of collaborative rule setting to the setting of boundaries within the mentorship. This author also asserts that the recommendations presented herein can be applied to other mentorships as long as there is a difference in power and a chance for multiple relationships to occur.

References

Ashforth, B. E. (2001). *Role transitions in organizational life: An identity-based perspective.* Mahwah, N.J.: Lawrence Erlbaum Associates, Inc.

Ashforth, B. E., Kreiner, G. E., & Fugate, M. (2000). All in a day's work: Boundaries and micro role transitions. *The Academy of Management Review, 25*(3), 472–491. Retrieved from http://www.jstor.org/stable/259305

Barnett, J. E. (2008). Mentoring, boundaries, and multiple relationships: Opportunities and challenges. *Mentoring & Tutoring: Partnership in Learning, 16*(1), 3–16. doi:10.1080/13611260701800900

Bazalgette, J. (2009). Leadership: The impact of the full human being in role. In E. Aram, R. Baxter & A. Nutkevitch (Eds.), *Adaptation and innovation: Theory, design and role-taking in group relations, conferences and their applications* (pp. 31–50). London, United Kingdom: Karnac Books.

Bulger, C. A., Matthews, R. A., & Hoffman, M. E. (2007). Work and personal life boundary management: Boundary strength, work/personal life balance, and the segmentation-integration continuum. *Journal of Occupational Health Psychology, 12*(4), 365–375. doi:10.1037/1076-8998.12.4.365

Clark, R. A., Harden, S. L., & Johnson, W. B. (2000). Mentor relationships in clinical psychology doctoral training: Results of a national survey. *Teaching of Psychology, 27*(4), 262–268. doi: 10.1207?s15328023TOP2704_04

Clark, S. (2000). Work/family border theory: A new theory of work/family balance. *Human Relations, 53*(6), 747–770. doi:10.1177/0018726700536001

Johnson, W. B., & Nelson, N. (1999). Mentor-protege relationships in graduate training: Some ethical concerns. *Ethics & Behavior, 9*(3), 189. doi: 10.12074/s15327019eb0903_1

Kossek, E. E., Lautsch, B. A., & Eaton, S. C. (2006). Telecommuting, control, and boundary management: Correlates of policy use and practice, job control, and work-family effectiveness. *Journal of Vocational Behavior, 68*(2), 347–367. doi:10.1016/j.jvb.2005.07.002

Lechuga, V. M. (2011). Faculty-graduate student mentoring relationships: Mentors' perceived roles and responsibilities. *Higher Education, 62*(6), 757–771. doi:10.1007/s10734-011-9416-0

Matthews, R. A., & Barnes-Farrell, J. L. (2010). Development and initial evaluation of an enhanced measure of boundary flexibility for the work and family domains. *Journal of Occupational Health Psychology, 15*(3), 330–346. Retrieved from http://search.ebscohost.com/login.aspx?direct=true&db=pdh&AN=ocp-15-3-330&site=ehost-live

Nippert-Eng, C. E. (1996a). *Home and work negotiating boundaries through everyday life.* Chicago, IL: University of Chicago Press.

Nippert-Eng, C. (1996b). Calendars and keys: The classification of "home" and "work." *Sociological Forum, 11*(3), 563–582. doi:10.1007/BF02408393

Noonan, M. J., Ballinger, R., & Black, R. (2007). Peer and faculty mentoring in doctoral education: Definitions, experiences, and expectations. *International Journal of Teaching & Learning in Higher Education, 19*(3). Retrieved from http://proxy.cityu.edu/login?url=http://search.ebscohost.com/login.aspx?direct=true&db=ehh&AN=33719133&site=ehost-live

Plaut, S. M. (2008). Sexual and nonsexual boundaries in professional relationships: Principles and teaching guidelines. *Sexual and Relationship Therapy, 23*(1), 85–94. doi: 10.1080/14681990701616624

Rankin, P. R. (2013). *Work/life boundary management in an integrative environment: A study of residence life professionals who live at their place of work.* ProQuest Dissertations and Theses. Retrieved from http://search.proquest.com/docview/1429526281?accountid=1230

Smith, D., & Fitzpatrick, M. (1995). Patient-therapist boundary issues: An integrative review of theory and research. *Professional Psychology, Research and Practice, 26*(5), 499–506. doi: 10.1037/0735-7028.26.5.499

Straus, S. E., Johnson, M. O., Marquez, C., & Feldman, M. D. (2013). Characteristics of successful and failed mentoring relationships: A qualitative study across two academic health centers. *Academic Medicine: Journal of the Association of American Medical Colleges, 88*(1), 82. doi: 10.1097/ACM.0b013e31827647a0

A New Era of Business Intelligence Education: Preparing Ethical Next-Generation Technology Leaders

Lindy Ryan, MAL
School of Applied Leadership

Abstract

Educators are responding to a sense of urgency to meet the changing leadership demands in information technology and data science by developing new academic programs. These programs are focused on continuous, prescriptive learning and an integrated education model between academia and industry. Preparing next-generation technology leaders includes technical competency and business acumen, but does not stop there. Educators must also recognize the ethical implications of the emerging big data era and foster the development of ethical leadership through a framework of competencies that includes emotional and cultural intelligence, adaptive and transformational leadership, and critical thinking.

Introduction

The term business intelligence (BI) was introduced in the early 1990s to describe the use of analytic applications for decision-making processes, such as reporting, querying, and predictive analytics (Watson & Wixom, 2007). Today, the confluence of emerging new market needs and capable new technologies has catapulted the information industry into a period of fluid, fast-paced change. This has resulted in a rapid reshaping of the skills and education needed by incoming business intelligence and business analytics (BA) professionals. The emergence of big data, which represents large quantities of new and unusual sources of data, paired with advanced computing technology and rare combinations of user skills (Wixom et al., 2014), has further influenced the need for change in next-generation academic efforts.

There has been significant contribution to the leadership literature on the identification of sharp criteria to address the need for improved educational curricula to prepare next-generation technology professionals, as well as for the need of a blended education model between academia and industry. While this paper addresses the leadership demands affected by technology and its influence on future technology leaders as organizations continue to become increasingly data-driven (or, data dependent), its primary purpose is to provide strategies for educators to address these changes to prepare ethical, next-generation technology leaders. As educators address the emerging leadership needs in the new technology era, they must begin by building a framework of competencies founded on ethics. Once this foundation is established, educators must foster the building of leadership competencies that include emotional and cultural intelligence, adaptive and transformational leadership, and critical thinking. These competencies equip graduates with the necessary skills to drive sustainable, ethical change in a rapidly evolving industry with the potential for significant data-driven consequences.

Ethical Implications of the Big Data Era

While many universities and organizations are starting academic programs and training initiatives to meet the needs of the technology industry, merely educating incoming knowledge workers is not the answer to developing future technology leaders. Gallager, Dadone, and Foster (2010) wrote that innovation cannot be a reactionary measure, and further, that reinvention is an intentional and proactive process designed to reimagine leadership potential. Developing leadership potential involves academic research, business acumen, and a process of developing the leaders from within to equip them with the leadership skills and competencies they need to be successful.

To be truly innovative, Phillips (2013) noted that leaders must be willing to be disruptive; they must break out into new technologies and new capabilities. Phillips further noted that at some point, even the most innovative can become stagnant if they are only improving on what has already come. Kotter (2008) said that creating a sense of urgency is the first step (of many) to avoid stagnation and achieve success in a rapidly changing world. To achieve this sense of urgency, leaders must identify and resolve issues that create obstacles to success; they must foster change initiatives, celebrate short-term wins that open pathways to larger goals, and incorporate changes into the organizational structure, processes, and culture (Kotter, 2008). While academia and industry respond to this sense of urgency on a larger scale through integrated education, today's educators must also embrace a sense of urgency in developing future technology leaders by fostering growth in critical leadership competencies.

The proliferation of big data in the past several years has raised concerns over privacy and the collection, storage, distribution, and use of sensitive information by organizations. The widespread and robust amount of data generated has led to an increased reliance upon data by businesses, and big data strategies are now a critical component of business objectives as organizations seek to maximize the value of information. However, while technology brings more opportunity to use data to inform business decisions, it also fosters the potential to use this data unethically (Nunan

& Di Domenico, 2013). Providing future technology leaders with a foundation in ethical accountability will support the emergence and nurturing of complementary leadership competencies in emotional and cultural intelligence, transformational and adaptive leadership, and critical thinking and decision making.

Developing Ethical Leaders

Developing leaders must be aware of their ethical responsibilities not only to the organization but also to the people inside the organization, those it affects, and society as a whole. Organizational structures (including requisite policies and codes of ethics) do not guarantee ethical behavior unless leaders actively demand that these policies are followed. Even then, ethical issues arise. Ethical leaders must have the courage to take action when the organization acts unethically, even if it damages profits or has an unfavorable impact on the business.

Freeman and Stewart (2006) encouraged leaders to have a "living conversation" (p. 4) about ethics and behaviors throughout all levels of the organization to provide a measure of accountability and transparency, reinforcing a culture of ethical responsibility. This conversation includes providing mechanisms to voice concerns and push back on organizational practices or activities perceived as unethical. Educators can help prepare future technology leaders to act as advocates in the ongoing ethics conversation by providing opportunities to develop emotional and cultural intelligence.

Emotional Intelligence

Emotional intelligence (referred to as EQ) is the ability to monitor one's feelings and those of others, and to use that information to guide thinking and action (Salovey & Salovey, 1990). Leaders must be aware of their decisions, mannerisms, and actions, and how these can be perceived by others (Mcabe, 2005). This awareness of self is a key function of emotional intelligence. Leaders who possess emotional intelligence can self-regulate and know which emotions they are feeling and why; recognize the link between their feelings and what they think, do, and say; recognize how their feelings affect their performance; and have a guiding awareness of their values and goals (Goleman, 1998). More important, ethical conduct is "essential for the proper functioning of society in general and business in particular" (Angelidis & Ibrahim, 2011, p. 115).

Studies by Angelidis and Ibrahim (2011) concluded that the ethical perspective of managers has a positive correlation with their levels of emotional intelligence, and that emotional intelligence provides a link between ethical understanding (the awareness and attention to ethical issues) and ethical behavior (the actions taken that support the former). Ultimately, the goal of increased emotional intelligence competency is awareness into the self and others, how actions and behaviors directly affect perceptions of a leader's ethical attitude and values, and how this reflects on the ethical behavior of an organization in its approach to big data.

The academic experience is charged with the objective of preparing future leaders through the accumulation of technical knowledge and skill set. Additionally, further core objectives of education have been de-scribed as developing the abilities of cognitive and intellectual ability, self-management and intrapersonal abilities (including adaptability), and relationship management and interpersonal abilities (Boyatzis, Stubbs, & Taylor, 2002). Horton-Deutsch and Sherwood (2008), too, noted that peda-gogies that integrate textbook learning with reflective learning are criti-cal to the development of emotionally competent leaders. Educators can help develop students' emotional intelligence by using a holistic approach to education; rather than relying on lecture-and-discussion methods, edu-cators should focus of learning rather than teaching and embed insights into the distinguishing characteristics of great managers from great lead-ers in curriculum and pedagogy (Boyatzis, Stubss, & Taylor, 2002). Further, educators should facilitate an accurate self-assessment of student emo-tional intelligence competency, and engage in development-oriented be-havior in the classroom to address areas of deficiency (Sheldon, Dunning, & Ames, 2013).

Cultural Competence

Finally, emerging technology leaders should be instructed in the responsiveness to a multicultural vision that assesses the cultural competence and empathy of leaders to help them thrive in diverse business environments. Cultural intelligence, or CQ, is a construct derived of Sternberg's integrative theoretical framework of different loci of intelligence as the "capability to function effectively in a variety of cultural contexts" (Livermore, 2011, p. 3). Freeman and Stewart (2006) further posited that ethical leaders can "understand why different people make different choices" (p. 6). A widespread understanding and insight into different cultures, motivations, and norms will provide leaders with the skills to make ethical decisions when dealing with the realities, opportunities, and challenges of working in diversity (Cortes & Wilkinson, 2009), and also provide them with insight into the behaviors and expectations of outside cultures (Moodian, 2009). Cultural intelligence is distinct from individual personality differences and has predictive validity in areas ranging from demographic characteristics to cross-cultural experience.

Leadership is the most important element in initiating a culturally intelligent perspective and diversity inclusion and awareness effort (Hubbard, 2004). Additionally—and perhaps more important—a top-down diversity leadership approach is a critical component of a diversity implementation within an organization (Ng & Sears, 2012). This includes the academic learning institution.

As leaders, educators can assist students in developing cultural intelligence by first and foremost demonstrating a commitment to diversity leadership. They must demonstrate actions to support, challenge, and champion the diversity process within their institution. Educators should foster further development of cultural intelligence within students by encouraging students to recognize diversity in everyday scenarios, ranging from direct interactions in a work or learning environment to virtual classroom, to casual interactions through various forms of social media and with peer groups.

Adaptive and Transformational Leadership

With the rapid rate of change, complexity, and uncertainty in the business intelligence industry, adaptive, transformational leadership is paramount to driving organizational success. The ability for organizations to thrive in new business environments is critical, and solutions to these challenges "reside in the collective intelligence" (Heifetz & Laurie,

2011, p. 58) of leaders. Heifetz and Laurie (2011) defined this trait requisite of successful leaders as that of adaptive leadership, which they also noted is "counterintuitive" (p. 59), primarily because leaders must be able to "see a context for change or create one" (p. 60), rather than respond to a need. Adaptive leadership, then, is about leading change that enables organizations to thrive. It is the practice of mobilization, and it occurs through experimentation and requires diversity (Heifetz, Linsky, & Grashow, 2009).

Because transformational leadership is "individually considerate" and provides followers with support, mentorship, and guidance (Bass & Riggio, 2006, p. 5), it is tied innately to the construct of emotional intelligence. This connection between transformational leadership and emotional intelligence has been supported by several empirical studies that report a positive correlation between the two, and analysis of study results has indicated that both emotional intelligence and transformational leadership are emotion-laden constructs (Lindebaum & Cartwright, 2010).

The principal difference between these two theories is that emotional intelligence is applied primarily to the leader, while adaptive leadership is applied primarily to the organization. However, adaptive leadership requires that a leader embrace a learning strategy to address challenges that are adaptive, or for which there are no known solutions and which require a shift in thinking (Granger & Hanover, 2012). This, in turn, denotes a need for emotional intelligence in the capacity to be self-aware and self-managing (Goleman, 2005). A transformational leader must shift perspectives to adapt to changes that are happening, and to leverage emotional intelligence skills to motivate and inspire others to engage when confronting a challenge, adjusting values, changing perceptions, and nurturing new habits—or, behaving ethically (Heifetz & Laurie, 2011).

Building on the competencies of emotional and cultural intelligence, educators can leverage these skills to build adaptive and transformational leaders by focusing on reflectivity and promoting self-aware leadership within the context of change. Mezriow's (1991) theory of transformative learning noted that critical reflection can transform the learner. And, as a learning strategy, reflective learning can help learners increase their "awareness of perceptions, reactions, and assumptions that limit thinking and foster conscious decisions" (Horton-Deutsch & Sherwood, 2008, p. 947) in a way that is congruent with values and drives organizational growth and positive change in society. This allows students to become more perceptive, less defensive, and more accepting of new ideas, leading to transformational leadership (Sherwood & Horton-Deutsch, 2008).

Critical Thinking

Leading critically is applying critical thinking skills to decision making and leadership actions (Jenkins, 2012). Future leaders begin with a limited amount of knowledge and gain new information by mastering the skills of reading, listening, and experiences—or, learning to observe, reason, imagine, and challenge—competencies that amount to critical thinking preparedness (Welton & Egmon, 2006).

Because critical thinking is a three-step process of discernment, analysis, and evaluation with assessing a situation or issue, critical thinking is an iterative and agile process of identifying an issue, reviewing its facets and characteristics (including potential complications, consequences, and merits), and systematically evaluating the scenarios and options discovered prior to initiating a responding action. Critical thinking is therefore an "art" (Paul & Elder, 2014, p. 41) that ensures one uses the best thinking for any circumstances. Together, the art and process of critical thinking leads to innovative decision making. Leveraging the inclusion of earned competency in emotional and cultural intelligence, the concept of psychological capital notes that a leader with confidence, intent, and optimism may display higher critical thinking skills (Luthans, Youssef, Sweetman, & Harms, 2013; Youssef & Luthans, 2007).

Leaders who exhibit strategic decision making analyze ideas in a non-superficial way to discover logical connections for reasoning and effective judgment (Patterson, 2011). Educators can help future technology leaders develop critical thinking skills by using inquiry-based teaching to encourage intellectual engagement. This method is intended to improve essential learning outcomes, like critical thinking and reasoning, which enhance cognitive performance and future competitiveness. It promotes student inquiry and discovery in an authentic context, and consists of elements including inquiry related to community need, subject-matter-aligned case study exercises, peer evaluation, individual accountability, and lecture content on key concepts (Greenwald & Quitadamo, 2014). Several studies exist that prove the applicability of the inquiry-based teaching model on development of critical thinking skills (Ernst & Monroe, 2006; Greenwald & Quitadamo, 2014). Moreover, critical thinking through a process of critical reflection prepares learners to "think and discriminate between beliefs that rest on empirical evidence and those that do not" (Horton-Deutsch & Sherwood, 2008, p. 948), and relies on the earlier discussed concept of reflection to drive higher thinking that includes self-awareness.

Vision of Future Leadership

Bennis and Townsend (2005) aptly stated that no two leaders are the same. However, developing future technology leaders from the foundation of ethics will establish an ethical framework for leadership behavior. It will also help incoming knowledge workers navigate the unintended consequences and inherent challenges present in an increasingly data-driven and analytic business environment (Buytendijk, 2013).

And while specific practices to prepare future leaders will vary for any given industry, the inclusion of a standard model of education on both technical and leadership skills; providing prescriptive, applicable, and practicable experience through an integrated learning model and educational and leadership opportunities; and recognizing that leadership is an ongoing process and that learning and growth happen perpetually provides educators with the framework needed to develop ethical, next-generation leaders, regardless of industry.

References

Angelidis, J., & Ibrahim, N. (2011). The impact of emotional intelligence on the ethical judgment of managers. *Journal of Business Ethics, 99,* 111–119.

Bass, B., & Riggio, R. (2006). *Transformational leadership* (2nd ed.). Mahwah, NJ: Lawrence Eribaum Associates, Inc.

Bennis, W., & Townsend, R. (2005). *Reinventing leadership: Strategies to empower the organization.* New York, NY: HarperBusiness.

Boyatzis, R. E., Stubbs, E. C., & Taylor, S. N. (2002). Learning cognitive and emotional Intelligence competencies through graduate management education. *Academy of Management Learning & Education, 1*(2), 150–162.

Buytendijk, F. (2013). *Big data analytics requires an ethical code of conduct.* Stamford, CT: Gartner.

Cortes, C., & Wilkinson, L. (2009). Developing and implementing a multicultural vision. In M. A. Moodian (Ed.), *Contemporary leadership and intercultural competence: Exploring the cross-cultural dynamics within organizations* (pp. 61–73). Thousand Oaks, CA: Sage Publications.

Ernst, J., & Monroe, M. The effects of environment-based education on students' critical thinking skills and disposition toward critical thinking. *Environmental Education Research,* (3), 429–443.

Freeman, R., & Stewart, L. (2006). *Developing ethical leadership.* Business Roundtable: Institute for Corporate Ethics. Retrieved from http://www.corporate-ethics.org/pdf/ethical_leadership.pdf

Goleman, D. (1998). *Working with emotional intelligence.* New York, NY: Bantam Books.

Goleman, D. (2005). *Emotional intelligence: Why it can matter more than IQ* (10th ed.). New York, NY: Bantam Books.

Granger, K., & Hanover, D. (2012). Transformational performance-based leadership: Addressing non-routine adaptive challenges. *Ivey Business Journal, 76*(1), 41–45.

Greenwald, R. (2014). A mind of their own: Using inquiry-based teaching to build critical thinking skills and intellectual engagement in an undergraduate neuroanatomy course. *Journal of Undergraduate Neuroscience Education,* (2), A100.

Heifetz, R., & Laurie, D. (2011). The work of leadership. *HBR's 10 must-reads on leadership* (pp. 57–78). Boston, MA: Harvard Business Review Press.

Heifetz, R., Linsky, M., & Grashow, A. (2009). *The practice of adaptive leadership: Tools and tactics for changing your organization and the world.* Boston, MA: Harvard Business Press.

Horton-Deutsch, S., & Sherwood, G. (2008). Reflection: An educational strategy to develop emotionally-competent nurse leaders. *Journal of Nursing Management, 16*(8), 946–954.

Jenkins, D. (2012). Global critical leadership: Educating global leaders with critical leadership competencies. *Journal of Leadership Studies, 6*(2), 95–101.

Kotter, J. (2008). *A sense of urgency.* Boston, MA: Harvard Business Press.

Lindebaum, D., & Cartwright, S. (2010). A critical examination of the relationship between emotional intelligence and transformational leadership. *Journal of Management Studies, 47*(7), 1317–1342.

Livermore, D. (2011). *The cultural intelligence difference: Master the one skill you can't do without in today's global economy.* New York, NY: Amacom.

Luthans, F., Youssef, C. M., Sweetman, D. S., Harms, P. D. (2013). Meeting the leadership challenge of employee well-being through relationship PsyCap and health PsyCap. *Journal of Leadership & Organizational Studies, 20*(1), 118–133.

McCabe, B. (2005). The disabling shadow of leadership. *British Journal of Administrative Management, 46,* 16–17.

Mezirow, J. (1991). *Transformative dimensions of adult learning.* San Francisco, CA: Jossey Bass.

Moodian, M. (2009). Journeys through the ecological niche: An introduction to and overview of the textbook. In Michael A. Moodian (Ed.), *Contemporary leadership and intercultural competence: Exploring the cross-cultural dynamics within organizations* (pp. 3–6). Thousand Oaks, CA: Sage Publications.

Ng, E., & Sears, G. (2012). CEO leadership styles and the implementation of organizational diversity practices: Moderating effects of social values and age. *Journal of Business Ethics, 105*(1), 41–52.

Nunan, D., & Di Domenico, M. (2013). Market research and the ethics of big data. *International Journal of Market Research, 55*(4), 2–13.

Patterson, F. J. (2011). Visualizing the critical thinking process. *Issues, 95,* 36–41.

Paul, R., & Elder, L. (2014). Learning the art of critical thinking. *Rotman Magazine,* 40–45.

Phillips, J. (2013). *Relentless innovation: What works, what doesn't—and what that means for your business.* New York, NY: McGraw-Hill.

Sheldon, O. J., Dunning, D., & Ames, D. R. (2013). Emotionally unskilled, unaware, and uninterested in learning more: Reactions to feedback about deficits in emotional intelligence. *Journal of Applied Psychology, 99*(1).

Sherwood, G., & Horton-Deutsch, S. (2008). Reflective practice: The route to transformative nursing leadership. In D. Freshwater, B. Taylor & G. Sherwood (Eds.), *An international textbook of reflective practice* (137–153). London: Blackwell/STTI.

Watson, H., & Wixom, B. (2007). The current state of business intelligence. *Computer, 40*(9), 96–99.

Wixom, B., Ariyachandra, T., Douglas, D., Goul, M., Gupta, B., Iyer, L., Kulkami, U., Phillips-Wren, G., Salovey, P., & Mayer, J. (1990). Emotional intelligence. *Imagination, Cognition, and Personality, 9*(3), 185–211.

Youssef, C. M., & Luthans, F. (2007). Positive organizational behavior in the workplace: The impact of hope, optimism, and resilience. *Journal of Management, 33*(5), 774–800.

Behavior Management for the Higher Education Leader

Rebecca C. Cory, PhD
School of Applied Leadership

Abstract

Student behavior in the adult classroom and on college and university campuses is rarely treated in a proactive way (Ragle & Paine, 2009). There is an underlying assumption that students know how to behave in the classroom and co-curricular settings. Student misbehavior is then treated in punitive ways, punishing students, using progressive discipline. This chapter includes discussions on prevention strategies, responses, and legal and ethical considerations of behavior management with the goal of helping academic leaders, faculty members, and others to consider how they can reduce student disruption.

Introduction

Since university and college students are adults, campus leaders and faculty members often assume that students know how to behave in the classroom and campus environments. However, since many students come from diverse backgrounds, without prior exposure to the college environment, some may not have the cultural context for appropriate behaviors in the campus environment. How students talk to authority figures and peers is dependent on their understanding of power and how to convey respect. Students need to be taught the culture of their college and of higher education environments in general. This chapter examines how university leaders can support faculty members and staff in creating a culture that supports positive behavior and minimizes disruptive behavior in the classroom and on campus.

Common examples of disruptive behavior include "tardiness and absenteeism, unpreparedness, inattention, personal disruption, distracting other students, inappropriate student demands, incivility towards the instructor, and academic dishonesty" (Marchand-Stenhoff, 2009, pp. 109–110). In a large-scale survey of students, the three most disruptive behaviors were "continuing to talk after being asked to stop . . . coming to class under the influence of alcohol or drugs [and] allowing a cell phone to ring" (Bjorklund & Rehling, 2010, p. 16). This chapter will address these types of behaviors. More violent behaviors will be briefly mentioned in a section on behavioral intervention teams.

Bayer and Braxton (2004) asserted that faculty members play the most crucial role in creating an environment of civility in their classroom. They also promoted the use of a code of conduct that binds both the faculty and students to specific civil actions in the classroom. Classroom behavior continues to be important, not just to create an adequate learning environment, but also because classroom disruption in the form of "disrespectful disruption and insolent inattention" can have a statistically significant impact on the persistence of students in higher education (Hirschy & Braxton, 2004, p. 71). Campus leaders who care about retention will strive to maintain the level of decorum that will lead to persistence of the students.

Prevention of Disruptive Behavior

In the Classroom

Appropriate behavior for a specific setting is learned. By being explicit in the communication of expectations, instructors can assist the students to learn the social norms of the classroom and prevent some common disruptive behaviors.

Disruptive behavior is not only a phenomenon in the brick-and-mortar classroom. One study showed that the greatest way to reduce disruptive behavior in the online classroom is to explicitly state behavioral expectations in the syllabus (Galbraith & Jones, 2010). Faculty members may want to consider articulating online etiquette or "netiquette" conventions in their opening statements. For those new to the online discussion forum, reminders of basic etiquette (e.g., using all capital letters is considered yelling, or that one should write in proper English and spell all words out fully, rather than in text-message code) for a classroom setting may assist students in acclimating to the environment and contributing to a positive learning experience with their behavior.

Research by Nordstrom, Bartels, and Bucy (2009) indicated that the clearest predictor of disruptive behavior in the classroom was a positive attitude toward that behavior. They theorize that reframing the behavior as negative or disruptive can assist the students in refraining from it. This research also supports the idea of outlining explicit expectations of behavior in order to prevent disruptions.

Instructors have many options for setting behavioral expectations. One option is for the instructor to engage in a group expectations activity. In this activity, the instructor asks their students to set a behavioral code for the class. As a member of the class, the instructor is able to influence the behavior code and make sure that the students' non-negotiable behaviors are incorporated in the code. This activity can be done with the whole class brainstorming together, or with every student writing his or her own list, sharing lists with their peers, and together selecting the themes.

Another option is to model behavioral expectations. Instructors should be explicit about their expectations for class. They should clarify which behaviors are unacceptable, and clearly state their policies on typical disruptive behaviors, such as cell phones, laptops, eating, and taking breaks. Faculty members should model the behaviors they want to see. For example, an instructor may want to start class by taking her cell phone out of her bag, and saying, "Let's all remember to turn our phones off" as they make a show of turning theirs off. This modeling will help the students see the behavior and recognize that the instructor is serious about promoting it. Additionally, faculty members should praise good behavior as they see it. For example, it can be helpful to say things like, "Wow, I'm so impressed that we are all ready to start right at two o'clock! Thank you all for being here on time." Students, like most humans, appreciate praise and will respond by being more likely to behave accordingly in the future.

Yet another way to set behavioral expectations is through good teaching practices. When students are engaged and feel supported in class, they feel a desire to participate and be positive. Good teaching practices include (a) ensuring that all teacher-led activities are engaging; (b) using a variety of teaching techniques to reach all types of learners; (c) providing a "map" for students to know where the class is going and to anticipate the day; (d) providing opportunities for students to interact with one another; and (e) ensuring that those opportunities are structured and appropriate.

And finally, instructors can set behavioral expectations by providing structure and accountability. For example, when assigning a group activity, faculty members can give each student a specific role in the group and give the group a specific product to produce during their time working together. Then, the instructor can circulate throughout the room, providing assistance and redirecting the students if they are off task. Providing this simple structure and accountability can increase time on task and reduce disruptions by the students.

On Campus

Preventing disruptive behavior outside the classroom requires similar skills and abilities to preventing it in the classroom. The difference is that for behavior outside of the classroom, all college or university employees are responsible for being explicit about expectations, modeling desired behavior, and praising good behavior. Because of the broad base of staff required to effectively create a culture of positive behavior on campus, leadership is crucial. Campus leaders need to enroll their staff in ensuring that the desired behaviors are the ones that are supported and modeled. Leaders must ensure that members of both the staff and faculty understand that they each are responsible for confronting students if they see disruptive or emergent behavior. Campus leaders should both explicitly state and model the behaviors they want in the staff and the students (Bayer & Braxton, 2004).

Campus leaders should also ensure that the physical spaces on campus are set up in ways that encourage positive behavior. This means keeping spaces neat and orderly, monitoring the noise in various spaces, putting in sound-reducing features when appropriate, and ensuring that broken furniture or equipment is removed or repaired. Creating a campus where students feel that the administration cares about them and about the environment can help support positive behavior on campus.

Responses to Disruptive Behavior

In the Classroom

Although prevention is the goal, it is also important for instructors to have a plan of action for how to respond to disruptive behavior when it happens. The first goal should always be for instructors to take care of themselves. Instructors cannot deal with disruptive behavior in appropriate and constructive ways if they are too flustered or angry to moderate themselves. Instructors should not confront a student or stay in a situation that they feel is dangerous. Therefore, they should remove themselves from situations if their presence is making matters worse. Instructors should know when to ask for help, either in the immediate situation of dealing with the disruptive behavior or processing a stressful situation after it happens.

Second, faculty members should remember that, in the classroom, they are in charge. They are responsible not only for the content of their classes but also for the learning environment that they cultivate. They should create and enforce a positive learning environment. It is up to the instructor to redirect students who are behaving in inappropriate ways, and even ask students to leave class if necessary. Faculty members should discern when they need to be direct. Sometimes, a simple "please stop" or "take that outside" can be enough to extinguish a behavior. Not confronting the behavior sends the message to the rest of the class that the behavior is acceptable. Faculty members should remember that it is okay, and even encouraged, to be direct.

Finally, when instructors need to confront a student, they may want to consider couching their confrontation in concern. For example, rather than saying, "You may not fall asleep in my class, get out!" the faculty member may have better success by saying to a student, "I'm concerned about your falling asleep in class because I'm afraid you may be missing important content. Are you OK?" Framing the confrontation in an "I'm concerned about your [behavior] because of the [impact]. Are you OK" gives the faculty member the ability to both confront the behavior and de-escalate the situation. The more specific one can be about the behavior, the easier it will be for the student to understand the problem.

On Campus

The response to disruptive behavior outside the classroom is similar to that inside the classroom. Campus leaders, faculty, and staff need to take care of themselves, remember who is in charge, and know when to be direct. The caring confrontation can go a long way in these situations as well. Campus leaders can support employees learning these conflict management skills. They can support a climate on campus that helps staff members support each other in confrontational situations. For example, some campuses have a pass phrase that if said casually means, "I need help." The employees can work that pass phrase into a conversation to ask their peers for help, without having to say, directly and in front of the student, "I'm in over my head."

Legal and Ethical Considerations

One important consideration in responding to disruptive behavior on campus is ensuring that students have due process. Due process means that legal proceedings are fair and that the alleged perpetrator of a disruption gets timely notice of the process and their right to be heard. Campus policies need to be followed and equally applied to all students. There should be opportunity for appeal if the student feels that the punishment is disproportionate to the disruption. In that event, students need to have fair notice of their hearing or review, and they need to have an opportunity for their side of the case to be reviewed (Dismissing Students, 2010). Students are also entitled to legal counsel if they could be facing criminal charges, in addition to the campus charges.

In addition to creating a fair and legal process for review of disruptive behavior, campus employees should always act in ethical ways when responding to student behavior. They should be discrete in the handling of confrontation, and should avoid threats of reprisal or punishment for students who want an appeal or representation for their hearings.

Teaching Behavior Management to Adult Educators

Current and future campus leaders should be trained on both preventing and responding to disruptive behavior on campus. Although behavior management is explicitly taught in K–12 education programs, there is little discussion of it outside of lessons on the judicial process in higher education or adult learning programs. Yet, disruptive behavior continues to be an issue on college and university campuses (Bayer & Braxton, 2004).

In recent years, many campuses have started behavioral intervention teams (BITs). These teams are charged with assessing and responding to tips or recommendations from faculty and staff who witness behavior they think is concerning. The teams often consist of campus security officers, academic and student services, deans, and representatives from risk management, human resources, and the counseling center. Many of these teams were formed in a post–Virginia Tech shooting era, where there is fear of the low-likelihood, high-risk occurrences, like a campus shooting.

BIT members can choose to respond to a situation with a continuum of responses, from monitoring the situation to a voluntary or involuntary leave for the student (HEMHA, n.d.). At many institutions, the BIT focuses on the prevention of a violent response by students. One factor that the HEMHA (n.d.) white paper on BIT revealed is that prevention of violence goes largely unnoticed, while a violent act that is carried out attracts attention. For a BIT to be effective, it must be organized to follow protocol and procedure in a systematic way. The team must have adequate training and guidance on what to do in specific scenarios.

Sokolow and Lewis (2009) indicated that "modern behavior intervention teams see their role as nominally to address threat, and primarily to support and provide resources to students" (p. 5). A campus that is well resourced (either on campus, or in the local community) for supporting all types of students' mental health needs, and for identifying and confronting students who need support, can take steps to avoid a catastrophic situation on campus. These teams, when functioning in a preventative mode, rather than a punitive one, can be a complement to the more punitive functionality of the typical campus judicial systems.

Because BITs have become more common and continue to increase after each high-profile violent act on campuses, future campus leaders need to be taught how to create or participate in these types of teams. Both prevention and response should be incorporated into classroom training. Courses like Legal Issues in Higher Education teach appropriate responses and legal details (such as due process) for responding, but there is little done in typical programs to teach prevention.

Bayer and Braxton (2004) promoted the notion of a campus committee on teaching integrity. The idea behind such a committee is to ensure that instructors are using the best practices in their classrooms and are not contributing to the disruptive behavior through process or procedure. Leaders on campuses can be integral in creating these committees and working with faculty to ensure that the committees have a positive effect.

Because university teaching is often done in an environment without outside observers, it is easy for faculty to slide in their own behavior. Faculty members need to be held to a code of conduct, and should be responsible for ensuring that they are not disruptive in the classroom. Students should be made aware of the code of conduct for teaching, and should have mechanisms for holding their instructors to that code. Braxton and Bayer (2004) published a ten-item code of conduct for faculty that includes elements like communicating details of the class content to the students, being fair and present in advising, and refraining from inappropriate relationships with the students. Such a code would make the behavioral expectations for faculty explicit and potentially cut back on disruptive behavior in class.

Training programs for faculty, whether through formal coursework or informal workshops, should assist in teaching excellent classroom management skills, including best practices in classroom instruction so that faculty can prevent disruptive behavior.

Conclusion

The prevention and response to disruptive behavior on campus is the collective responsibility of campus leaders, faculty, and staff. Proper training in classroom management and teaching techniques can assist faculty in maintaining proper decorum in their classes. Campus leaders need to model desired behaviors and communicate expectations effectively. BITs and committees that support teaching integrity can further promote a positive campus environment.

References

Bayer, A. E., & Braxton, J. M. (2004). Conclusions and recommendations: Avenues for addressing teaching and learning improprieties. *New Directions for Teaching & Learning, 2004*(99), 89–95.

Bjorklund, W. L., & Rehling, D. L. (2010). Student perceptions of classroom incivility. *College Teaching, 58*(1), 15–18.

Bjorklund, W. L., & Rehling, D. L. (2011). Incivility beyond the classroom walls. *Insight: A Journal of Scholarly Teaching*, 628–636.

Braxton, J. M., & Bayer, A. E. (2004). Toward a code of conduct for undergraduate teaching. *New Directions for Teaching & Learning, 2004*(99), 47–55.

Dismissing Students. (2010). *Campus Legal Advisor, 10*(11), 16.

Galbraith, M. W., & Jones, M. S. (2010). Understanding incivility in online teaching. *MPAEA Journal of Adult Education, 39*(2), 1–10.

HEMHA. (n.d.) Balancing safety and support on campus: A guide for campus teams. A Higher Education Mental Health Alliance (HEMHA) Project.

Hirschy, A. S., & Braxton, J. M. (2004). Effects of student classroom incivilities on students. *New Directions for Teaching & Learning, 2004*(99), 67–76.

Marchand-Stenhoff, S. (2009). *Academic incivility in higher education.* (Order No. 3386703, Indiana University). ProQuest Dissertations and Theses, 154. (304899583)

Nordstrom, C. R., Bartels, L. K., & Bucy, J. (2009). Predicting and curbing classroom incivility in higher education. *College Student Journal, 43*(1), 74–85.

Ragle, J. D., & Paine, G. E. (2009). The disturbing student and the judicial process. *New Directions for Student Services*, (128), 23–36. doi:10.1002/ss.339

Sokolow, B. A., & Lewis, W. S. (2009). 2nd generation behavioral intervention best practices (a white paper). National Center for Higher Education Risk Management.